REFORMING THE HOUSEHOLD OF GOD

REFORMING THE HOUSEHOLD OF GOD

Paul's Models of Belonging

ALLISON L. GRAY

Paulist Press
New York / Mahwah, NJ

Cover image by Studio_G/Shutterstock.com
Cover and book design by Lynn Else

Library of Congress Cataloging-in-Publication Data
Names: Gray, Allison L., 1983– author.
Title: Reforming the household of God : Paul's models of belonging / Allison L. Gray.
Description: New York / Mahwah, NJ : Paulist Press, [2022] | Includes index.
Identifiers: LCCN 2022018979 (print) | LCCN 2022018980 (ebook) | ISBN 9780809155569 (paperback) | ISBN 9781587689536 (ebook)
Subjects: LCSH: Bible. Epistles of Paul—Criticism, interpretation, etc. | Identity (Psychology)—Religious aspects—Christianity—Biblical teaching. | Identification (Religion)—Biblical teaching. | Belonging (Social psychology)—Biblical teaching.
Classification: LCC BS2655.I33 G73 2022 (print) | LCC BS2655.I33 (ebook) | DDC 227/.06—dc23/eng/20220803
LC record available at https://lccn.loc.gov/2022018979
LC ebook record available at https://lccn.loc.gov/2022018980

ISBN 978-0-8091-5556-9 (paperback)
ISBN 978-1-58768-953-6 (e-book)

Published by Paulist Press
997 Macarthur Boulevard
Mahwah, New Jersey 07430
www.paulistpress.com

Printed and bound in the
United States of America

CONTENTS

ACKNOWLEDGMENTS

This book takes its shape from the many communities to which I belong. My writing companions offered feedback and unconditional support, especially Katie Duda, Julia Kowalski, Katharine Mershon, Lauren Osborne, and Lindsey Wieck. Colleagues at my university, particularly my chair Todd Hanneken, have helped me carve out the time to read, think, and write. Christopher Frechette, my acquisitions editor at Paulist Press, has been a champion of this project since its inception. I am also grateful for the encouragement of Kate Aultman in the Sponsored Projects, Academic Research, and Compliance office at St. Mary's University, and Alicia Cordoba Tait, Beirne Director of the St. Mary's University Center for Catholic Studies, who expressed their enthusiastic support for this project in its nascent form. Alicia invited me to speak on a panel at the 2019 Crossroads Symposium about the role of Catholic higher education in responding to child sex abuse in the Catholic Church. I very much appreciated the opportunity to meet and think with representatives from SNAP, the Lay Commission on Clergy Sexual Abuse of Minors in the Archdiocese of San Antonio, and the U.S. Bishops' Secretariat of Child and Youth Protection. The university also awarded me a generous Internal Faculty Research Grant in 2019, which supported several key activities that led to this monograph.

With the support of the grant, I was able to travel to Holden Village in Chelan, Washington, during the summer of 2019. The Village staff and guests who gathered each morning for Bible study formed a prayerful thinking community and fueled a week's worth of rich conversations about these Pauline images, their perils and promise in contemporary U.S. Christian life. The wisdom and questions all the participants shared helped refine my understanding of what this book might be able to accomplish. I am especially grateful to Jakob Rinderknecht, former Village potter and the one who suggested I apply to join the summer teaching faculty. Jakob's friendship and serious engagement with this project have contributed to my sense of belonging in the field of academic theology.

My students have had the greatest impact on my thinking about Pauline metaphors. Working with theology master's students, many of whom serve in parish ministry and adult faith formation, has helped direct my attention to particular ways the ideas from my home discipline of biblical studies can have a profound impact in the lives of faith communities. The initial inspiration for this project came from the graduate students in my courses on the Gospels, and I hope the book might prove helpful in their teaching. In the fall 2019 semester, I taught a new undergraduate course called New Testament Themes: Kinship and Family. My theology department colleagues were encouraging as I designed a class that would put Pauline material alongside contemporary case studies, to "test out" the format of the book. The students were phenomenal. Classroom discussions covered difficult topics, from the experiences of military personnel to public debates about Kaepernick's protest to child sex abuse in the Catholic Church. Students consistently held respectful space for one another to share and learn in the classroom community. They offered insights from disciplines across the liberal arts, enriching my thinking about this book and shoring up my love for interdisciplinary teaching and learning. I also found their creativity inspiring. Their final projects explored how kinship metaphors have been deployed to create belonging in Navajo tribes, police units, the music industry, the Marvel Comic Universe, and among immigrant populations. Students' openness and genuine interest in the questions raised by Paul's metaphors sustained my hope that this book will find a receptive and curious audience.

My deepest gratitude is due to Kaitlynn Moody, my student research assistant and conversation partner about all things Paul (and Alysia Montaño) from 2019 to 2021. Kaitlynn conducts her own scholarly inquiry from a place of deep care and concern for those who experience marginalization. It has been a privilege to study the Bible and belonging in her company.

Allison L. Gray
St. Mary's University, San Antonio
October 2021

INTRODUCTION

What does it mean to be a Christian? The New Testament letter writer Paul offers a whole collection of metaphors to explain Christian identity, including athlete, slave, soldier, body, and child. These familiar images capture our imagination, but we may have only a vague notion of what each one really meant in practice in Paul's day. Digging into the historical and contemporary realities that have shaped the interpretation of each image can open new paths forward, allowing us to consider how culture and controversy affect our reading and our living. How can each metaphor speak to us today as we discern what it means to belong together in Christian community?

Paul's letters let us catch a glimpse of everyday life in early church communities. People from different backgrounds—Jew, Gentile, free, enslaved, rich, poor, male, female—gathered together to read sacred texts, to worship, to learn from teachers, and to provide support for one another. Surprising gospel claims about Jesus's death and resurrection, his identity as the Messiah promised in Hebrew Scriptures, inspired them to be joyful, generous, and welcoming. Daily life raised questions about how much to follow the advice of traveling missionaries, how much to adhere to teachings from existing religious traditions, and whether or not to trust letters they received.

There were disagreements about who was in charge, about which texts to read and teach, about who should speak up and who should remain silent, about the right way to live out a shared faith. Some disagreements even appear to have led to a breakdown of social bonds, within the community or between the community and wider society. Together with epistle authors like Paul, these earliest Christ-believers[1] explored many dimensions of what it means to belong together as brothers and sisters in a single "body of Christ" (1 Cor 12). Throughout the book, I use *Christ-believers* to refer to the earliest communities, including those Paul taught. There is no incontrovertible evidence showing that the name was used consistently in the first century CE, and Paul himself does not use the term *Christians* for his followers, though he does emphasize that their shared belief in Christ is what ties them together.

Church communities in these early centuries adapted to changing circumstances, weathering conflict and unexpected historical developments. Although they were different from one another, they carried their practices and their hope for unity forward. The New Testament in our Bibles collects many pieces of the cherished correspondence that guided those early believers. Today biblical scholars and members of Christian faith communities continue to read these ancient letters and peer through the window they create into the past. Like window glass, though, the letters also offer us a reflection of ourselves, the readers. We can see aspects of our own experience in these texts; Christians today also face questions, doubts, triumphs, and surprises that challenge our ability to be in community. We Christians in the United States in the twenty-first century face many significant challenges to our sense of a shared identity.

I write from my vantage point as a white woman, a cradle Catholic, and a scholar of the New Testament and early Christian literature, trained in the academic study of religion. Within my own religious tradition, a number of interrelated issues suggest that the U.S. Catholic Church falls short in attempts to create a hospitable and vibrant community to which people feel they can belong as their full selves. Laypeople are leaving the Church. When asked about their religious affiliation, an increasing number of young people identify themselves as "nones," a shift reflected in declining attendance and participation at the parish level. Most "nones" are not irreligious, but they practice some form of personal spirituality and do not identify with an institutional religion.[2] People from the LGBTQ+ community, those who disagree with Church teachings about contraception and abortion, and those who face racism, sexism, or other discrimination within Catholic communities do not experience the Church as a place where they are welcomed.

There is a crisis of church leadership, on multiple fronts. Many religious orders and diocesan priests are aging, with fewer younger people taking on vocations to the priesthood or religious life.[3] At the Amazonian synod in October 2019, local bishops were mindful of how priest shortages make it difficult for the faithful to have access to the sacraments. The bishops engaged in serious conversations about the possibility of ordaining married men to the priesthood and expanding the diaconate to include women, on the model of the early churches.[4] Those who argue for women's ordination often cite the dearth of men's vocations as one sign of the Church's need. Creating more prominent roles for laypeople is another possible way forward. The university where I teach was founded by the Marianist order, an order like many others in which religious vocations are on the decline. Marianists are actively seeking ways to increase lay support for the order's charism, especially at their three institutions of Catholic higher education: St. Mary's University, University of Dayton, and Chaminade University.[5] The COVID-19 global pandemic has created an even greater strain on priests and parish leaders, including the many laypeople like my graduate students whose paid or volunteer labor keeps parish life viable. The need for physical distancing has led to a shift in the ways we gather as a Church, with a proliferation of Masses and community events streaming online.

Perhaps most importantly at this moment, the Catholic Church as a whole must dismantle and reimagine structures of leadership and power that facilitated the sex abuse crisis and its cover-up.[6] Ensuring the safety of all members in the church community is crucial, and it requires abusers and those who sheltered them be held accountable. In this way we can secure justice for survivors of abuse. To the extent that clericalism has contributed to the lack of oversight and abuses of power, it is essential that any reformation of church leadership incorporate more significant roles for laypeople.

Many of these *concerns*—attrition, a leadership vacuum, and a need for structures that ensure accountability—apply in other Christian communities in the United States. What's more, the social space that shapes U.S. Catholics' conceptions of Pauline metaphors also shapes the conceptions of Christians who belong to other denominations. In the interest of ecumenical cooperation and flourishing, I intend for the arguments of this book to benefit all contemporary U.S. Christian communities. If the household of God that is the living Church is to flourish as a space where all can belong, we need to meet the major challenges we face as Christians with a commitment to compassionate listening, a willingness to engage in difficult or even painful conversations, and a genuine dedication to taking action that serves our siblings in the human family. For crucial conversations about lay leadership, institutional reform, and community belonging to take place, the faithful must first feel empowered to see and articulate connections between their lived experiences and the foundational texts that are part of the authoritative canon of Scripture. We have to grapple with those New Testament letters that talk about what it means to belong.

PAUL AND THE POWER OF IMAGES

Paul's letters incorporated powerful, enduring metaphors that helped create communities in the first and second centuries. These metaphors have shaped existing models of church community: we are children of God, we are the Body of Christ, we are athletes running a race, we are soldiers in a battle for salvation. Do those Pauline images still hold meaningful answers to our questions about belonging as brothers and sisters? Can they offer advice about reforming the kinship that has been broken by abuses and mistrust? How can readers today interpret Paul's letters in ways that acknowledge the importance of history but also honor the integrity of ourselves as persons?

Some historical context will be useful in our work of examining and engaging the Pauline material.[7] Paul, née Saul, was born in the city of Tarsus, probably roughly around the same time as Jesus was born. Like Jesus, Paul was raised as a Jew, and he identifies himself as belonging to the tribe of Benjamin (Rom 11:1); in his letters he explains, "I advanced in Judaism beyond many among my people of the same age, for I was far more zealous for the traditions of my ancestors" (Gal 1:14). After the death and resurrection of Jesus, Paul confronted those who claimed that Jesus was the Jewish Messiah, rejecting their claim as nonsensical and blasphemous. But then came a turning point. Paul writes that God "reveal[ed] his Son to me" (Gal 1:16). This revelation or visionary experience led him to stop persecuting Christ-believers and instead join their number, taking up work as an itinerant missionary and "apostle to the Gentiles" in Greek cities of the Roman Empire.

Between roughly 40 and 60 CE, Paul traveled to urban centers in the provinces of Arabia, Judea, Asia Minor, Pontus and Bithynia, Macedonia, Achaea, and Italia, preaching to Gentiles so that they could join Jewish Christ-believers in identifying Jesus as the Greek *Christos* or Hebrew *Messiah* promised in the Jewish Scriptures. He delivered his message with a sense of urgency, fully expecting that the resurrected Jesus would return imminently for the day of final judgment. Exhorting his audiences to believe in Jesus the Christ, Paul also called upon both Jewish and Gentile Christ-believers to live as brothers and sisters in a new creation, serving one another and building up the community using their individual spiritual gifts for the common good. He called this community an *ekklēsia*, a Greek term literally meaning "assembly" and that we today usually translate as "church." At its root, the word refers to those who have been "called out" (*ek* plus *kaleō*), which reflects Paul's own apostolic task and his conception of the new people he sought to create, those who have been called and set apart.

As he traveled from community to community, Paul maintained a robust network of fellowship with the help of missionary partners (his "fellow soldiers" and "coworkers") and his many epistles. His partners were men and women, Jew and Gentile, slave and free, which likely influenced his famous statement in Galatians 3:28 that all are one in Christ.[8] Biblical scholars largely agree that Paul's letters were occasional in nature, meaning that he wrote them in response to particular occasions, situations, or questions that had arisen in Christ-believing communities. Like most writers of his time, Paul appears to have relied on a scribe or *amanuensis* (secretary) to whom he could orally dictate his letters.[9] He infrequently remarks on adding certain sentences in his "own hand" (e.g., Gal 6:11), which we may take as a sign that this was unusual. Paul's letters also generally adhere to a standard ancient epistolary format. He opens with a prescript that identifies the letter's sender(s) and addressee(s) and offers a wish for the recipients' well-being. Where most Greco-Roman writers would use the greeting *chairein*, literally "rejoice" or "be greeted," Paul substitutes the formula *charis kai eirēnē*, "grace and peace" (e.g., Rom 1:7; 1 Cor 1:3). A typical letter body would begin with an expression of thanksgiving, then proceed to a discussion of the main issues at stake. Paul's letters demonstrate that such discussions could be brief (Philemon) or lengthy (Romans), depending on the needs of the reading and listening audience. Like all authors, he makes modifications to the letter form when it seems expedient, for example omitting a thanksgiving in his agitated address to the Galatian communities. Paul's letters, in accord with epistolary standards of his time, would usually conclude with practical advice or *paraenesis* and personal greetings from those in his company to the addressee(s).

When a letter from Paul arrived in the *ekklēsia*, perhaps delivered by a fellow missionary, one of the literate members of the community would have read it aloud to individuals and groups, likely multiple times.[10] These letters were listened to, discussed, preserved, and eventually gathered into a Mediterranean-wide letter collection that made up the Pauline corpus. Subsequent reception of this Pauline material in churches and scholarly circles has tended to recognized three classes of letters: undisputed epistles, Deutero-Pauline epistles, and the Pastoral Epistles. The so-called undisputed letters are those that the majority of scholars agree were written by the historical Paul during his lifetime. These seven letters are Romans, 1 and 2 Corinthians, Galatians, Philippians, 1 Thessalonians, and Philemon. Even within the group of seven letters we call undisputed, there are debates about whether some of the letters might be composite documents. Various partition theories for 1 Corinthians and Philippians, for example, point out literary seams and rhetorical infelicities in the letters that might indicate a later editorial hand blended multiple letter sources into a single document.

The historical authorship of three letters—2 Thessalonians, Ephesians, and Colossians—is regularly debated. Many scholars, with careful attention to details like vocabulary choice and theological inconsistencies, believe that these letters were written by later Christian authors but attributed to Paul. This would accord with a practice called pseudepigraphy, literally "false (Greek *pseudo*) attribution." Those who study education in the ancient world point out that writing a speech or letter *as though you are some other figure* was a common part of rhetorical training. The exercise, called *prosopopoeia*, would allow students to imagine themselves as Alexander the Great encouraging his troops before a particular battle or Pericles delivering a speech of consolation to the Athenians, to develop their imaginations and their ability to construct a persuasive composition using situationally appropriate evidence and rhetorical style.[11] It is not a stretch to imagine that some leaders and devotees in the early Christian communities of the Mediterranean could have turned to prosopopoetic imitation of the important evangelist Paul, imagining how he might address pressing issues in their own times and places. There is even more consensus that the letters 1 and 2 Timothy and Titus were probably pseudepigraphic compositions, perhaps composed in a third generation removed from Paul's lifetime. Many scholars date these letters to the early second century, by which time the growing *ekklēsia* had begun to solidify an institutional structure and established place within Greco-Roman society. Following scholarly convention, I will refer to these letters as the Pastoral Epistles and their author as the Pastor, in recognition of his clear concern for shepherding the community to which he belongs.[12]

Across all these texts that make up the collection of Pauline epistles in the New Testament, readers encounter rhetorical finesse, emotional depth, compelling theological reflection, and powerful imagery. The letters are rich texts, replete with figurative language, especially metaphors that were designed to create belonging: athlete, slave, soldier, body, and child. We Christians today hear these metaphors so often in liturgical contexts and in homilies that we may read over them or take them for granted. We forget that they are radical, imaginative claims about who we are and how we belong together. It is also easy to overlook the fact that our contemporary historical circumstances affect the way we understand these images. What if we examine, with intention, the ways our experiences and expectations play off of Paul's language? How might some comparative work illuminate new ways of belonging, new paths forward toward greater unity? In writing this book, I hope to enable and encourage thoughtful conversation about the power of New Testament metaphor for reflecting experience, determining identity, forming community, and reimagining church structures today.

ASSUMPTIONS AND METHODS

My approach to the Pauline corpus is first and most profoundly shaped by my own academic position. I am a scholar in the academic field of biblical studies, teaching both undergraduate and graduate students in a theology department at a small Catholic liberal arts university. One of my foundational assumptions is that studying the historical context of New Testament writings and other early Christian literature can provide necessary insight into the texts. As an important 1965 Catholic document on divine revelation, *Dei Verbum*, points out, the scholar's historical awareness helps illuminate the biblical texts:

> The interpreter must investigate what meaning the sacred writer intended to express and actually expressed in particular circumstances by using contemporary literary forms in

> accordance with the situation of his own time and culture. For the correct understanding of what the sacred author wanted to assert, due attention must be paid to the customary and characteristic styles of feeling, speaking, and narrating which prevailed at the time of the sacred writer, and to the patterns men normally employed at that period in their everyday dealings with one another. (no. 12)[13]

That is, the more we as readers can attempt to acclimate ourselves to the author's world, the more we may discover, not only about what the author teaches but how he chooses to teach and why.[14] This approach to reading, grounded in the historical critical method and literary criticism, is not shared by all Christian denominations in the United States; in particular, groups that assert biblical inerrancy and take a more fundamentalist view of Scripture as divinely inspired may find some of my arguments do not accord with what they have learned in the sermons and Bible studies of their home churches. I would invite such readers, as I invite my students, to approach unfamiliar ways of reading with an open mind and an eye for how different hermeneutical methods might shed light on new or surprising aspects of these familiar texts.

Because the history of New Testament texts does not stop when they are written down, or even once they are grouped together and identified as a collection, I also examine the reception history of the Bible. Reception history considers the long centuries of biblical interpretation by all sorts of people and groups, in scholarly, theological, artistic, liturgical, political, and devotional circles. Knowing how people have read and applied Paul's teachings tells us about Paul's impact. The New Testament epistles are still living guides for many communities today, so we can and should consider our own moment in reception history. What are we drawn to read, what repels us, and why? How does our history affect our reading practices?

Historical understanding alone is not sufficient. Questions and tools from other fields of research provide us with new ways of engaging, interrogating, and appreciating biblical texts. Literary criticism helps biblical scholars recognize an important function of figurative language like Paul's: not only do metaphors reflect an author's historical reality, but the metaphors we use to describe a community and its members can profoundly shape the experiences and expectations of individuals within that community. If we hear that Paul identifies himself as a slave of Jesus Christ (Rom 1:1), our real-world understandings of enslavement bump up against how we think of Jesus. Is he a slaveholder? If we claim to be children of God, we are locating ourselves within a household power dynamic, drawing on our own conceptions of family and childhood to make quick assumptions about our potential, our interconnectedness as family members, and our authority or lack thereof. Do children really have the power to influence community life?

Literary interpretation also shows us that language is imperfect and metaphors are slippery. They can make a theological teaching more relatable, but taken literally, they might distort that teaching. Anna Rebecca Solevåg points out that the act of Pauline interpretation is additionally complicated by the presence of figurative and literal statements used side by side:

> Early Christian texts employ the metaphors of childbearing, slavery, and marriage in a discursive context in which literal slavery, marriage, and childbearing are integral parts of everyday life. It is not only the metaphorical side of slavery, marriage, and childbearing that we encounter in the New Testament; we find numerous references to these social realities.…What shape does the social context give the theological metaphor, and how did the theologized concept shape kyriarchal family organization?[15]

Metaphors are tools and can be used to outline and model a course of action. Whether said action bears fruits for good or ill depends on a whole host of factors, many of which are tied to historical and social setting. The sheer variety of ways people have interpreted Paul's words throughout history illustrate how challenging it is to pin metaphors down and find agreement among readers about what they might/can/should mean.

One more insight from literary criticism is crucial: the Bible can be read intertextually. Ancient authors and today's readers all carry other texts with us when we read and write. This applies to things like art, statues, songs—anything we encounter that can be interpreted—which we might not ordinarily identify as "texts." We use these "intertexts" to help ourselves interpret stories or create new pieces of literature. By knowing more about the intertexts Paul and his readers might have shared, we can better understand how Paul's letters might have been received among early Christ-believers. We should also be mindful that the New Testament itself is an omnipresent intertext for readers and communities today.

Readings from social-scientific, feminist, and postcolonial scholars appear throughout this book. Thinkers working with sociological theory remind us to attend to class, status, race, and social position; their interpretations highlight ways these factors influenced early Christian beliefs, practices, and texts, as well as the ways positionality and identity affect readers today. Feminist hermeneutics, which are highly varied, point us toward readings that are mindful of women's experiences, whether we are thinking about women in the ancient world or contemporary women who belong to communities that read the New Testament. Many feminist biblical scholars also address the impact of intersectionality by taking a multidimensional approach to analysis and accounting for intersecting identities based in, for example, both race *and* gender.[16] Most draw our attention to the effort of imagination and revisioning that are involved in reading the Bible as a text that can liberate women. Postcolonial critics insist that we must also read the New Testament and its interpretations through a lens that recognizes power structures, especially the forces of empire and colonization. Postcolonial hermeneutics helps biblical scholars attend to the positionality and concerns of New Testament authors and their readers who live(d) under hegemonic structures.

The methodological approach I adopt is broadly comparative, relying on case studies to capture moments in the reception history of Paul, from his lifetime to the present. The case studies presented here are meant to be suggestive rather than exhaustive. They direct our attention to important questions about the way Pauline metaphors and their continued use in Christian communities matter. While I have selected cases that have inspired conversation in my community and classroom, it is my hope that readers will continue the interpretive project and propose additional comparanda in their own ongoing discussions. The rationale for taking a comparative approach is twofold.

First, giving attention to how a kinship metaphor was used in the first-century Mediterranean world and how the same metaphor can bear a different meaning in contemporary U.S. life can illuminate the fact that we readers are responsible for cocreating the meaning of a text with its author. The "gap" between an epistle writer and today's epistle readers can therefore become a fruitful space for exploring different interpretations rather than seeming merely like an obstacle to understanding. Furthermore the contemporary world is not the only context that has called for a retooling or reimagining of New Testament metaphors. To help illustrate the constant mutability of kinship language, each chapter draws on case studies from the early Christian world of late antiquity, the second to sixth centuries of the Common Era. I hope these ancient adaptations and transformations might serve as models for today's responses.

Second, an attempt to account for how metaphors function in varied historical settings can, I hope, open us to new possibilities for the Church we would like to build. Rather than taking the text's meaning as fixed, a "given" that can only be embodied in one form of community life, we might be able to imagine how changes in our interpretive context or an emphasis on different aspects of meaning will renew the vitality of a text or render a certain image harmful. Tapping into the creative power of metaphor can free us as readers and as embodied Church, so that the New Testament re-forms us into a household that might yet be a liberating space for all God's people.

METAPHORS FOR BELONGING

This book examines five key Pauline metaphors, their interpretation, and their potential in today's U.S. Christian communities: athlete, slave, soldier, body, and child. Each part of the book focuses on one image, taking it as a jumping-off point to explore whether the same relational models that shaped early Christ-believing community life can or should be at work today. I will begin each part with a chapter that discusses why these metaphors were effective and sometimes even revolutionary for first- and second-century Christian communities. Readers will encounter comparative literary and philosophical analysis built into a rich portrait of each metaphor and its use in Greco-Roman and Hebrew Bible texts. The second chapter in each part examines multiple historical moments in which Paul's metaphors were interpreted for a new context, to illustrate how interpretation is affected by sociocultural realities. In each case the chapter will turn to address a selection of contemporary case studies that invite U.S. Christians to reimagine the continued use of Pauline metaphors.

Part 1 explores the idea of a Christian as an athlete who will receive the crown of salvation. I examine how the authors of martyrologies adapted this metaphor to help early Christians conceptualize the kinds of moral strength and endurance required to die for the faith. Turning to contemporary case studies featuring athletes and injustices they face, I propose questions about the importance of collective action by Christian "athletes" today.

In Part 2, we turn to Paul's figurative language about slavery and a discussion of ancient slavery. Examining how Pauline teaching was used in the United States to justify slaveholding, we conclude with a discussion of ongoing racial injustice, wage slavery, and sex trafficking, challenging the continued use of "slave of Christ" in today's Church.

Part 3 studies how Paul links evangelization and faithfulness with military life, calling Christ-believers "soldiers." We examine Roman military realities, including soldiers' participation in imperial cult and Roman colonialism, then turn to ways Christians in later centuries adapted Paul's images to portray Christ as an imperial leader. Contemporary case studies focus on moral injury and mental health among U.S. military personnel, with proposed questions for the Church, which can provide spiritual and material care for survivors.

Paul's famous image body of Christ is the focus of Part 4. Ancient medical teachings and literary comparanda help illuminate his choice of bodily imagery for community belonging. Turning to the third and fourth centuries, we explore how the real bodies of ascetics affected readings of Paul. Today's disability justice movement and emphasis on self-care help identify new questions and pathways for U.S. Christians as embodied persons in community.

Part 5 addresses kinship and family language in Paul's letters, turning to the metaphorical household of God and the view that Christ-believers are children of God. Paul's imagery is situated in the context of ancient educational practices and physical household spaces. We look at how the "child" image helped theologians in the fourth and fifth centuries conceptualize episcopal power and catechesis. Finally, we imagine how the terrible crisis of child sex abuse in today's churches might galvanize us to reject the idea that laypeople must remain powerless "children" in the Church.

READING AHEAD

At its heart, this is a project about biblical interpretation. The early Christian authors whose writings eventually became the New Testament were themselves grappling with questions about what it meant to live as community and how they should define themselves in light of the life, death, and resurrection of Jesus. What would such a community look or feel like, who was invited, who was excluded, and what was the best way to talk about relationships or fellowship? Within the field of biblical studies, scholars recognize that interpretation is an ongoing process with profound effects. When readers encounter early Christian texts, those readers change and are changed by the images and metaphors in those texts. Readers bring themselves and their experiences to each act of reading and interpreting.

Images from Paul's letters reverberate in many parts of contemporary life: politics, gender roles, church hierarchy, interfaith and ecumenical dialogue, personal spirituality...the list goes on. Therefore this biblical studies project is also written for contemporary communities who live in the world created through interpretation of these texts. Although New Testament epistles invite Christians to see themselves cooperating as linked members of the Body of Christ (1 Cor 12), shifting historical circumstances may require us to revise what belonging means in God's household. This book raises questions and offers practical suggestions for "reforming" the living household of God through a more conscious and careful use of Pauline metaphors.

PART 1

ATHLETES COMPETING FOR A CROWN

Athletic Training as a Force for Belonging

> *The mission of the CYO Athletics is: To offer to all youth sports and recreation programs emphasizing friendly competition through good sportsmanship modeled by adult participants. To invite all participants, Catholic and otherwise, youth and adults, to share in the life of their faith community.*[1]

The mission statement for Catholic Youth Organization (CYO) Athletics highlights the organization's primary values: participation, sportsmanship, adults setting an example for young people, and extending an invitation to join a community of faith. The link between athletics and faith is, practically speaking, a matter of the CYO's connection to the institutional Catholic Church. Founded in Chicago in 1930, the CYO was conceived by auxiliary Bishop James Bernard Sheil. CYO chapters spread rapidly, and "by 1935, Catholic dioceses from across the nation, including New York, San Francisco, Cincinnati, Salt Lake City, Milwaukee, and Louisville, modeled their own youth organizations after Chicago's."[2]

Sheil (1886–1969) was a Chicago native and avid amateur athlete. When he became a priest, he worked as a chaplain serving both military and prison populations before being appointed a bishop and later vicar general. He established the CYO largely to address issues of juvenile delinquency, believing that structured athletic programs provided a healthy outlet for youthful energy and could combat some of the pernicious influences that undercut civic engagement and democratic values.[3] Obligations to God, country, and church featured equally in early versions of the CYO pledge, which participants would recite before matches.[4] Ideals of masculinity were embedded in these statements, as well, with participants pledging to "promote, by word and example, clean, wholesome, and manly sport."[5]

To some extent, the CYO drew inspiration from the YMCA (Young Men's Christian Association), an organization founded in the late nineteenth century in England that opened its first U.S. chapters in the 1850s. The YMCA exemplified a rising form of Protestant evangelism, prevalent until the 1930s. It encouraged a perfection of mind and body, especially among men, as part of the path to salvation, blending faith and sports as mutually beneficial for personal spiritual growth.[6] From the beginning, however, the CYO functioned as a group that supported not just applying athletic discipline to one's faith life, but also positive interracial interaction and cooperation. The link between athletics and faith in the city of Chicago had a not insignificant effect of unifying different ethnic groups, even as the wider social situation was characterized by redlining policies and opposition to racial integration in neighborhoods and schools. As Timothy B. Neary points out in his book about the early history of the CYO, "Although it did not stop racism and racial segregation within the city's Catholic churches or neighborhoods, the CYO made significant contributions to inter-racialism in Chicago during the Great Depression, World War II, and immediate postwar period."[7]

At the beginning of the twentieth century, Catholic parishes in the city were "national parishes," organized by national origin or ethnic group. Sheil, together with Chicago Archbishop George William Mundelein (1872–1939), worked toward a goal of a blended American

Catholicism. They tried to emphasize civic values and church unity over ethnic identity. The fully racially integrated nature of the CYO was a part of this larger project of creating belonging for the Catholic Church in the United States and for Black Catholics within the U.S. Catholic Church. Through the CYO, Chicago's Irish American Catholics, who ran the city's political machine, were encouraged to develop meaningful, mutually beneficial relationships with Black Catholics, based on their shared Catholic identity. As a result, many Black Catholics rose to prominent positions as ward committee members, citywide officers, and managerial personnel in local businesses.[8] Athletics transformed the community.

This idea that athletic training could be a force for belonging and unification in the Christian life of faith did not originate in the 1930s. New Testament authors in the first and second centuries creatively drew upon images of athletes and athletic victory to help audiences envision what is required to form and sustain a cohesive community. Pauline epistles describe the ideal Christ-believer figuratively: she is a disciplined, upstanding athlete, competing in a contest of cosmic proportions and hoping to achieve spiritual victory alongside her fellow believers. The metaphorical New Testament athlete, competing for a crown of salvation, both reflects and challenges aspects of the wider cultural context. The Pauline athletic metaphor takes on double duty in carving out a hybrid space for the Christ-believers to belong. It may overturn cultural expectations of athletes and competition or galvanize the believers to transform themselves.

After examining the use of athletic metaphors in the New Testament Pauline epistles in chapter 1, I will turn in chapter 2 to a later moment in Christian history: the third and fourth centuries. Identifying distinctive features of the Christian experience in that period, I will analyze how changed cultural context affected interpretation of the Pauline athletic imagery and its power for creating belonging in Christian community. Finally, I will introduce a few case studies from the contemporary United States and address potential directions for understanding practical implications for today's U.S. Christian churches.

Chapter 1

RUNNING THE RACE

THE IMAGE IN THE UNDISPUTED PAULINE EPISTLES

From his position in prison, surrounded by members of the imperial guard, Paul writes to the early Christ-believers in Philippi. This Greek city in Macedonia had come under Roman control in 148 BCE. After 30 BCE, Octavian (later the Emperor Augustus) reclassified it as a Roman colony and settled military veterans there. By the time Paul wrote to the Philippian *ekklēsia* in the late 50s or early 60s CE,[1] the city was populated by native Macedonians, the descendants of Roman veterans, and Greeks. Local diversity was reflected in the presence of various religious groups, including Jews, Greek and Roman polytheists, and some Christ-believers. Paul offered words of encouragement to the community of Christ-believers he had helped to found, exhorting them to face struggles that would come their way and strive together on behalf of the gospel:

> Live your life in a manner worthy of the gospel of Christ, so that, whether I come and see you or am absent and hear about you, I will know that you are standing firm in one spirit, striving side by side with one mind for the faith of the gospel, and are in no way intimidated by your opponents. For them this is evidence of their destruction, but of your salvation. And this is God's doing. For he has graciously granted you

> the privilege not only of believing in Christ, but of suffering for him as well—since you are having the same struggle that you saw I had and now hear that I still have. (Phil 1:27–30)

Though it is not evident in the NRSV English translation quoted above, Paul is drawing on a multivalent athletic metaphor to characterize the Philippians' ideal behavior.

He connects the Christ-believers' tasks of daily living to a larger struggle for salvation using the image of athletic competition. Paul invites the Philippians to "strive together" using the verb *sunathleō* (1:27). The prefix *sun-* ("together, with") is attached to *athleō*, the verb for competing in an athletic contest. In Paul's imagination the Philippians' striving is an athletic feat that prepares them for military-style success against enemies. They are to be teammates, cooperating to defeat their opponents or to achieve a common goal. Paul's readers in the first-century Mediterranean world would have been familiar with the idea of athletes striving to defeat opponents in the context of some larger struggle. Lucian of Samosata (ca. 125–post 180 CE), a Greek satirist living in the Roman Empire, captured the way Greeks thought about athletics and warfare. He wrote an imagined dialogue between two figures of the sixth-century BCE *Anacharsis.* Solon the famous Greek wise man answers questions posed by Anacharsis, a foreigner who observes Greek youths exercising in the gymnasium and wonders why they are wasting their time with such foolish pursuits. Anacharsis is particularly disgusted by the wrestlers wallowing in the mud. However, in response to Anacharsis's disdain, Solon insists that the young men are in fact preparing to defend their cities in battle. While practicing the physical skills that will make them ready for warfare, they are also learning the discipline that will allow them to work together and engage in difficult pursuits with both individual and collective excellence.[2]

Paul similarly highlights the importance of competing together rather than fighting against one another. The togetherness embedded in the verb *sunathleō* is a feature of this letter, with Paul applying the *sun-* prefix twelve times to eight nouns or verbs.[3] Later in the letter, he insists that communal efforts can prevent or repair harmful divisions in the community. He notes that two women who are leaders in the city's *ekklēsia*, Euodia and Syntyche, have distinguished themselves by their act of striving together with Paul. Their past cooperation is held up as a model for their future behavior. The two women have supported

Paul's missionary evangelizing efforts through prayer, financial means, and active imitation. This complex of activities he calls "the work of the gospel" (Phil 4:3). If there has been some rift or disagreement between them,[4] the larger context of their shared struggle should remind them to "be of the same mind in the Lord" (Phil 4:2).

Paul exhorts all members of the Philippian assembly to "be of the same mind," recommending a sort of internal training or conditioning and shifting attention from physicality to internal disposition (Phil 2:1–2). This shift, too, had precedents in first-century literature and society. In particular, Stoic philosophers used athletic images and the concept of discipline to describe how a person could gain control of their passions, those drives that can either lead to impulsive behavior or can be governed by the rational mind. Troels Engberg-Pedersen has convincingly demonstrated that Paul's use of athletic imagery and the *agōn* motif closely echoes Stoic usage.[5] Seneca, a Roman contemporary of Paul, reflects on endurance as a moral virtue common to athletes and gladiators, one that they actively employ in their training.[6] The famous Stoic philosopher Epictetus, a man formerly enslaved, and Philo, an Alexandrian Jewish philosopher, both employ athletic metaphors to describe self-discipline and ways of cultivating moral excellence. Philo emphasizes the role of Jewish law and Scripture as guides for the athlete in training. As Robert Paul Seesengood points out, from a postcolonial perspective it should not surprise us that scholars and thinkers like Epictetus, Philo, and Paul, who likely felt displaced or disconnected from the structures of Roman imperial power, nevertheless used the language and images of the dominant society to describe themselves and their ideals. As he puts it, "Can it be coincidental that those with threatened or ambiguous cultural identities are those who choose metaphors rooted in competition in order to demonstrate or articulate a desire for an integrated community?"[7] Paul applies athletic imagery in an ethical and spiritual context, artfully rendering his teachings legible to a broad swath of society while simultaneously inviting his audience to reconsider the value of athleticism.

In the Letter to the Philippians, the appeal to train the thoughts precedes the famous hymn about Christ's humiliation and exaltation, implying that the shared mind is a mindset or attitude of humility that would enable members of the community to prioritize care for others over concern for the self.[8] Like athletes, they should condition their thoughts to work together. Community leaders like Euodia and Syntyche are clearly meant to focus on their shared experience of Christ's love and of the Spirit. They are to be united in faith and thereby empowered for the challenging work of sustaining community.

Paul emphasizes in Philippians 1:30 that the Christ-believers are not struggling alone but are joining in an ongoing contest that he began and that he continues alongside them. The "struggle" the Philippians share with Paul is an *agōn*. This Greek term refers to a competition, contest, race, or fight. It was often used in a literal sense to describe athletic contests in which athletes could prove their mettle. In this letter, Paul speaks of a figurative *agōn* in an attempt to explain that there is something important at stake for Christ-believers living in community. Those who are called to see themselves as athletes engaged in the contest are providing evidence of their fellowship with Christ, the source of salvation (Phil 1:28).

In other letters, Paul indicates that the contest is public. Paul blends the language of athletic discipline and gladiatorial spectacle, carving out a place for Christ-believers in Greco-Roman discourse about competition and victory.[9] He writes to the Corinthians that "God has exhibited us apostles as last of all, as though sentenced to death, because we have become a spectacle to the world, to angels and to mortals" (1 Cor 4:9). The word *spectacle* (Greek *theatron*) is a term that also commonly referred to a space where entertainment, performances, and spectacles happened, such as a Roman arena. Gladiatorial fights were also identified as "spectacles." Contrary to today's popular representations, gladiators were seldom killed in the arena, although they were sometimes pressed into service to kill prisoners. These professional athletes were specially trained in ritualized forms of fighting, using specific combinations of weapons and armor, and gladiators were organized into classes based on skill.[10] The gladiator's trainer or *lanista* earned money for each bout and could exact a high price if a gladiator were seriously injured or killed in a show fight. Many gladiators who frequently won their contests gained celebrity status. There were a few female gladiators, a fact partly brought to our attention by the Emperor Septimius Severus, who issued a decree in 200 CE banning them.[11] For the most part, these publicly visible and publicly acclaimed athletes were male, and their performance in public spectacles and games was a popular form of entertainment. In Paul's interpretation, the Christ-believers also undertake their struggle on a public stage, before worldly and supernatural eyes.

The Philippians must be prepared for opposition when they enter their contest. What sorts of real opposition would Christ-believers have faced in a Roman city? In Philippi, a city with strong ties to the Roman military, opposition likely entailed pressure to participate in various forms of Roman civic cult. All citizens of the empire were encouraged to sacrifice to the gods, especially to the Capitoline triad of Jupiter, Juno, and Minerva. Such sacrifices would curry divine favor and help to ensure protection and prosperity for all the empire's citizens and subjects. Even if Christ-believers did not perform or subsidize the sacrifices, they might have been urged to participate in communal meals that used the meat of the sacrificial victims or to purchase such meat in the public market.[12] Some participation in the imperial cult was probably also expected. Away from the imperial center at Rome, many communities practiced a form of emperor cult that involved active worship of the living emperor. For monotheistic Christ-believers, all of these routine civic activities would have constituted idolatry. Unlike the Jews who had a long-established religion and were therefore granted exemptions, the novel cult around Christ was considered a form of superstitious atheism, and Christians may have experienced pressure or even punishment for failing to participate. An athlete's self-discipline and strong community support would be required to remain faithful in this environment.

Paul promises that faithfulness will be rewarded. He describes the Christ-believers' heavenly reward in 1 Corinthians, where he equates the athlete running in a race with a person entering a contest (*agōnizomai*) and competing for a prize (Greek *brabeion*) (1 Cor 9:24–25). Paul refers both to a general prize and specifically to the "crown" (Greek *stephanos*) that the victor in a literal athletic contest would receive. In the Greek and Roman regions of the Mediterranean, crowns were indeed awarded for athletic excellence. The crowns were often woven from leaves of plants associated with various deities: olive for Athena/Minerva, myrtle for Aphrodite/Venus, laurel for Apollo and Dionysus/Bacchus. Some crowns were more permanent, made from gold or bronze. Victors in the Olympian games would earn these crowns, which served as symbols of glory and success, and public lists of victors in the Olympic and Isthmian games are still extant. Emperors and military commanders were crowned as part of the triumphal celebration, acknowledging their victory. Crowns could also be awarded to civic benefactors to reflect their honor, a form of social capital in the Greco-Roman world; as J. R. Harrison points out, this practice was one way of creating incentives for wealthy elites to provide for their fellow citizens.[13] It also reflects the omnipresence of an agonistic lens through which many people in the Roman Empire viewed all their communal endeavors. Paul's images of crowned athletes would have been very familiar to his early readers because of public crowning ceremonies that took place in civic centers, and because crowns and wreaths decorated civic monuments to emperors, athletes, and local benefactors.

Given the glory, honor, and public reputation associated with crowns, Paul's use of the image conveys that the stakes in the Christ-believers' contest are high, and the competition is accordingly fierce. Paul asks the Corinthians, whose city regularly hosted the Isthmian games, "Do you not know that in a race the runners all compete, but only one receives the prize? Run in such a way that you may win it" (1 Cor 9:24). By promising that their efforts will be rewarded, he reinforces the exhortation he offers to his readers to stay the course. Endurance or perseverance is an essential quality for the Christian athlete.

Paul recommends endurance throughout his letters, noting for the Corinthians that the testing they undergo is overseen by God, and "he will not let you be tested beyond your strength, but with the testing he will also provide the way out so that you may be able to endure it" (1 Cor 10:13). The test, a *peirasmos*, is literally a trial that requires Christ-believers to *hypopherō*, bear up or endure. The *peirasmos* here is set by God, but the term can also refer to an instance of temptation or to an attempt to learn about someone or something. The implication in 1 Corinthians is perhaps that the athletic competition will reveal a deeper truth about the steadfastness and character of the Christ-believers. Their fundamental character is of the utmost importance.

One effect of focusing on character is greater democratization and the potential for increasing belonging.[14] Athletes' bodies in the ancient world were gendered bodies, an observation that is significant for our understanding of the athletic metaphor in the Pauline epistles and how this metaphor might have signified for women among Paul's earliest readers. In classical Greek city-states, athletes were male, members of the elite classes who received athletic training as part of their education. Their training took place in the gymnasium, a space named for the fact that those training were *gymnos*, or nude. When involved in athletic pursuits, then, male bodies were on display, participating in a public performance of Greek masculinity. Evidence from ancient art (paintings on pottery, mosaics, and frescoes) reinforces what we read in classical texts: the ideal body was athletic and male.

Since victory in the Pauline sense does not depend on actual physical bodies and the limits placed on them by Roman society, individuals excluded from real athletic contests, like women and slaves, may nevertheless participate in this Christian competition. For the Pauline crown is not an earthly but an eschatological prize. It will be given to the victors on the Day of the Lord (1 Thess 5:2) or the Day of Christ (Phil 2:16).[15] The Day of the Lord is shorthand for the time of final judgment (e.g., Isa 2:9–19), a complex idea in the Hebrew Bible and noncanonical Jewish literature, especially from the second temple period. Paul's references to the Day of the Lord reflect a particular strain of early Christ-believing eschatology that equates the final judgment with the Parousia, or second coming of Jesus. The Greek term *parousia* is an equivalent of the Latin *adventus*. It is literally an "arrival," and the term was used to refer to the festive occasion when an emperor or ruler would make a formal state visit to a city or region and be welcomed by a delegation of local leaders. It could also be applied to the visit of an imperial administrator who was arriving to make announcements, bestow favors, or enact Roman justice.[16] Picking up on the political overtones of the Parousia, Paul explains that Jesus's inevitable and impending return will signify the onset of the final judgment. At this point, the wicked will face punishment and the righteous will be rewarded. Not all will be victorious, because the race is not actually against other athletes, but against vices, transgressions, and lapses that would lead to a negative outcome at the Parousia.

In light of that imminent final judgment, Paul informs the Corinthians that "athletes exercise self-control in all things; they do it to receive a perishable prize [*brabeion*], but we an imperishable one" (1 Cor 9:25, altered translation).[17] He argues from the lesser to the greater: If even an earthly reward can inspire people to commit to monumental efforts and virtuous conduct, how much more should the Christ-believers be inspired, knowing they are going to receive a heavenly reward? There is also an implicit critique here: Greek and Roman practices of crowning are empty and meaningless when compared to the reward that awaits Christ-believers.

The victory Paul envisions seems to belong to the community rather than a single individual. He insists in 1 Corinthians that the Christ-believers are all participating in a single race, with a single goal. This aligns with the case for unity he presents to Corinth, where there appears to have been an issue of factionalism or division between elites and members of the lower classes (1 Cor 11:17–19).[18] Elsewhere Paul describes the victor's crown as a prize he will accept on behalf of the community, insisting that his own success is contingent upon their collective steadfastness. In 1 Thessalonians 2:19, his ability to earn the crown depends on the conduct of the community he has founded. They will be the source of his joy and his crown (*stephanos*) at the time of judgment, which will furnish him an occasion for boasting. Paul also addresses the Philippians as "my joy and crown" (Phil 4:1). By claiming the crown that is a result of their labor, he appoints himself as a representative of the community and as their benefactor. His collectivist expectation only reinforces the sense that communal efforts and shared striving will determine the outcome for the whole group.

Like Paul the community's representative, an ancient athlete could become a focal point for corporate identity or public concern. As early as the Olympic competitions, athletes were celebrated as delegates of their individual *poleis*, with the victors bringing honor to their hometowns. In the imperial period, makeshift communities grew up around particular athletes or teams, like modern-day fandoms. For example, the archaeological record preserves lead *defixiones*, or curse tablets, wishing injury or at least defeat upon competing teams of horses and chariot drivers in citywide chariot races.[19] In the Christ-believing communities, to belong is to know that one's failures and successes affect other community members.

Ultimately, however, Paul teaches that the victory belongs to Christ because of God. Christ is the victor in every trial, even overcoming sin and death, and he shares that victory with the Christ-believers. In a shocking reversal of typical social expectations, however, Christ obtains this victory through his humiliating, shameful passion and death. That is, the terms of the contest are being rewritten. Christ also empowers his followers to compete in this upside-down contest and to obtain the reward, which is given to them by God through Christ (1 Cor 15:57). In Philippians 3, Paul writes that he himself is only able to continue striving to reach the goal "because Christ Jesus has made me his own" (v. 12). It is because of God's generosity that both Christ and the Philippian Christ-believers may be exalted. God graciously gave (Greek *charizō*) Christ an exalted position and glorious name (Phil 2:9), in the same way that he graciously gave (Greek *charizō*) the Philippians an opportunity to stand fast in their suffering (Phil 1:29). As Paul explains in Romans, God's election of the community "depends not on human will or exertion [lit. "running," Greek *trechō*], but on God who shows mercy" (Rom 9:16).

Although time is short and the contest is already happening, entering the contest requires preparation and training. Paul explains that the ideal Christ-believing athlete undertakes *askēsis*—training or discipline. This was a basic expectation in Paul's cultural context. As Cavan Concannon puts it, "Greek athletics were embedded in an ideology that focused on Greek concerns about beauty, the body, self-control, education, and agonistic competition."[20] The resulting body was athletic: it should have key external, physical attributes, yes, but these were thought to reflect on internal traits the athlete possessed. For example, athletes were to be well-muscled and toned, their care for their physical bodies indicating that they possessed exemplary masculine virtues of self-control and discipline.

Greek and Latin authors extolled the many virtues that could be gained through athletic training. Dion of Prusa or Dio Chrysostom (literally "Golden Mouth") was a renowned Greek orator who lived circa 40–120 CE.[21] Among his orations are two praising the famous boxer Melancomas, whose early death Dio views as a tragic loss. While praising Melancomas's physical prowess, the orator consistently remarks on the qualities of soul the boxer had obtained as a result of his athletic training and discipline:

> It was his good fortune to come of an illustrious family, to possess beauty, and, in addition, courage, physical strength, and self-control—things that are certainly the greatest blessings. But what was indeed the most surprising thing about a man is to have remained undefeated not only by his opponents but also by toil and heat and gluttony and sensuality; for the man who is going to prove inferior to none of his opponents must first be undefeated by these things.[22]

Not only is his physical success impressive, but his self-mastery is even more worthy of praise. Note that Dio Chrysostom implies a hierarchy of disciplinary achievements; first a man must master himself and his passions, then he can master external opponents. Paul seems to think similarly about a Christian's aiming at virtues. Learning to control oneself is a prerequisite for engaging external threats. For Dio

Chrysostom and for Paul, *askēsis* is the key concept linking the athlete to moral excellence.

Paul describes the transformative effects training has for the individual and the community. He recounts his personal journey through humiliation toward eschatological exaltation in Philippians 3, creating a parallel between his trajectory and the trajectory described in the hymn of Philippians 2. He encourages the Philippians to become imitators of him and therefore of Christ (Phil 3:17). Their collective *askēsis* will only bind them more closely together. At 1 Corinthians 9:25, he emphasizes the self-control, or *enkrateia*, that athletes must cultivate. Self-control is required to build each other up and avoid causing harm. Robert Paul Seesengood explains how this dimension of athletic discipline functions: "Athletic metaphors refer to the self-denial and struggle necessary for individuals to live in harmonious community."[23] For example, some members of the community may need to control or limit their own activities to avoid harming other members. When Paul writes about eating food that has been sacrificed to idols (1 Cor 8), he exhorts the Corinthians to recognize that their actions might create stumbling blocks for their fellow believers.

So although the cosmic *agōn* is against supernatural opponents, Paul points to an additional source of danger: self-sabotage. If the athlete does not approach his training and discipline with the proper seriousness, his efforts may be in vain (1 Cor 9:26–27). The human body with its desires and tendencies toward vice is also a site of athletic struggle. This seems to be an especially important message for the Corinthians, some of whom appear to have believed that their baptism and participation in the Spirit meant they were above bodily concerns (e.g., 1 Cor 8:9, 11–12). Paul describes his own approach as though he is a boxer, writing, "So I do not run aimlessly, nor do I box as though beating the air; but I punish my body and enslave it, so that after proclaiming to others I myself should not be disqualified." He echoes the concern about remaining in the contest in 2 Corinthians, where he employs the terminology of being "thrown down," used to describe the pin that defeats a wrestler (2 Cor 4:8–9). The point is maintaining the proper focus to avoid defeat. The Galatian Christ-believers, too, need to focus on the race at hand, which they "were running well," and not allow themselves to be derailed or tripped up (Gal 5:7). In Philippians, Paul attempts to reassure himself and his readers that "it is by your holding fast to the word of life that I can boast on the day of Christ that I did not run in vain or labor in vain" (Phil 2:16). Sustained, collective effort is required to ensure that the Christ-believers arrive at the Parousia as victors.

He expresses more anxiety about "running in vain" in Galatians, but this time because of divisions within the Christ-believing community (Gal 2:2). Paul says he had traveled to Jerusalem and presented there the gospel he was teaching to Gentiles, a gospel that allowed them to join the community of Christ-believers without undergoing circumcision, even though some Christ-believers considered circumcision a prerequisite for belonging. The letter seems to indicate that disagreement between Paul and some Jerusalem authorities had the potential to undermine his teaching, despite his conviction that the gospel he preaches has divine sanction.[24] He insists he did not need approval from leaders like Peter/Cephas and James. Nevertheless, cooperation was desirable so that his preaching would increase Jewish and Gentile unity rather than schism. The effort he expended to ensure that Gentile Christ-believers could achieve full belonging in the community is figuratively participation in a race; his evangelizing work is a part of the *agōn* that he undertakes on behalf of others.

The same athletic discipline that allows an athlete to remain in the *agōn* should also allow that athlete to cultivate single-mindedness and consistent adherence to the goal. In Philippians 3:13–14, he articulates a mission statement of sorts: leaving behind what has already been accomplished and achieved, he continues to push forward to the prize (*brabeion*) that still lies ahead. Although he has already gained much and created a number of Christ-believing communities, he recognizes that he cannot be finished with his evangelizing mission; it is, in his words, better for him to remain so that he may offer support and exhortation to the Christ-believers (Phil 1:24–25). Although elsewhere Paul talks about becoming all things to all people for the sake of the gospel, when the choice is between the gospel and personal gratification, the gospel must take priority.

Weaving together all these images and qualities associated with the ancient athlete, the authentic Pauline epistles fashion a web of meaning, creating multiple points of entry into the Christ-believing community for ancient readers. He consistently calls upon these figurative athletes to keep their larger goals in mind and to cooperate with one another. He offers opportunities to participate in training and takes on the role of a coach urging teammates to look ahead to the eternal consequences that accompany their current struggle. As a leader of the community, he invites the Christ-believers to draw inspiration from their shared experience of Paul's own striving and his willingness to exert himself on their behalf. They are to follow his example as he himself follows the example of Christ. They must participate daily in the cultivation of qualities like courage, endurance, and self-discipline to achieve their aim: the crown of victory that is salvation.

THE METAPHOR IN OTHER EPISTLES ATTRIBUTED TO PAUL

The Pastoral Epistles pick up the athletic imagery and develop it in a slightly different direction, specifically applying the language of an athlete's struggle to leaders in the growing *ekklēsia*. In the early second century, the Pastor is responding in part to what has become increasingly apparent among the Christ-believers: Jesus has not yet returned, the Parousia has been delayed. While Paul appears to have expected that the Day of the Lord was imminent and the eschatological prize or crown would be conferred upon Christ-believers soon, the Pastor must encourage the figurative Christ-believing athletes not just to strive but to sustain their efforts. While earlier assemblies could justify separating themselves from the ordinary operations of society, long-term resistance of the status quo is more challenging and more costly. Leaders appointed in the community also need encouragement because they serve as guides, exemplars, and enforcers. The Pastor indicates that athletic endurance is needed in order to maintain the communities of Christ-believers as they acclimate to being a Church in the world yet not entirely of the world.

In 1 Timothy, the Pastor exhorts Timothy to perform well in the ongoing struggle. He specifically uses the verb form of *agōn* to describe the young leader's efforts: "But as for you, man of God, shun all this; pursue righteousness, godliness, faith, love, endurance, gentleness. Fight [*agōnizou*] the good fight [*agōn*] of the faith; take hold of the eternal life, to which you were called and for which you made the good confession in the presence of many witnesses" (1 Tim 6:11–12). Here the Pastor picks up the Pauline image of the Christian athlete as spectacle, competing in the public view. Timothy is meant to reject false teachings and their associated practical ills, such as pursuing wealth and denying one's faith (1 Tim 6:3–10). The Pastor mentions making a "good confession" (*homologia*) before witnesses, referring to a profession of faith or acknowledgment of his identity as a Christ-believer.[25] Pointing back to Timothy's commitment to the faith and linking it to the athlete's reward of eternal life, the Pastor indicates that Timothy's effective leadership is fundamental to his salvation.

The letter indicates that endurance, Greek *hypomonē*, is a crucial quality for this leader. There is of course a need for patience and perseverance while waiting for the Parousia. The call to endure also implies the existence of hardships that must be put up with. The Pastorals mention several problems or obstacles that might present hardship for Timothy and the other Christ-believers. There are individuals who have turned away from teachings or practices that the Pastor considers proper (e.g., Hymenaeus and Philetus in 2 Tim 2:17–18). Their dissension is envisioned as sowing discord in the community and as leading the wrongdoers toward eschatological danger (2 Tim 3:1–9). The behavior of community members is also apparently a source of trouble, in the sense that some Christ-believers are drawing negative public attention to the group. Different constituencies, divided by gender, age, and social position, are instructed to conduct themselves in ways that will avoid public censure. The Pastor specifies that an *episkopos* (community overseer or bishop) "must be well thought of by outsiders" (1 Tim 3:7), women are forbidden from teaching (1 Tim 2:12), and young widows are censured for behaving inappropriately in public (1 Tim 5:13–14).

The *agōn* as envisioned by the Pastor has another dimension in 1 Timothy. Near the beginning of the letter, before launching into a set of specific instructions for community life, the Pastor writes in direct address: "I am giving you these instructions, Timothy, my child, in accordance with the prophecies made earlier about you, so that by following them you may fight the good fight, having faith and a good conscience" (1 Tim 1:18–19). Instead of *agōn*, the Greek term translated as "fight" here is more martial: *strateia*, Greek for a military engagement or campaign. As noted above, there was a close connection between athletes and soldiers in the ancient world, with many individuals engaging in both pursuits and a popular perception of athletics as preparation for military life. But what should we make of this athletic-martial overlap in the Pastorals?

The Pastor seems to be situating the Christ-believers and their athletic evangelizing efforts within a specific political and religious battle.

As Christ-believing groups grew and became more publicly visible, they may have experienced (or at least perceived) more public opposition from other members of their wider communities. In fact, around the time the Pastorals were composed (ca. 111 CE), the Emperor Trajan issued an important rescript that reflects imperial attitudes toward Christians. Pliny, who was from 111 to 113 CE the governor of Bithynia and Pontus in what is now northern Turkey, sent Trajan a letter inquiring about how to deal with accusations against Christians in his region. After a series of investigations that included the torture of "two female slaves who were called deaconesses," Pliny determined that Christians gathered for worship and meals did not appear to be doing anything threatening beyond participating in a "superstition." He nevertheless took issue with their regular refusals to sacrifice on behalf of the emperor and asked Trajan how to proceed when he received accusations that people in the area were Christians. Should he prosecute them on the basis of their religious identity, or seek out some other criminal justification? What if the accusations were submitted anonymously? The emperor responds by agreeing that Pliny should punish those Christians who refuse to recant their allegiance to Christ and who fail to perform public sacrifices to the Roman gods. However, he insists they be punished only on account of their actions, not on the basis of anonymous accusations. Accepting anonymous tips is, as Trajan puts it, not in keeping with modern times.[26]

Regardless of Trajan's measured and progressive response, it is entirely plausible that the Pastor and his community were experiencing local resistance or considered themselves to be in danger. The perceived opposition is presented in 1 Timothy as evidence of a battle that Christ-believers must engage in some fashion. The Pastor's use of athletic imagery around the *agōn* seems like his way of exhorting the believers to prepare themselves, through discipline, for endurance. In this later time period, that endurance is directed outward.

Timothy's athletic prowess and ability to endure are envisioned as different from those of an average Christ-believer. The metaphor here is specifically being applied to a leader in the *ekklēsia*, and he is presumably meant to set an example in the same way Paul had done. In the imagined scenario of the letter, the youthful Timothy's authority in the community seems to have been questioned by other leaders, perhaps especially those who are older. However, the Pastor insists Timothy's youth is not an obstacle, because he has been brought up with the wisdom of the gospel and the entire faith since his childhood (2 Tim 1:5). The letters themselves represent endorsement from the recognized leader Paul, much like contemporary letters of recommendation. Applying the image of athletic excellence to Timothy rather than all believers, the Pastor renders it newly and differently meaningful for a community where authority is concentrated in specific individuals rather than diffused, as in the undisputed Pauline epistles.

The Pastor associates athletic victory with living out one's faith properly or correctly. Timothy is warned that "in the case of an athlete, no one is crowned without competing according to the rules" (2 Tim 2:5). In the context of this letter, the Pastor, in the voice of Paul, is arguing for a single correct form of the gospel proclamation. The rules, then, are Pauline teachings, those that the Pastor considers authoritative. He encourages his young compatriot and fellow missionary to stay faithful to the gospel message he received, preserving the received tradition even in the face of opposition from competing teachers, other interpreters, and social pressure. By characterizing Pauline teachings as the rules of an athletic contest, the Pastor implies that variant teachings will result in a failure to gain the hoped-for eschatological reward. This is not totally dissimilar to the expectations outlined in the undisputed Pauline epistles. Both Paul and the Pastor are talking about the gospel as a unified message presented by particular teachers. Yet the Pastor attaches more specifics to the concept of "competing according to the rules," also building in comments about internal disposition and moral conduct.[27] The new setting, in which a second generation must take over community leadership, seems to have inspired the increased emphasis on competing lawfully.

If the rules are followed properly, the letter suggests, an eschatological reward is practically guaranteed. The Pastor applies the expectations or rules to his own mission by situating Paul's foundational missionary work within an *agōn*. Writing as Paul, he says, "I have fought the good fight, I have finished the race, I have kept the faith. From now on there is reserved for me the crown of righteousness, which the Lord, the righteous judge, will give me on that day, and not only to me but also to all who have longed for his appearing" (2 Tim 4:7–8). Note that here the author expresses certainty about receiving the crown that has been reserved, as though it is already earned. Linking the crown to righteousness, the Pastor demands that the believer conform to or imitate Christ, who is a righteous judge of the contest. This is presumably to be accomplished, as the rest of the letter describes, through adhering to right teaching and various forms of acceptable behavior, including particular models of leadership in the household and the *ekklēsia*. It must also involve actively combating other forms of teaching, portrayed in this letter as heterodox and dangerous (2 Tim 2:14–26). Most significantly, Christ's role has shifted. He is no longer sharing in the struggle with the Christ-believers, but he is the judge setting the challenge and assessing their performance.

One example from the Deutero-Pauline epistle to the Colossians highlights another familiar athletic image, with a twist.[28] Colossians 4:12 describes prayer as an agonistic act, saying that Epaphras the slave of Christ Jesus "is always wrestling in his prayers on your behalf, so that you may stand mature and fully assured in everything that God wills." This seems to stretch the metaphor beyond sense. Although athletes can represent their cities and regions, it is unclear how one athlete's wrestling allows other people to stand mature. Even the idea that an individual's self-discipline develops virtues that may benefit the community is not fully helpful here. Yet by highlighting prayer, the author shifts the *agōn* into a fully spiritual realm, where the athlete might indeed serve as a benefactor whose struggle bears fruit for members of their community.

EFFECTS OF THE IMAGE FOR EARLY AUDIENCES

Like biblical interpreters today, New Testament authors were drawing upon existing symbols and realities to communicate fundamental aspects of their religious belief system and to recommend a particular way of life for the burgeoning Christ-believing community. Within this wider cultural context, the earliest readers and hearers of Deutero-Pauline and Pastoral epistles likely accepted the use of the athletic metaphor as a tool for creating and sustaining a community. To "strive together" in an athletic contest, to join in a collective *agōn*, would have created a sense of fellowship and belonging among the Christ-believers, based on their internal disposition as well as their outward behavior. Whether they are sending Timothy, *episkopoi*, and deacons forward as representatives or stepping onto the field of play themselves, early Christ-believers could feel assured that their self-discipline would result in an eternal reward. Until the day of judgment arrived, their collective efforts at *askēsis* would bear more immediate fruits in the form of virtue, honor, and steadiness, and these desirable qualities formed the basis of a shared ideal vision for community life that might be respected by those outside the community itself.

Chapter 2

PUBLIC VICTORY

AFTERLIFE OF THE IMAGE: EARLY CHRISTIAN INTERPRETATIONS

Significant cultural transformations in subsequent centuries affected the interpretation of the Pauline athlete competing for a crown. In particular, shifting roles for Christian women and acts of violent persecution challenged theologians and interpreters to reconsider what it meant to belong to a Christian community. As new individuals and groups sought belonging and claimed space within the Christian *ekklēsia*, readings of the Pauline athletic metaphors changed to suit new circumstances and new needs.

ECCLESIOLOGY: A FORENSIC MODEL OF MARTYRS AS ATHLETES

Martyrdom provided one lens through which to view Pauline athletic metaphors of endurance and victory. Early Christian martyrs were frequently depicted as engaged in a dangerous *agōn*, one where the reward for victory was eternal life. This struggle took place in public, as a form of spectacle entertainment that subjected Christian bodies and beliefs to scrutiny. The martyrs are literally "witnesses" (Greek *martyres*) providing "testimony" (Greek *martyria*) to their faith in Christ. The title of witness is already figurative, invoking the forensic context of a courtroom and trial, where the martyr can be questioned, prosecuted, and punished on account of their testimony, but where the testimony also serves to amplify belief in the wider community.[1] Whether the trial scenes in martyr accounts are real or to some extent imagined, the authors frequently conflate the martyr-witnesses with athletes by drawing on athletic ideas of disciplined training, self-control, and exemplary endurance of hardships, even death. How did the experiences of and narratives about martyrs shape contemporaneous Christian interpretations of the Pauline athletic metaphors?

One early text, the *Martyrdom of Polycarp*, straightforwardly portrays its eighty-six-year-old hero as an athlete. Polycarp was a bishop in the port city of Smyrna (modern-day Izmir in Turkey). Tradition held that he was a follower of John the disciple of Jesus, the purported author of the Gospel of John. Most scholars agree that Polycarp lived circa 69–156 CE, though the church historian Eusebius records his death as occurring in 166 CE. The text itself is difficult to date, since the extant manuscripts are all quite late, from the tenth century forward, but scholarly opinions hold that its composition likely happened in the second or third century. According to the martyrology, Polycarp faced off against opponents in the arena, fulfilled his duty to his community, and endured physical hardship (torture) in order to achieve an ultimate victory.

Polycarp is tested in many ways during his trial and execution, but through it all he stands as a challenger who defeats every opponent. The main contest or struggle takes place in a forensic scenario: Polycarp, like his historical contemporaries, is encouraged to swear an oath of loyalty and make an offering to the *genius* of the emperor. Remember that sacrifices to the Capitoline triad—Jupiter, Juno, and Minerva—on behalf of the emperor were considered a means of preserving the safety of all citizens and subjects and were thus a standard part of civic life in the empire. Because he refuses, Polycarp is identified as an atheist, a dangerous charge that implied sedition and betrayal. Roman authority figures in the city come out against him and threaten him with death. The bishop displays key athletic virtues. He will not back down from the fight. He stands trial before a city official, who offers him every opportunity to swear the oath and make the sacrifice, but Polycarp remains steadfast in his faith, refusing to budge. As Polycarp enters the arena, a voice from heaven exhorts him to "be a man." This command, using the Greek verb *andrizein*, highlights one of the major traits associated with ancient athletes: manliness or manly virtue.

Famous female martyrs Perpetua and Felicitas of Carthage similarly demonstrate the athlete's singlemindedness and courage.[2] Though both are mothers, Perpetua leaves her infant son with family members to become a martyr, simultaneously turning down another family bond when she refuses her aged father's request that she return home. Felicitas, eight months pregnant in prison, prays for God to enable her to be martyred with her compatriots, and so she gives birth to her infant prematurely, two days before the planned execution. Lynn H. Cohick and Amy Brown Hughes point out that "defiance of conventional expectations for familial *pietas*, or faithful rendering of family obligations, is especially evident in the female martyrs' stories."[3] The singlemindedness of a female martyr stands out against the backdrop of the status quo, which expected women would care for family members within the household, stewarding family wealth and resources through making advantageous marriage alliances. In effect, these women illustrate an alternative form of familial belonging, creating for martyrs a community in which belonging depended not on blood or marriage but on a shared spiritual struggle, culminating in steadfast commitment and endurance.

Arena spectacle, which Paul references figuratively, is a reality for Perpetua. Before her contest with wild beasts, Perpetua experiences four visions that seem to reflect a Pauline spiritualization of her real ordeal. The first reveals that her true adversary is not a worldly opponent or a political oppressor, but the devil himself. Her vision, of a ladder that enables her to crush the head of a serpent and reach a shepherd who offers her refreshment, solidifies Perpetua's sense that when she enters the arena, she will be engaging in a high-stakes cosmic *agōn*. The fourth vision confirms that she will be victorious over the devil, represented in the vision by an Egyptian gladiator whom she defeats and on whose head she steps. In this vision, Perpetua records, she "became a man." This statement bears a striking resemblance to the command Polycarp hears to "be a man." Both martyrs' stories paint courage as a manly athletic quality, reflecting Roman cultural assumptions about virtue and gender. As Gail P. C. Streete points out, though, Perpetua bucks against gendered norms only to a certain extent. She displays a "feminine" concern for her modesty in the arena: "The woman with a man's courage, a male in her dreams, was used as a tool to promote bravery in martyrdom for both men and women, while at the same time preserving feminine decorum."[4] Emphasizing the internal, virtue-focused valence of Pauline athletic imagery helps Christians reading the martyrology make sense of this woman who is victorious in a stereotypically masculine space.

The martyr Blandina, an enslaved Christian woman violently tortured and executed in the Roman province of Gaul at the end of the second century (177 CE), is directly identified as a "noble athlete." Before the eyes of her torturers and the Christian onlookers (including those who later read the martyrdom), Blandina is transformed into Christ. The church historian Eusebius writes that through her endurance she demonstrates that, "small and weak and despised as she was, she had put on the great and invincible athlete, Christ; she had overcome the adversary in many contests, and through the struggle had gained the crown of immortality."[5] The cluster of Pauline images—athlete, contest against the adversary, crown, participation in Christ's victory—provide a template for interpreting Blandina's suffering and death.

According to the martyrological accounts, Perpetua, Felicitas, and Blandina literally embody and reproduce the passion of Jesus. Cohick and Hughes sum up the power of Perpetua's physical testimony in terms that emphasize her victory over death, a sharing in the victory of Christ: "Perpetua highlights the image of Christ victorious in his battle with death. In every case, the female body is the place where Christ shows his victory."[6] Although the ideal athletic body in Paul's time was male and masculine, women in later centuries could mimic the ultimate ideal body, Christ's, through martyrdom as *imitatio Christi*. In Streete's terms, martyrdom offered a sort of "equal opportunity" for men and women from different social classes, all of whom were empowered by Christ's example to participate in the cosmic struggle.[7]

Cohick and Hughes remind us that very few Christians were martyred in the second century, but "the image of the martyr became a key figure around which Christians explained their worldview and its opposition to aspects of Roman culture."[8] Even if the martyrs were exemplary but not really imitable, their stories were considered instructive. Candida Moss rightly points out that martyrdom can be seen as a set of discursive practices that render experiences of persecution meaningful.[9] The martyr's single-minded devotion to a Christ-believing identity lent her an athlete's self-control and enabled perseverance in the *agōn*.

A SHIFT IN THEOLOGICAL ANTHROPOLOGY AND BELONGING

As early Christian martyrologies illustrate, the Pauline metaphors recommending athletic *askēsis* as a spiritual practice could be applied to help make sense of corporal punishment. Athletic training in the Pauline corpus referred largely to internal conditioning, acclimating oneself to think of Christ and the community more than of oneself. Martyrologies put the spiritual athlete to the test in a forensic setting and reframed the individual struggle and search for salvation as a spiritually meaningful battle. This reinforced the emphasis on athletic training and preparation but moved away from collective and communal striving to center on individuals. Pointing to intense physical suffering or renunciation as the main ways a person could demonstrate their athletic discipline created a new way of thinking about Christian community but also set the bar for entry and belonging quite high, to some extent undermining the democratization of Paul's figurative athlete.

CONTEMPORARY CULTURAL CONTEXT AND NEW INTERPRETATIONS

Let us return to our initial consideration of CYO athletics, having thought more carefully about Pauline athletic metaphors and the afterlife of athletic imagery in the early centuries of Christian life. The application of this cluster of Pauline metaphors to a Christian community cannot be separated from cultural context. And the cultural context—in the parlance of biblical studies, the "intertexts"—evoked in a reading or hearing audience, may bring in transformative associations, for good or for ill.

At the time of its founding, the CYO drew on highly gendered stereotypes of masculinity to emphasize the claim that an athletic outlet was necessary for character formation.[10] The Reverend Gerald Scanlan, a CYO official, put it this way: "What we are endeavoring to do, is translate and emphasize through this sport [boxing], the fundamental advantages and requirements of clean-living, self-sacrifice and sportsmanship to equip our boys in the battle of life in their fight against the scourge of present-day indifferentism and the false standards of soft existence and easy money."[11] In a striking echo of Pauline Christian anthropology, Scanlan here insists that athletic discipline leads to the cultivation of desirable traits that improve the athlete's chances of prevailing in an *agōn* between Church and culture. Even contemporary scholars analyzing the CYO's history import agonistic language. In the conclusion to his chapter on Sheil, Neary writes, "The CYO *fought against* crime, bigotry, materialism, Communism, and secularism."[12] Another chapter in the book centers entirely around "The Fight outside the Ring: Antiracism in the CYO."[13]

Belonging, for Sheil the founder, hinged on a conscious cultivation of American pluralism. As Neary puts it, "Sheil's CYO exploited the appeal of mass popular culture, specifically sports and leisure, while at the same time invoking the language of Americanism to advance a civic culture based on communal values."[14] For Catholics in the 1930s and 1940s, those communal values included social action inspired by Pope Pius XI's papal encyclical *Quadragessimo Anno*. To justify increasing protections for the basic rights of workers and supporting social services, Chicago Catholics referred to a fundamentally Pauline model of a single Church body with many interdependent members (1 Cor 12). The interpretation of Pauline "body of Christ" metaphors as calls for corporatism and racial justice, an interpretation espoused by Chicago Catholic leaders Mundelein and Sheil, were shaped by the historical climate: Franklin Roosevelt's New Deal program, increasing racial diversity in U.S. urban centers, and the rise of labor unions.

Today's CYO reflects our historical period. As of July 26, 2020, the San Antonio CYO website, under the heading "Evangelization," offers the following statement, which I quote in full:

> The Mission of the SA Archdiocese CYO athletic Program is to empower athletic leaders to animate gospel values in catholic youth Sports, encouraging young people to live as disciples of Jesus Christ.
>
> In a world that focuses on a win-at-all cost attitude, where professional athletes have moved from role model to entertainer, and when kids are just not having fun anymore, catholic youth sports should be offering more:

> A safe, healthy place to play, physically, emotionally, spiritually and intellectually;
> A place where lessons are learned in winning and lessons are learned in losing;
> A place where all are welcomed and respected for who they are, for what they can or cannot do;
> A place where Catholic gospel values, character, and faith matter;
> A place where GOD is present.[15]

The statement expresses concern for the character of participants and an interest in preserving play for young people. The statement also assumes CYO coaches and participants will ground their practices in a holistic view of the person and of personal formation. Intriguingly, the statement's authors have set the CYO view of athletics over and against the view of athletics in "the world," reflecting two assumptions: (1) professional athletes are celebrities rather than role models and (2) cultural values associated with sport stand in opposition not only to the preferred view of athletics, but to Christian discipleship.

Instead of adopting a wholly negative view of contemporary U.S. athletics, perhaps modern Christian institutions, organizations, and people of faith can seek out fruitful resonances and dissonances between our perception of sports or athletes and the Pauline invitation to be athletes competing for a crown. Where can our own cultural context facilitate reflection on community life and ways of belonging, with each other and in the world? In what follows, I propose some possibilities.

COLIN KAEPERNICK

Athletes in the contemporary United States have a range of experiences that both overlap with and differ significantly from the experiences of athletes in the first century CE. Perhaps most strikingly, athletes in contemporary society garner a level of attention and public scrutiny that is unmatched by anything in the ancient world. Social media accounts and a rapid news cycle provide the public with an illusion of uninterrupted access to highly personal details of these athletes' lives. The public visibility comes with a conflicting set of expectations.

Athletes should be community minded, philanthropic, and socially engaged role models, while at the same time remaining unobjectionable and nonconfrontational, "staying in their lane" of sport.

To protest police shootings of unarmed Black men, NFL player Colin Kaepernick of the San Francisco 49ers took a seat while the U.S. national anthem was played before a game. Subsequently he began kneeling during the anthem, and other players picked up the symbolic action as a sign of solidarity. Immediately, news outlets and celebrities began commenting on the act of protest. Responses to Kaepernick's protest were mixed, but different constituencies in society reacted immediately and with strong emotion.

Other professional and amateur athletes also began kneeling in protest. High school and elementary school players adopted the practice in various cities throughout the country. Some active duty military personnel and veterans objected to Kaepernick's kneeling as a challenge to patriotism, while others defended players' rights to free speech and protest. Even the then president, Donald Trump, offered an opinion, suggesting that players who did not show their support for the flag and military personnel should be fired.[16] In the aftermath, the NFL instituted new rules that require players who are on the field to stand for the playing of the anthem. If players violated this rule, the team would be fined, and coaches and team owners were free to pass the fine along to individual players. Some players chose to remain in the locker room while the anthem was played, but kneeling on the field subsided during NFL games. February 2019 conversations among players and civil rights groups pointed out that players might be able to contest these rules on the grounds that they violate players' rights to organize and threaten the bargaining power of unions.

After George Floyd, a Black man, was killed by police in May 2020, a national outcry reignited the NFL debate. Ten days after Floyd's death, a group of Black NFL players released a video statement identifying themselves as the NFL and requesting that the NFL "condemn racism and a systemic oppression of Black people…[and] admit wrong in silencing our players from peacefully protesting."[17] In what appears to have been a response to the players' video, Roger Goodell, the NFL commissioner, issued a June 5, 2020, statement that made a striking reversal. Goodell used the NFL Twitter account to circulate a video of himself, in which he said the following: "We, the National Football League, condemn racism and the systematic oppression of Black people.

We the National Football League admit we were wrong for not listening to NFL players earlier and encourage all to speak out and peacefully protest."[18] The statement received mixed reviews, which is perhaps unsurprising.[19] Others criticized Goodell for not going far enough, noting that he had not apologized to Colin Kaepernick; a Harris poll of one thousand people, conducted the week of June 7, indicated that 61 percent of Americans thought Goodell owed Kaepernick an apology.[20] As protests about Floyd's death continued into a fourth week throughout the nation, Goodell gave a June 15th ESPN interview in which he said he would support any team that wanted to sign Kaepernick.[21] On July 7, 2020, Kaepernick signed a contract with Disney, the parent company of ESPN, to produce various forms of content that explore issues of racial justice. Kaepernick's protest, the initial public backlash, and a subsequent shift to growing public support raise a number of important questions about expectations placed on athletes in the United States. A question Neary posed about the CYO remains relevant here: "How important were sports to race relations?" He writes that "throughout the twentieth century, sports repeatedly symbolized and dramatized issues of race relations and racial justice, particularly for African Americans."[22] When professional athletics are inseparable from questions of racial justice and human dignity in our nation, Pauline metaphors about human endurance and the cultivation of virtue can take on new valence.

In U.S. Christian churches, there may be a temptation to fall back on the Pastor's model of policing the behavior of ourselves and others in order to ensure that we are "well thought of by outsiders" (1 Tim 3:7). Who among us is currently enduring needless suffering—because of racism, sexism, ableism—and what can we who are comfortable do to make space for their belonging, even when it makes us unpopular with outsiders? When the figurative athletes in our own communities speak out for the sake of justice, causing discomfort and stirring debate, can we operate from a position that assumes they speak with courage and goodwill rather than malice? It is necessary for the Church as a community to recognize the struggles of the most marginalized as our own struggle, not as a side issue for others to handle. Part of white Christians' work toward racial justice and equity involves openly acknowledging and discussing the role of positionality and privilege in shaping our comfortable definitions of what it looks like to be Christian. That work will enable us to recognize forms of virtue forged in an *agōn* that not all of us have experienced alike. When we encounter a disconnect between the Deutero-Pauline call for good conduct and the Pauline call to prioritize what builds up the community even if it costs us (1 Cor 10:23), what texts do we choose to read and teach in our communities?

COMPENSATION FOR COLLEGE ATHLETES

While most people in the United States look to athletes to provide some benefit to the public, at least on the level of entertainment, we are less likely to take action on behalf of those athletes, to see ourselves as engaged in reciprocal relationship with them beyond basic monetary exchange. Recent years have seen increasingly public debates about college athletes receiving financial compensation. Those who favor pay for players note that colleges and universities receive highly lucrative endorsement deals and broadcasting contracts, as well as prestige and donations from wealthy alumni, without passing those benefits along to the young players. The National Collegiate Athletics Association (NCAA) sets limits on the amount of compensation (grants-in-aid) student-athletes can receive. Founded as the Intercollegiate Athletics Association of the United States in 1906, the NCAA was originally set up to deal with injury rates among athletes. In the 1950s the association's focus shifted to finances, specifically the increasing cost of recruiting players.[23]

The compensation these students typically receive, in the form of scholarships that cover some portion of tuition, room, board, and books, can vary wildly in actual monetary value, depending on costs at a particular institution. The scholarships also frequently do not cover the full cost of attendance, given additional school fees. While players are characterized as student-athletes and academics are ostensibly prioritized, the NCAA has set limits on a student-athlete's ability to transfer between schools, with penalties including having to sit out a year of game play. Nevertheless, because they are classified as students, college athletes are not protected by labor laws; they cannot organize to participate in collective bargaining. As Allen Sanderson and John Siegfried point out, students who play college sports are in an unusual position relative not only to professional athletes but to their college peers: "Student-athletes appear to be the only category on a campus where an outside organization (the NCAA) is granted power to dictate compensation and hours of work."[24] Additionally these students may experience limits on their ability to seek other employment and even their freedom of speech. Racial justice is also an important part of the equation:

> When thinking about who benefits from the current arrangements, it is worth remembering that the vast majority of star Division I football and men's basketball players are African-Americans, many from low-income families.... Lower-income (on average) minority athletes are "taxed" to provide benefits to other people who are overwhelmingly white and from higher socioeconomic strata.[25]

The NCAA maintains a monopoly on the professional prospects of student-athletes as well, by means of agreements with the NFL and NBA, which implement lower-limit age restrictions in their hiring practices, leaving young athletes who wish to play after high school with few alternatives outside of college.[26] A series of lawsuits from 2009 forward have reflected players' demands: to be compensated for the use of their likenesses, to be viewed as employees, and to be allowed to organize players' unions. One case, *O'Bannon vs. NCAA*, acknowledged in a 2015 decision that student-athletes' labor is a primary product in an industry of $11 billion per year and noted that the NCAA's activity violated antitrust laws, but nevertheless set a cap on the amount college athletes can earn (an appeal in the Ninth Circuit resulted in that additional compensation being rejected; students can earn up to the full cost of attendance).[27]

In October 2019, the NCAA announced their determination to allow college players to earn money from the use of their names and likenesses. On April 29, 2020, the NCAA Board of Governors issued specific rules to this end. Athletes can profit from their name, image, and likeness, in the form of accepting third-party endorsements or promotions. They still may not receive this profit in the form of compensation from their college or university, and school or conference logos cannot be used.[28] The new rules underwent review by groups representing all three collegiate sports divisions, and a working group from the NCAA was formed to interface with Congress to help ensure consistent applicability throughout the nation.[29] The new rules went into effect in July 2021 and applied beginning in the 2021–22 academic year.

U.S. Christians reading the Pauline literature might benefit from bringing a few insights from the experiences of college athletes to our interpretation: training is rigorous, its results benefit many, and those who participate in any form of *askēsis* require support. In particular, those whose efforts benefit the community deserve support from that community, even if it requires the community to reconfigure itself and its conception of authority. College athletes, whose efforts sustain a massive (and massively profitable) industry, are requesting ongoing compensation. Within church communities, we face our own issues of exploitative demands for volunteer labor. Meanwhile most structures of governance within the institutional church lack mechanisms for ensuring that those doing the work have fair and equal access to institutional power. When Paul (1 Thess 2:1) identifies himself as the representative of the community, the one who will accept the crown on their behalf, we should think of equivalents in our own churches. Who is receiving credit for collaborative work? Whose contributions are ignored, undervalued, or erased? On an individual level, how can we engage in corrective conversations with those who do not recognize or compensate the work of others? Can those of us with power step aside to make room for others or use our positions to advocate on their behalf?

FOOTBALL PLAYERS AND CTE

Concerns for players go well beyond issues of compensation. For a long time, the heaviest cost of the massive sports-entertainment complex has been borne by the athletes who suffer serious and life-altering brain injury. These physical burdens were not prominent in the public eye before 2004, but awareness of the problem has been increasing. One metric is cases of Chronic Traumatic Encephalopathy (CTE); this debilitating brain disease results in a buildup of Tau proteins in certain areas of the brain and has been connected to symptoms like dementia, mood swings, impulse control, and suicidal thoughts. It usually manifests years after the initial injury or injuries and is commonly found among military veterans and athletes.[30]

In recent years, more information about high incidence of traumatic brain injuries among professional athletes has come to light. Researchers at the VA-BU-CLF Brain Bank, housed at Boston University School of Medicine, found in 2018 that "190 of 202 football players (94%) studied who played in college or the NFL have been diagnosed with CTE. Among players who played in college but did not play professionally, CTE was diagnosed in 86% (57 of 66)."[31] A 2019 study by the Brain Bank, published in the *Annals of Neurology*, noted that increased time spent playing was correlated with increased risk of developing severe forms of the disease. This study examined the brains of 266 deceased former amateur or professional football players and found that only 16 percent had no evidence of CTE.[32] An important limitation applies to all these studies: findings at the VA-BU-CLF Brain Bank are based on brains that have been donated by the deceased or their family members, which means they come from a self-selected population who already suspect the presence of the disease.

Some working groups are seeking new ways to test for CTE in living people. One study involved injecting members of a control group and a test group with a marker that attached to the Tau protein, making it visible in a PET scan. The test group was made up of twenty-six former players, aged forty to sixty-nine. The authors noted in their *New England Journal of Medicine* article that abnormal levels of the protein were found in the players' brains in areas associated with CTE.[33] The study holds promise for being able to compare those with minor traumatic brain injuries to those whose injuries come from football, to more accurately assess the level of risk.

While new tests are being developed, concern for younger athletes is also rising, and there are public debates about the safety of collision sports for young people. In October 2019, for example, New York state lawmakers heard from various constituents about a proposed bill that would ban children twelve and under from playing tackle football, because of the high number of head injuries that can occur and may lead to damage, including CTE.[34] Even where laws are not in place, an increasing number of safety regulations at the league and school level aim to limit cases of head injury and concussion. Major athletic organizations have not only instituted new rules, they have also directed financial resources toward prevention, research, and care. As early as 2014, the NCAA offered $70 million to cover settlement costs in head-injury related lawsuits brought in the state of Illinois.[35] The NFL, too, has responded to medical findings: "In 2016, the NFL pledged $100 million in support for independent medical research and engineering advancements in neuroscience related topics."[36]

These athletes' injuries and our failure to protect them are part of our cultural context. These considerations can help us ask new questions when we read a passage like 2 Timothy 2:5, "And in the case of an athlete, no one is crowned without competing according to the rules." The rules of play in football benefit audiences but harm players. What existing or missing rules are causing harm to members of our broader community, and who benefits from the status quo? Within the Church itself, if we identify groups who are bearing an outsized cost, can we also explore policies or protections that can alleviate their burdens, leaving them free to experience the community as a place of welcome, not of pain or death? Perhaps we can explore our attachment to rules and the power dynamics they create in light of Paul's vision of Jesus in the *agōn*; Jesus reframes the very terms of the competition in Philippians 2:5–11, overturning cultural expectations about what victory and belonging look like. Are we willing to do the same?

FIGHTING DISCRIMINATION TOGETHER

Physical injury, denigration, and public disregard are not the only types of harm athletes experience. Discrimination on the basis of gender draws our attention to divisions within athletic communities, as well as opportunities for collaboration. Debates over whether or not to allow transgender athletes to compete on teams that align with their gender identity are taking place at all levels, from elementary schools to professional athletics.[37] Even when athletes are not excluded on the basis of gender, they often face other forms of gender-based discrimination. Despite increasing protections offered to women in college athletics under Title IX, massive disparities continue in amateur and professional sports leagues. Women in sport have made significant strides that illustrate the power of collective bargaining and of identifying themselves as members of a community of female athletes.

The U.S. women's soccer team has long been asking to receive pay and perquisites equal to what players on the men's team receive. To some extent, the disparity is due to a different pay structure for the men and women, which creates differences in base salary and game-play compensation. Another major difference can be attributed to vastly unequal

World Cup bonuses, a $400 million pot for thirty-two men's teams versus $30 million for twenty-four women's teams. Those bonuses are set by FIFA, the body that governs soccer worldwide. The U.S. Women's National Team Players Association filed a lawsuit against the national governing body, U.S. Soccer, in 2019. Their case alleged gender discrimination that violates the Equal Pay Act and Title VII of the Civil Rights Act. This step built on an earlier, stalled complaint five players had lodged with the Equal Employment Opportunity Commission in 2016, which had not yet led to any action. In May 2020, a federal judge rejected some segments of the players' lawsuit, most importantly their call for equal pay. On Judge Klausner's interpretation, the different pay structure the women's team had agreed to in their collective bargaining agreement meant "plaintiffs cannot now retroactively deem their CBA [collective bargaining agreement] worse than the MNT [Men's National Team] CBA by reference to what they would have made had they been paid under the MNT's pay-to-play structure when they themselves rejected such a structure."[38] Players have vowed to continue pushing for greater equality as some parts of the lawsuit focused on travel and hotel accommodations move forward, and they filed an appeal for the case to move up to the Ninth Circuit on May 9, 2020.[39] In September 2021, the U.S. Soccer Federation decided to offer the men's and women's players the same contract proposals, unifying them under a single collective bargaining agreement and pay structure.[40]

Female athletes in U.S. track and field have made significant strides to combat gender discrimination. Olympic track and field athlete Alysia Montaño published a *New York Times* op-ed and launched a social media campaign that put pressure on companies like Nike to ensure that female athletes with endorsement deals would receive uninterrupted sponsorship through pregnancy and early maternity.[41] Fellow highly decorated Olympian Allyson Felix similarly shared her frustrations with Nike's policies, including their refusal to contractually guarantee she would not be penalized if she did not perform at her best in months surrounding childbirth.[42] As a result of public scrutiny and outcry, Nike announced a new maternity policy on August 12, 2019, which would guarantee pay protections for eighteen months surrounding pregnancy.

These instances of collective organizing and coordinated action may chart a way forward toward greater gender equality in sports. And the athletes themselves think of their power and influence in collaborative terms. As soccer star Megan Rapinoe stated in 2019,

> We very much believe it is our responsibility, not only for our team and for future US players, but for players around the world—and frankly women all around the world—to feel like they have an ally in standing up for themselves, and fighting for what they believe in, and fighting for what they deserve and for what they feel like they have earned.[43]

Similarly, Felix described the reaction to her opinion piece in positive terms that noted she received outreach and support from others: "I think there's definitely a shared experience there, and I think there's power in coming together, power of the collective. I think the more voices that come out, you know, change is happening."[44] In early 2020, Montaño founded a nonprofit organization, &Mother, with Molly Dickers, to continue advocating for "a working world where mothers are supported as leaders and sought after as employees. Where the value of mothers in the workforce has become intrinsic such that new structural norms facilitate the needs of the modern family."[45] The organization has already advocated successfully for lactation spaces, childcare, and family-friendly housing options at competition spaces, including the 2020 Tokyo Olympics.[46]

The coordinated efforts and public campaigns happening in contemporary U.S. athletics might help Christian communities read Pauline athletic imagery with new eyes. Paul praises the Philippians for "striving side by side" (Phil 1:27) for the sake of the gospel. Today's Church can take real athletes as models for collective action, with an emphasis on *action*. Catholic social teaching, for example, demands we prioritize care for "the least of these" (Matt 25:40), the marginalized and underresourced in our world. Where can church communities take direct action to engage in real fellowship and cooperation with our brothers and sisters who make demands for full inclusion? Where might such action need to involve participation in legislative and judicial processes? Female athletes have demonstrated the power of individual stories to capture attention and inspire advocacy, even to create space for new communities where those excluded may belong; this power should be familiar to us who espouse a faith grounded in biblical stories. An important first action step is to welcome stories from voices that have been silenced in the Church. In the work of listening and advocating, we may discover the grounds of an *agōn* where we can strive side by side.

PERIL AND PROMISE: ATHLETES IN THE HOUSEHOLD OF GOD

These case studies highlight a few of the distinctive cultural expectations U.S. Christians who approach Paul's letters may hold about athletes and the struggles athletes face. In his own time and place, Paul marshalled a complex of athletic metaphors, grounded in real experiences of sport and competition at the time, to describe the discipline, cooperation, focus, and endurance that Christ-believers must cultivate in order to sustain a healthy community. Christian readers in the second through fourth centuries drew on slightly different facets of the athlete metaphor that enabled them to align their own lived experiences with some aspects of the Pauline message. Through interpretation and application, Christians rendered these metaphors meaningful in new ways. Today, the real experiences of athletes can help Christian communities in the United States identify opportunities to transition from the comfortable space of a spiritual *agōn* to spaces in which we take action alongside those who find themselves excluded or exploited. Reimagining ourselves as Pauline athletes, we can discipline ourselves to enter the arena on behalf of others, focus on a shared goal of living the gospel, and strive together by exercising community care. Who belongs in the contest and for whom can the contest create belonging?

Next, we turn our attention from athletics to another arena: the social realm of citizenship, status, and freedom. In exploring Paul's polarizing image "slave of Christ" and its cultural resonances from his own time to its reverberations in U.S. Christianity today, we will keep an eye on central questions about belonging, exclusion, and power.

PART 2

SLAVE OF CHRIST, CITIZEN OF THE EMPIRE

Power, Freedom, and Belonging

In the appendix to *Narrative of the Life of Frederick Douglass, an American Slave, Written by Himself*, Frederick Douglass offered a scathing and justified critique of American Christianity:

> What I have said respecting and against religion, I mean strictly to apply to the *slaveholding religion* of this land, and with no possible reference to Christianity proper; for, between the Christianity of this land, and the Christianity of Christ, I recognize the widest possible difference—so wide, that to receive the one as good, pure, and holy, is of necessity to reject the other as bad, corrupt, and wicked. To be the friend of the one, is of necessity to be the enemy of the other. I love the pure, peaceable, and impartial Christianity of Christ: I

> therefore hate the corrupt, slaveholding, women-whipping, cradle-plundering, partial and hypocritical Christianity of this land. Indeed, I can see no reason, but the most deceitful one, for calling the religion of this land Christianity. I look upon it as the climax of all misnomers, the boldest of all frauds, and the grossest of all libels.[1]

Douglass describes what he has observed and experienced, enumerating acts of violence and oppression perpetrated by slaveholders. He highlights instances of physical and sexual assault alongside insidious abuses like depriving enslaved people of access to education. The slaveholders who perpetrate these horrendous acts not only insist on their Christian identity but further insist that their very mistreatment of enslaved persons is in line with Christian teaching and scriptural precedent. Douglass remarks that he is judging the nature of American Christianity by observing and assessing its fruits. He clarifies, "I mean by the religion of this land, that which is revealed in the words, deeds, and actions, of those bodies, north and south, calling themselves Christian churches, and yet in union with slaveholders. It is against religion, as presented by these bodies, that I have felt it my duty to testify."[2] He appears to be drawing on a combination of gospel statements about how to recognize people who truly belong to God (e.g., Matt 7:16–20) and the idea of "fruits of the spirit," an important image in Paul's letters (e.g., Gal 5:22–23).

Douglass's argument that the Christianity of American slaveholders is not the Christianity of Christ likely appeals to contemporary white U.S. Christian communities who wish to distance their vision of the household of God from the slaveholding households of their seventeenth-, eighteenth-, and nineteenth-century predecessors. And indeed, most modern interpretations of Jesus's words in the Gospels tend to emphasize universalism, reconciliation, and the idea that Christ's sacrificial death is redemptive for all. Yet what Douglass calls Christian hypocrisy or false Christianity may actually be less distant from the Christianity of Paul than we would like to admit. After all Paul did not advocate for the abolition of slavery in his day, taking the institution of slavery for granted as a part of life in the Christ-believing communities of his time.

Generations of slaveholders pointed to the Pauline epistles as evidence that slavery was not only permitted but divinely ordained and entirely justified in Christian society. Paul's decision to return a runaway enslaved person to his enslaver featured prominently in arguments justifying the passage of the Fugitive Slave Law of 1850.[3] Other epistolary statements explicitly instructing slaves to be obedient to their masters were quoted in proslavery arguments and even in didactic sermons directed at enslaved Christians.[4] On an even more basic level, Paul's habit of proposing dichotomies to persuade his audiences to choose freedom over slavery, faith over the law, or life over death fed into some Christians' certainty that the phenotypic expressions of melanin, light or dark, had spiritual significance: "Such polarized color symbolism easily was identified with other Christian moral and ontological dualisms, that is, spirit and matter, mind and body, good and evil, God and the devil, being and nonbeing, qua 'light' versus 'darkness.'"[5]

The legacy of American slaveholding Christianity still reverberates in U.S. churches today, and the passages and teachings that earlier American Christians used to justify the institution of slavery are still held up as authoritative texts in today's communities. These fraught and dangerous texts include parts of the undisputed Pauline letters and other epistles attributed to Paul. These next two chapters will examine whether the Pauline image "slave of Christ," with its powerful initial impact and its damaging history of interpretation, can or should be part of the contemporary U.S. Christian toolbox for creating belonging in the household of God.

Pauline letters in the New Testament both address the realia of first-century slavery and deploy the figurative idea of slavery to Christ as a positive marker for belonging and authority within the Christian community. Chapter 3 will draw out how Paul's image "slave of Christ" might have been read and understood by his earliest audiences. While Paul appears to advocate for a spiritual enslavement that can overturn his readers' conventional ideas about power, rights, and social obligations, a closer study of the undisputed letters reveals that he does not envision overturning the historical institution of slavery. And later letters included in the Pauline corpus use the image in ways that reinforce the hierarchical divisions between free and enslaved members of the Christian community.

Chapter 4 focuses on the history of reception of Pauline teachings about slavery, real and figurative. Among early interpreters of the second to fourth centuries, the writings of bishops like Ignatius of Antioch, Gregory of Nyssa, and John Chrysostom are taken to represent a range of Christian attitudes toward the institution of slavery and ideas about Christian obligations to enslaved persons (themselves Christian or not). Homilies and letters by these theologians illuminate developments in theological anthropology and ecclesiology, both abstract principles and their real-world consequences in a hierarchical, institutional church. The latter part of the chapter examines ongoing phenomena that restrict the freedoms of individuals: wage slavery, debt bondage, and human trafficking. (How) can the Pauline image of a "slave of Christ" facilitate or obstruct belonging for the individuals who experience the oppressive impact of such systemic injustices? The chapter poses some essential questions for modern Christian communities that hold the Pauline epistles as authoritative texts while seeking to create genuinely welcoming spaces for oppressed and marginalized persons.

Chapter 3

SLAVE OF CHRIST JESUS

THE IMAGE IN THE UNDISPUTED PAULINE EPISTLES

One of Paul's shortest letters is also a deeply personal piece of writing, addressed primarily to a single individual and concentrated on a single issue. Paul composed the Letter to Philemon from prison, probably in the mid- to late 50s CE.[1] The opening offers greetings to Philemon, "dear friend and co-worker," as well as to Apphia, Archippus, and "the church in your house" (Phlm 1–2).[2] If the *ekklēsia* meets in Philemon's home, he is probably one of the wealthier members of the Christ-believing community in his city, Colossae (its population relocated to what is now Honaz in the twelfth century). At the end of the letter, Paul sends greetings on behalf of some people who are with him (Phlm 23–24); although he primarily addresses Philemon, by mentioning all these other believers Paul suggests the central matter is of concern for the Christ-believing community as a whole.

As Paul explains, the letter is about the possibility of reconciliation between Philemon and Onesimus:

> I am appealing to you for my child, Onesimus, whose father I have become during my imprisonment. Formerly he was useless to you, but now he is indeed useful both to you and to me. I am sending him, that is, my own heart, back to you. I wanted to keep him with me, so that he might be of service

> to me in your place during my imprisonment for the gospel; but I preferred to do nothing without your consent, in order that your good deed might be voluntary and not something forced. Perhaps this is the reason he was separated from you for a while, so that you might have him back forever, no longer as a slave but more than a slave, a beloved brother—especially to me but how much more to you, both in the flesh and in the Lord. (Phlm 10–16)

What might strike a reader first is the deep care Paul has for Onesimus. He is Paul's "child" and "heart," someone who has brought great comfort during a challenging time. Paul, who often writes from a position of self-assured authority, shows deference to Philemon, hinting that the man had found Onesimus "useless" and indicating that Philemon has the power to decide Onesimus's fate.[3] What is not mentioned until the final line of the passage is the reason Paul feels the need to appeal to Philemon on Onesimus's behalf: Onesimus is an enslaved member of Philemon's household, subject to the enslaver's whims.[4]

While Paul can suggest Philemon consider Onesimus "a beloved brother," all the language around the proposal reflects awareness of the real power dynamics between a slaveholder and an enslaved person. Indeed, the very genre of the letter seems to situate Paul as an *amicus domini* (a "friend of the master").[5] Onesimus is in a precarious position, and Paul seems to think sending him with this letter of recommendation and his apostolic approval could alleviate the hardship Onesimus might otherwise face. Hans-Josef Klauck has identified key elements of ancient letters intended to serve a recommending or mediating function, and he notes that emphasis on the strength of the personal relationship between the sender and addressee, and the sender and recommended, are commonplace in the genre.[6] This can help explain why Paul repeatedly inserts himself and his desires into the discussion.

The letter also reflects Paul's awareness of the financial stakes of Onesimus's situation. He urges Philemon, "If he [Onesimus] has wronged you in any way, or owes you anything, charge that to my account. I, Paul, am writing this with my own hand: I will repay it" (Phlm 18–19). As an enslaved person traveling without the consent or knowledge of Philemon, Onesimus could have been held responsible for the expense of his lost labor or any additional debts accrued. To drive his own authority home, Paul puts Philemon's feet to the fire, writing, "I say nothing about your owing me even your own self" (Phlm 19). Paul here seems to pit Philemon's personal and religious obligations to his religious patron over against his financial concerns as a slaveholder. In any event, the language certainly indicates that Paul and his readers shared an understanding of the negative consequences awaiting an enslaved person at the hands of an angry slaveholder.

Therefore it seems strange that at the beginning of a different letter, Paul poses the following rhetorical questions: "Am I now seeking human approval, or God's approval? Or am I trying to please people? If I were still pleasing people, I would not be a slave of Christ" (Gal 1:10, alt. trans.). Paul insists he is not compelled by the opinions of others but is motivated only by a desire to gain God's approval. So committed is he to God alone that he characterizes himself as a slave of Christ. It is clear he intends this to be a positive self-description. Given Paul's apparent awareness of the economic and interpersonal dangers that a real enslaved person like Onesimus would face, how should we make sense of his willing adoption of "slave of Christ" as a desirable figurative title for himself? Why does he extend the title as a mark of honor to other Christ-believers, like Timothy in Philippians 1:1?

Paul and his earliest readers all belonged to a society in which slaveholding and the forced labor of enslaved persons were major drivers of the economy, and the letters reflect this context.[7] The Greek term for an enslaved person is *doulos*, and it appears twenty-eight times in the letters attributed to Paul. A shockingly large number of contemporary English-language Bibles translate the term as "servant" instead of "slave" when it appears to be used figuratively. This translation choice obscures Paul's reliance upon slavery as a significant concept and may also distract readers from enslaved people's lived reality.[8] That reality was exploitative and destructive.

Slavery in the first-century Roman Empire involved many kinds of labor, both skilled and unskilled, both urban and rural. While some enslaved people in the position of *oikonomos*, or "household manager,"[9] might have been responsible for managing public affairs and household funds as formal representatives, the majority were denied access to and control of resources and had the lowest possible social standing. Peter Hunt explains that "a Roman noble may have kept a couple of highly educated, well-treated Greek slaves as status symbols and tutors to his children. But over a thousand slaves may have spent their lives doing hard manual labor on his farms scattered across the Italian countryside."[10]

With intersectionality in mind, we note that while no enslaved people had the right of bodily autonomy, physical and sexual abuses were particularly aimed at enslaved girls and women: "Even if they could not produce legitimate heirs, female slaves' reproductive capacity was useful, since they could regenerate the slave population and thus contribute to the increased wealth of the owner."[11] The common denominator for all enslaved persons is summed up in a quotation from Aristotle's *Politics*: "For anyone who, despite being human, is by nature not his own but someone else's is a natural slave. And he is someone else's when, despite being human, he is a piece of property."[12]

Individuals became enslaved persons in the ancient world in a variety of ways. Keith Bradley explains that the Roman Empire relied on four main sources for enslaved labor, with no one source ever emerging as predominant. Sometimes people were captured in the wake of war, or through piracy, which today we might best describe as kidnapping and trafficking. Infants who had been exposed due to a family's inability to provide care (for a whole variety of reasons) would often end up as enslaved persons. And reproduction within the enslaved population made Roman slavery a multigenerational system.[13] The modern scholar Orlando Patterson notes the additional and destructive dimension of natal alienation, or the fact that enslaved people

> lack all the other rights that other people acquire with *birth*: their claims on their parents, their relations with siblings, and their links with and prestige deriving from ancestors. In fact, slaves have parents and sometimes have siblings, children, and wives; they remain socially dead because they cannot acquire any such claims or establish any formally recognized relationship other than the subordinating relationship with their masters.[14]

To "be a slave" (Greek *douleuō*) would for Paul and his readers carry two major implications in regard to that relationship with the putative master or slaveholder. To be a slave is to be subjected to the control and demands of another, to be subordinate. The verb can also mean "to act or conduct oneself as one in total service to another," a more expansive definition that could be applied to people who were not literally enslaved.[15]

Paul does draw upon that expansive idea of subordination. Given that in Paul's context an enslaved person was subject to the demands of another's authority, it should not surprise us that when Paul does draw his readers' attention to the negative aspects of slavery, he seems to be focusing on people's attachments or commitments to various power structures that he sees as getting in the way of relationship with God. To be subordinate to something other than Christ is to be wrongly attached. In particular, he encourages the Christ-believers to think of a spiritual state analogous to literal enslavement. People might be slaves to sin, a condition with disastrous consequences: "Do you not know that if you present yourselves to anyone as obedient slaves, you are slaves of the one whom you obey, either of sin, which leads to death, or of obedience, which leads to righteousness?" (Rom 6:16). They can also be enslaved to "beings that by nature are not gods" (Gal 4:8), probably a reference to prior acts of polytheistic religious worship among Gentiles who have now become Christ-believers.[16] He goes on to discourage the Galatians from turning back to these "elemental spirits" (Gal 4:9). The phrase "elemental spirits," or sometimes "rudiments," as in foundational principles, is *stoicheia*, a Greek term that biblical scholars think refers to quasi-demonic powers that have oppressive authority over Jews and Gentiles alike. Paul even describes creation itself as "subjected" and in "bondage," in contrast to "the freedom of the glory of the children of God" (Rom 8:20–21).

Turning to the meaning of *douleuō* that signifies total service, we begin to see how Paul can imagine that the title "slave of Christ" is a positive designation for himself and other Christ-believers. For Jewish Christ-believers and those Gentile "god-fearers" familiar with the Jewish Scriptures, the title "servant/slave of God" (Hebrew *'ebed*) might have called up memories of honorable ancestors Moses and Joshua.[17] In his letter to the Galatians, Paul draws in particular upon another patriarch's story that would presumably have been familiar for many of his readers. In his retelling, each element takes on symbolic meaning, transforming the story into an allegory about aligning yourself with what will benefit rather than harm you (as Paul sees it). He recounts that

> Abraham had two sons, one by a slave woman and the other by a free woman....Now this is an allegory: these women are two covenants....Now you, my friends, are children of the promise, like Isaac. But just as at that time the child who was born according to the flesh persecuted the child who was born according to the Spirit, so it is now. But what does the

> scripture say? "Drive out the slave and her child; for the child of the slave will not share the inheritance with the child of the free woman." So then, friends, we are children, not of the slave but of the free woman. For freedom Christ has set us free. Stand firm, therefore, and do not submit again to the yoke of slavery. (Gal 4:22, 24; 4:28—5:1)

Paul understands the power of a good story, especially a story that could be put to persuasive use. As is his usual practice, Paul constructs a dichotomy, or a set of paired opposite concepts. Given a choice between slavery and freedom, he rightly imagines his readers will choose to identify themselves as free. The intended implication of this retelling of Genesis 16 and 21, of course, is that freedom is in every way to be preferred to slavery, a terrible condition that will result in hard labor under a heavy yoke and the inability to inherit. Any savvy reader will choose to "stand firm" and be free rather than becoming a slave! In this case, Paul relies on common knowledge of slavery's horrors and the assumption that no person would desire to be enslaved.

To the extent that Christ's saving death or the individual's Christ-belief frees a person from enslavement to these other forces, Paul and his readers might have seen Christ as manumitting human beings. Manumission was the formal process by which enslaved persons became free. It could be initiated by the slave owner during his lifetime or upon his death, in his will.[18] Rarely an enslaved person might purchase their freedom.[19] It effected a change of legal status. Under Roman law, the formerly enslaved person was newly classified as a freeperson, with new rights and legal protections but without citizenship. In very rare cases, as for the Greek philosopher and formerly enslaved Epictetus, manumission could lead to great upward social mobility.[20] More typically, formerly enslaved persons continued as clients of their former enslaver, who now served as their patron. Certain groups, like enslaved people who had committed a crime or who had served as gladiators, were limited in their social mobility, acquiring upon manumission not the status of freedmen, but of defeated foreigners.[21] In the case of some enslaved women who were manumitted so that their former enslavers could marry them, freedom came with a price. Although a typical Roman marriage contract allowed the bride to retain control of the property she brought into the marriage and to initiate divorce proceedings,[22] many formerly enslaved women entered into marriages without those rights.[23] Manumission did not always carry a guarantee that slavery would not enter the picture again; for example, the Senatus Consultum Claudianum of 52 CE decreed that the children of a free woman and an enslaved man might be enslaved, and the free woman herself could be socially demoted to the status of a freedwoman (as though formerly enslaved).[24] Paul, too, appears to consider a Christ-believer's newly gained freedom as partial or somehow tenuous, depending upon the believer's subsequent choices. He admonishes the Galatians: "For freedom Christ has set us free. Stand firm, therefore, and do not submit again to a yoke of slavery" (Gal 5:1).

The movement from slavery to freedom can be more or less complete in Paul's reckoning, depending on the passage, but it is always an undeniably positive shift. In Galatians 4:1–7, Paul lays out his argument that the new Christ-believers were formerly enslaved but have now become God's adoptive children and heirs. Paul explicitly acknowledges that "both, the minor and the slave, lack the capacity of self-determination"[25] and must "remain under guardians and trustees until the date set by the father" (Gal 4:2). In this section of the letter, Paul insists that the believers have gained a new and more powerful social status within the metaphorical household of which God is the head. As children they will eventually have the right to inherit and to exercise their own authority, something that would never apply to enslaved people. In Romans 7:6, the move from slavery to freedom is instead a symbolic rebirth: "But now we are discharged from the law, dead to that which held us captive, so that we are slaves not under the old written code but in the new life of the Spirit."

Having been freed from slavery to negative forces, Christ-believers are to think of themselves as slaves of Christ, proposing yet again a positive image of enslavement. Paul describes himself this way in Galatians, as we have seen, but also in the very first line of his letter to the Romans, where he is "Paul, a slave of Jesus Christ, called to be an apostle" (Rom 1:1, alt. trans.). He goes on to note that he and his coworkers have "received grace and apostleship to bring about the obedience of faith among all the Gentiles for the sake of his name, including yourselves who are called to belong to Jesus Christ" (Rom 1:5–6). By a sort of transitive property, Paul seeks to cultivate in others the same obedience to Christ that he himself models in his role as metaphorical slave. Indeed we see that he thinks others are or can become slaves of Christ. He and Timothy are both "slaves of Christ Jesus" (Phil 1:1, alt. trans.). The general principle is outlined in 1 Corinthians, where Paul writes, "For whoever was called in the Lord as a slave is a freed person belonging to the Lord, just as whoever was free when called is a slave of Christ. You were bought with a price; do not become slaves of human masters" (1 Cor 7:22–23).

How would the idea of being a "slave of Christ" facilitate belonging in the figurative household of God? To identify a person as the slave of someone else would have implied belonging in the sense of ownership. Several times Paul uses a formulation that could refer to enslaved persons as active and even honored members of the Christ-believing community. In his long list of greetings at the end of Romans, he includes "those who belong to the family of Aristobulus" and "who belong to the family of Narcissus" (Rom 16:10–11). In 1 Corinthians, he mentions "Chloe's people" as messengers who have alerted him to divisions in the Corinthian community (1 Cor 1:11). Remembering that enslaved people were considered the property of the slaveowners, perhaps these agents were enslaved. Yet they seem to be in a position with some authority and Paul trusts their word. Indeed, in the ancient world the power of an enslaved person was linked to and derived from the power of the slaveowner. So if Chloe was someone Paul trusted, he would also trust the enslaved people in her household.

On a spiritual level, such authority "transferred" from the enslaver to enslaved person makes it possible for Paul to treat the title "slave of God" or "slave of Christ" as a positive indicator of power. That is, this connection to an all-powerful God renders God's slave powerful. He even speaks of enslavement as conferring an "advantage" (*karpos*, literally "fruit") on the believer in Romans: "But now that you have been freed from sin and enslaved to God, the advantage you get is sanctification. The end is eternal life" (Rom 6:22). In perhaps the most striking application of the slavery metaphor, Paul indicates that Christ, too,

> emptied himself,
> taking the form of a slave,
> being born in human likeness.
> And being found in human form,
> he humbled himself
> and became obedient to the point of death—
> even death on a cross. (Phil 2:7–8)

Here Christ is enslaved to God, making God a slaveowner who demands total obedience. Noting that Christ becomes a slave when he takes on human form, Chris L. de Wet suggests "the fundamental principle in the hymn is that by becoming human, Christ himself became heteronomous [ruled by another, versus autonomous]—corporeal heteronomy is a condition of humanity in the hymn."[26] The implication is that all Christ-believers must become totally obedient to God, by choice. In the famous "Philippians hymn" (Phil 2:6–11), it is Christ's *kenosis*, or self-emptying, that leads to his exaltation at the hands of God, and Paul encourages his readers to imitate Christ's willingness to take on "the form of a slave" in order to advance God's glory (Phil 2:11).

The Christ-believers owe God absolute religious devotion and service. Paul praises the Thessalonian Christ-believers for having "turned to God from idols, to serve [*douleuō*] a living and true God" (1 Thess 1:9). He also envisions someone who serves as completing actions that support cooperative living in community. Those who "cause dissensions and offenses, in opposition to the teaching that you have learned...such people do not serve our Lord Christ, but their own appetites, and by smooth talk and flattery they deceive the hearts of the simple-minded" (Rom 16:17–18). On the other side of the coin, someone who "serves Christ is acceptable to God and has human approval" (Rom 14:18). In addition to acts of worship and right conduct, Paul seems to expect that the believers will have an attitudinal shift, telling the Romans, "Do not lag in zeal, be ardent in spirit, serve the Lord" (Rom 12:11). In their freedom, members of the Christ-believing community take on the service and devotion expected from enslaved persons.

In summary Paul purposely depicts leadership within the early Christ-believing groups as a form of slavery, marked by absolute loyalty to Christ. At the same time, Paul overturns conventional ideas of authority and power by making those who are factually enslaved persons into slaves of Christ, thereby elevating their status, and demanding that people in Christian leadership positions—whether literally free or enslaved—serve as slaves to the community.

Many scholars, ministers, and theologians have sought to defend Paul's apparent insensitivity toward real enslaved persons on the grounds that within a Christ-believing community, typical enslaver-enslaved dynamics are not meant to apply. After all, some say, Philemon is to consider Onesimus a brother (Phlm 16), and Paul famously writes, "There is no longer Jew or Greek, there is no longer slave or free, there is no longer male and female; for all of you are one in Christ Jesus" (Gal 3:28). Paul's use of the slavery metaphor could have helped the earliest readers envision a new kind of relationship for enslaved people and slaveholders within a Christ-believing community. If both free and enslaved persons fall under the ultimate authority of Christ and God, they might take on a more mutual view of obligation and relationship under Christ's authority. And some Christ-believing communities do seem to have put Paul's egalitarian vision into (limited) practice. The correspondence between Pliny and Trajan, often cited as proof that early Christ-believers were not a political threat to Roman society, also contains evidence of the treatment of some enslaved persons in the first century CE and in Christian communities of that time. Pliny tells Trajan that he has questioned "two female slaves, who were called deaconesses."[27] The fact that enslaved women could hold the position of deaconess, appointed to a leadership role in the Bithynian Christian community, appears to show that the Christians did not fully abide by the expected power structures of their time and location.

Yet the picture is not so clear, for Pliny also reports that he extracted their testimony through torture, a method he could not have used had they been freepersons or Roman citizens. Under Roman law, enslaved people could be subjected to coercive interrogation tactics that could not legally be imposed on citizens. The laws put very minimal limits on the torture of the enslaved, prohibiting only castration and holding slaveholders liable for instances of homicide.[28] Even a rank in the institutional hierarchy of the Christian community did not protect enslaved persons from heinous treatment in the justice system. In fact, Paul's topsy-turvy claim that leaders become slaves serves to reinforce the patriarchal power structure of the ancient Roman household, simply replacing the powerful human man at the top of the hierarchy with Christ. Along with Jeremy Punt, we may recognize in this patriarchal context the "ominous" nature of Paul's seemingly touching reference to Onesimus as his child, "considering that it was made in a world where an adult male slave's lack of honour and dignity was underscored by the perception of him as παῖς or *puer* ('little one' or 'boy')."[29]

Paul's claim to be a "slave of Christ" is undeniably metaphorical. He attempts to use the figurative enslaved person to restructure power dynamics within Christian communities. At various points Paul seems to hint at actual egalitarianism for free and enslaved persons within the faith community, but he never goes so far as to suggest that slavery as an institution should be abolished or that Christ-believers should make abolition a social goal. Instead, Paul turns the institution that caused real pain and suffering for a large number of enslaved persons into an image that he uses to outline his own ideas about devotion, submission, and affiliation. Whether this truly facilitated a sense of belonging for enslaved persons in the early Christ-believing groups is, unfortunately, a piece of history we cannot retrieve.

THE IMAGE IN OTHER EPISTLES ATTRIBUTED TO PAUL

Following Paul's usage of the title "slave" as emblematic of Christian devotion, the authors of the Deutero-Pauline epistles apply the title to various coworkers of Paul. Epaphras is a "slave of Christ Jesus" (Col 4:12, alt. trans.) who is called Paul's "beloved fellow slave" (*syndoulos*, Col 1:7, alt. trans.). In the same letter, the author speaks of Tychicus with a string of positive epithets: "a beloved brother, a faithful minister, and a fellow slave [*syndoulos*] in the Lord" (Col 4:7, alt. trans.). The new term "fellow slave" would indicate belonging in the same household, under the control of the same master. Like Paul, Tychicus and Epaphras are subordinate to Christ above all, and their devotion to Christ gives them authoritative status in the Christian community.

Actual enslaved persons are in view more frequently in these later letters than in the undisputed Paulines. From a sociological perspective, this affirms what we might have expected from a study of the Letter to Philemon: the early Christian movement did not engage in an abolitionist project, even when they realized the Parousia was delayed. When these letters address enslaved persons, the author(s) give instructions about conduct and attitudes, both in the household and before God. The enslaved members of the community are encouraged to serve (*douleuō*) their human enslavers as though serving Christ:

> Slaves, obey your earthly masters [lit. "lords," *kyrioi*] with fear and trembling, in singleness of heart, as you obey Christ; not only while being watched, and in order to please them, but as slaves of Christ, doing the will of God from the heart. Render service with enthusiasm, as to the Lord [*kyrios*] and

> not to men and women, knowing that whatever good we do, we will receive the same again from the Lord, whether we are slaves or free. (Eph 6:5–8)[30]

Not only is the real Christian household equated with God's household, but enslaved persons are to imagine that their service and devotion to an earthly *kyrios* is really service to Christ *Kyrios*. For those literally enslaved, metaphor and reality begin to merge. That is, the real domestic space and the figurative divine household are collapsed into a single location where enslaved people always owe service.

Yet the corresponding command given to slaveholders shifts attention primarily to the metaphorical enslavement of all believers, reminding them to treat enslaved persons well because "both of you have the same Master in heaven, and with him there is no partiality" (Eph 6:9). Colossians 3:11 reiterates Pauline teaching about a new social status for those who believe in Christ, where "there is no longer Greek and Jew, circumcised and uncircumcised, barbarian, Scythian, slave and free; but Christ is all and in all!" While a conceptual shift is encouraged, there is no language recommending actual steps slaveholders could take to create practical equality with the enslaved members of their households.

In the early second century, the Pastor deploys the figurative title "slave" as an honorific for Paul and his coworkers. Titus 1:1 identifies Paul as "a slave of God and an apostle of Jesus Christ" (alt. trans.). Pairing these two titles in the epistolary prescript, the Pastor sets the tone for the letter, which highlights the importance of devotion to proper teaching and the orderly management of households. Second Timothy 2:24–25 describes the most essential qualities for a member of the community, noting that "the Lord's slave must not be quarrelsome but kindly to everyone, an apt teacher, patient, correcting opponents with gentleness" (alt. trans.). Right conduct and right teaching are benchmarks for the believer-as-enslaved-person.

As in the undisputed letters, the alternative is to be figuratively enslaved to negative things. The Letter to Titus advises against being slaves to "drink," and bemoans a time when the letter's putative authors were "slaves to various passions and pleasures, passing our days in malice and envy, despicable, hating one another" (Titus 2:3; 3:3). The Pastor aims to keep community members from participating in vices, especially vices that could ruin the reputation of the Christians in the public eye (Titus

2:15, "Let no one look down on you"). Such attention to community conduct is a slight shift from Paul, who used the dichotomy between slavery and freedom to discourage alternative religious practices (Gal 4:8–9) or allegiance to sin and death (Rom 6:16).

In line with this concern for right behavior and decorum, we also find a more specific and decorum-focused guideline for slaveholders in the Pastoral Epistles. First Timothy forbids extreme mistreatment, namely "man stealing," using coercion or force to put someone into an enslaved position, on the grounds that this practice is "contrary to the sound teaching" of the community (1 Tim 1:10). Although cruel treatment may be outlawed, the letters absolutely do not envision equality for enslaved persons. In fact, 1 Timothy places the onus on enslaved people to protect the community from ill repute. The enslaved are to "regard their masters as worthy of all honor, so that the name of God and the teaching may not be blasphemed" (1 Tim 6:1–2). The author not only wields public opinion as a threat, he also suggests that it is an act of devotion to serve. Since the slaveholders are Christians, the enslaved "must serve them [masters] all the more, since those who benefit by their service are believers and beloved." While it could be argued that in the undisputed epistles Paul uses figurative slavery to render enslaved and free persons relative equals under the lordship of Christ, passages like this in the Pastoral Epistles show that within a generation the Christian communities have repurposed the image to reinforce existing social norms.[31]

It is worth noting briefly that the authors of the Catholic Epistles, which were never attributed to Paul, also reflect a similar early Christian use of "slave of God" and "slave of Christ" as positive titles. These authors call themselves "slave of God and of the Lord Jesus Christ" (Jas 1:1, alt. trans.), "slave and apostle of Jesus Christ" (2 Pet 1:1, alt. trans.), and "slave of Jesus Christ and brother of James" (Jude 1, alt. trans.). The Letter 1 Peter also addresses all Christ-believers with this admonition: "As slaves of God, live as free people, yet do not use your freedom as a pretext for evil" (1 Pet 2:16, alt. trans.).

The metaphorical title "slave of God/slave of Christ" is a ubiquitous honorific for members of the Christ-believing communities in the first and early second centuries. Paradoxically, self-identifying as a slave in this context indicates possession of authority and confers legitimacy. The title designates leadership and, in the later letters attributed to Paul, alignment with right teaching and right behavior. Its frequent appearance in the New Testament letters almost certainly reflects its perceived effectiveness for conveying to readers a clear understanding of the loyalty, devotion, and submission expected of Christ-believers in the divine household.

EFFECTS OF THE IMAGE FOR EARLY AUDIENCES

One major challenge scholars of slavery in antiquity face is a lack of the kinds of sources that would give us firsthand information about an enslaved person's experience of hearing the title "slave of Christ" held up as an honorific. Peter Hunt, in his 2018 book, *Ancient Greek and Roman Slavery*, sums it up clearly:

> Ideally, scholars of ancient slavery would have copious evidence by masters and by slaves, both male and female, as well as by people who were neither masters nor slaves. The most obvious bias in our surviving evidence, however, is that wealthy men, slaveholders almost without exception, produced virtually all of it. In their writing, they occasionally reveal their thoughts about slavery in general and about their own slaves in particular. They sometimes even represent the lives and words of slaves: for example, slaves play important roles in Greek tragedies. But it was wealthy free men who wrote these plays. Rarely do we hear directly from women and almost never from slaves themselves.... This bias in our sources makes it hard to avoid a top-down view of ancient slavery and limits our insight into slaves' perspectives or the active role slaves sometimes played in shaping their lives.[32]

In biblical interpretation, the same problem holds. The authors of the New Testament epistles are not, to the best of our knowledge, enslaved persons, and so the attitudes of people like Paul and the Pastor toward literal and figurative slavery reflect an external perspective that almost certainly does not capture how those enslaved experienced their own lives, relationships, and spirituality. Would an enslaved person choose to talk about "belonging to" Christ? Despite apparently positive ideas about what it means to be a slave of Christ, Paul and his imitators do not seek to undermine or abolish slavery as a system. And we today bring our own collection of questions and assumptions to any discussion of "slaves of Christ" in Pauline literature.

Chapter 4

SLAVES IN AN OPPRESSIVE EMPIRE

AFTERLIFE OF THE IMAGE: EARLY CHRISTIAN INTERPRETATIONS

The Pauline letters deployed the image of the Christ-believer as the "slave of Christ" in an attempt to inculcate in all members of the community, regardless of social status or social position, an attitude of humble and dedicated service to Jesus the Lord. As noted in the previous chapter, in practice this vision of radical equality did not result in the abolition of slavery or substantially change the quotidian experiences of enslaved persons, who by and large continued to suffer from a lack of autonomy and natal alienation under Christ-believing slaveholders. In the centuries following Paul's writing, the Christians of late antiquity either followed Paul's socially conservative approach and maintained the status quo or, less frequently, proposed abolishing slavery on the basis of Pauline and other scriptural teachings about fundamental anthropology. The case studies discussed below illustrate the bifurcated nature of theological teachings about the institution of slavery in the early Church.

A COMMUNITY OF EQUALS: ANTHROPOLOGICAL CLAIMS

In fourth-century Cappadocia, the women of one prominent Christian family transformed their estate into a religious retreat of sorts. Within their household at Annesi, the wealthy homeowners formed a domestic Christian community. The community's leaders were Macrina the Younger and her mother, Emmelia, who could trace their family's Christian identity back to conversion under Gregory Thaumaturgus (ca. 210–270 CE), the wonderworking bishop of Neocaesarea. They shared responsibility for household management and religious education with the enslaved women of the household and with other local elites, including one daughter of a Roman senator.[1] These women from a variety of socioeconomic backgrounds apparently shared their lives and resources in common and dedicated their time to religious formation and ascetic living.

Gregory of Nyssa, Macrina's younger brother and a Christian bishop in his own right, extolled the women's way of life, in part because of their ability to create this community of equals. As an observer he noted that all the women conducted themselves in such a holy way that it was nearly impossible to think of them as regular human beings. He wrote, "Just as by death souls are freed from the body and released from the cares of this life, so their life was separated from these things, divorced from all mortal vanity and attuned to an imitation of the existence of the angels."[2] Whether enslaved or free, all of the women could take part in this angelic life of devotion and piety. Gregory was writing a biography of his sister and spent much of the text praising Macrina's rejection of the family's wealth, so the detail of manumitting enslaved members of the household could have been a way of highlighting Macrina's absolute nonattachment to earthly concerns and creature comforts. But readers should not gloss over his apparently casual mention of formerly enslaved women becoming full participants in the Christian life of the family and community. It is surprising for the time period, yet Gregory appeared to take for granted that these women could make a valuable contribution to the religious life of the community, being equal in spiritual stature to their free companions. And elsewhere in his writings Gregory pushed for the abolition of slavery not only in Christian households but in the universal Church.

Gregory's *Homily IV on Ecclesiastes* addresses slavery first indirectly, commenting on the biblical verse Ecclesiastes 2:7. There the Teacher (Qoheleth) states, "I bought male and female slaves, and had slaves who were born in my house; I also had great possessions of herds and flocks, more than any who had been before me in Jerusalem." Gregory notes that the Teacher betrays an excessive pride when he decides to lump enslaved human beings in with flocks as a source of wealth. He poses a question to the biblical author: "How can you who are equal in all things have superiority so that as man, you consider yourself as man's ruler and say, 'I have servants and maidens' as if they were goats or cattle?"[3] Pointing back to Genesis 1:26, where human beings are given dominion over animals, Gregory explains to his audience that this dominion cannot extend to the control or subjugation of fellow human beings. This is consistent with the anthropological claim at the start of Genesis 1:26, namely that human beings are made in the image of God: How can one person be the master of another who is created equal? For Gregory this is nonsensical. Demanding power over other human beings is basically claiming you are equal to God, the only one who should exercise total dominical authority.

In a 1993 commentary on the homily, Lionel Wickham makes the point that Gregory's discussion of slavery should be considered in the broader context of this homily series, where Gregory is discussing the right relationship between people and God, and the ways that sin disrupts that relationship. He explains,

> Slavery is, of course, an issue for public conscience and morality, and Gregory's arguments are, in the end, arguments for the abolition of slavery. But Gregory treats the matter in the domain of private conscience.... Gregory is not generalizing to the condemnation of a social system as such, so far as I can see. What he has to say is consistent with the toleration of the system, provided that the absolute claims of God are recognized.[4]

Wickham has a point that Gregory uses slaveholding as an example of extreme human pridefulness and therefore a violation of the proper order and relationship between humans and God. Yet perhaps closer attention to Gregory's interpretations of Pauline teachings can shed more light on his conception that Christianity and slavery are generally incompatible.

Within the homily, Gregory goes further and reminds his readers that even God does not use divine authority to enslave people but in fact "called us back to freedom when we were slaves of sin."[5] Here Gregory relies on a Pauline teaching from Galatians 4—5. Ilaria Ramelli argues that Gregory takes seriously Galatians 3:27–28, not only in terms of equality between men and women, but also between enslaved and free persons in the Christian community. Her argument revolves in part around his use of the Greek term *homotimos*, "worthy of equal honor" or "of equal dignity." She writes,

> Remarkably, the word ὁμότιμος [*homotimos*] (which he uses to indicate that God endowed masters and slaves with the same dignity, so nobody can be a slave of a fellow human and Christian masters should free their slaves, and to indicate that Macrina, her mother, and her siblings made themselves "of equal dignity" with their former slaves) is the same term that he and Basil use to designate the equal dignity of man and woman and that Gregory Nazianzen employs to declare that Theosebia had the very same ecclesiastical dignity of a ἱερεύς [priest].[6]

This summary draws attention to a few key points in Gregory's theological approach to slavery. As noted above, his view of equality traces back to the theological anthropology of the creation story in Genesis 1:1—2:4a. His argument also relies on an eschatological belief that all persons will ultimately be drawn to God, and that this final realization of equality should have an impact on the way Christians treat each other now. If all persons have the same ultimate end or telos, a social status like enslavement is not only not natural, it is inherently unjust. Christians should work for abolition in the period of "already but not yet" they inhabit.

HIERARCHICAL STRUCTURES: ECCLESIOLOGICAL IMPACT

While abolitionist movements of later periods adopted many of these same interpretive tactics, early Christian arguments against the institution of slavery were not widely accepted or successful. De Wet notes that even Gregory's fellow Cappadocians, Basil of Caesarea and Gregory of Nazianzus, only asserted that people should treat the enslaved humanely, without questioning the entire institution of slavery.[7] The vast majority of early Christian theologians followed Paul's lead in not pushing back against the status quo in their slave-owning economy and society. For example, Clement of Alexandria (ca. 150–ca. 215 CE) argued that the humanity of enslaved persons must be respected but made no move to recommend an end to slavery.[8] At the same time as a few Christian writers advocated for the abolition of slavery, others were constructing an institutional church that relied on the labor and subjugation of enslaved persons and articulating theological positions to support their practices.

Ignatius of Antioch, writing in the early second century CE, advised his Christian contemporaries on household management, appearing to echo the author of the letters 1 and 2 Timothy and Titus. Assuming that the Christians would be judged on the basis of their orderly way of life, which might even attract more converts, Ignatius reminded women, children, and the enslaved to be obedient to male heads of household. Slaves "were even forbidden to ask their fellow-believers to make charitable contributions toward the sum they required to buy their freedom."[9] Ignatius seems to be attempting to reinforce the status quo of his contemporary slave-owning society when he advises, "Do not treat slaves (whether male [*douloi*] or female [*doulai*]) contemptuously, but neither let them become conceited; instead, let them serve all the more faithfully to the glory of God, that they may obtain from God a better freedom. They should not have a strong desire to be set free at the church's expense, lest they be found to be slaves of lust."[10] He treats slavery as a given and even suggests that those enslaved persons seeking freedom are incurring some risk to their ability to serve God well if they can no longer demonstrate their obedience to earthly masters. To the extent that he tied the survival and even growth of the Christian movement to social propriety, Ignatius understood slavery and freedom as less significant than Christian identity. The Christians would be judged by how well they carried out the duties associated with their social stations.

Historians in the latter half of the twentieth century often argued that the number of enslaved persons in the Roman Empire dwindled in the fourth through sixth centuries; there were fewer imperial expansionist wars that would have led to the enslavement of noncitizens. But more recently scholars have proposed a different understanding of what happened during this period. Historian Averil Cameron points out that in the late Roman Empire, large numbers of enslaved persons were held on the estates of landowners, and "when such landowners became Christian, they sometimes sold their property in order to use the wealth for Christian purposes, in which case the slaves were sold too."[11] As an example she points to Melania the Younger (ca. 383–ca. 439), who is revered as a saint and praised for renouncing her wealth (including the enslaved) on the basis of her faith. In a great stroke of irony, when Melania presented herself to the governor of Alexandria to plead on the behalf of some Egyptian holy men, she announced, "I am So-and-So's daughter and So-and-So's wife. I am Christ's slave."[12] Enslaved persons also continued to work in rural agriculture alongside freepersons, all subordinate to the wealthy landowners. Cameron notes that it is somewhat unclear "how slaves related to *coloni*, technically free tenants who were, in many areas, theoretically tied to their particular estates by imperial legislation, and over whom the landlords had rights which can look very much like the rights of owner over slave."[13] Unsurprisingly many Christian landowners and the bishops managing church estates relied on enslaved persons for labor.

The expectation of continued social stratification was reinforced in sermons interpreting the Pauline letters for this later audience. John Chrysostom, for example, had a generally negative view of slavery,[14] yet he continued using Paul's idea that each person has a choice of remaining enslaved to sin and death or becoming a slave of God and Christ. One major implication of this view comes from de Wet: "Just as reward and punishment are used to manipulate the behavior of institutional slaves, so the teachings of eternal life, judgment, and hell are supposed to influence the behavior of slaves of God and slaves of sin."[15] In his book-length study of Chrysostom, *Preaching Bondage: John Chrysostom and the Discourse of Slavery in Early Christianity*, de Wet demonstrates that the Constantinopolitan bishop considered slavery a consequence of the human fall into sin. In his homily on 1 Corinthians, Chrysostom explains, "From the beginning, God made only one form of government, placing man over woman, but after our race ran aground into much disorder, other forms of rule appeared, that of slaveholders, that of secular governors."[16] He apparently extrapolates from the Pauline idea that all individuals were enslaved to sin and death, necessitating the introduction of the law through Moses (e.g., Paul in Gal 3:23–26). This anthropological point could have had positive practical implications for enslaved people in the fourth and fifth centuries. After all, Chrysostom appears to suggest that the institution of slavery is not a natural human state desired by God. Rather, it is a historical development. However he does not suggest Christians take any steps to abolish the institution of slavery immediately, instead advising that if Christians need enslaved persons, they should have no more than one or two, or they should manumit their slaves after teaching them a trade.[17] That is, he seems more concerned with the ability of wealthy Christians to show restraint and generosity than he is with the experiences of enslaved persons who might desire freedom.

Furthermore, Chrysostom's teachings about how to be a properly obedient figurative "slave of God" reflected and amplified his understanding of slaveowners disciplining actual enslaved persons whose obedience faltered. Equating God to an ideal slaveowner, Chrysostom asks, "Is it not a sign of goodness to punish, and of cruelty not to punish, and is it not so in the case of God? Since he is good, he has therefore prepared a hell."[18] Note that when human social conditions are used as a lens for understanding divine power and motivations, the Pauline texts can be used to argue not just that human Christ-believers should serve Christ as if they were enslaved to him, but that God and Christ are rightly understood as slaveowners. It was a small step from this conception to a view that slaveowners should wield God-like power and to Douglass's experience of American Christianity, where "the dealers in the bodies and souls of men erect their stand in the presence of the pulpit, and they mutually help each other. The dealer gives his blood-stained gold to support the pulpit, and the pulpit, in return, covers his infernal business with the garb of Christianity."[19]

Chrysostom's largely figurative and yet uncritical approach to the institution of slavery is illustrative of what became the dominant Christian position for at least another millennium and a half.[20] As the image of an imperial Christ-God became entrenched, Paul's idea of a "slave of

Christ" similarly became less likely to create a sense of empowerment and more likely to reinforce existing social hierarchies that disenfranchised those who were already most vulnerable.

CONTEMPORARY CULTURAL CONTEXT AND NEW INTERPRETATIONS

Many authors, including New Testament scholars, have pointed out the historical connections between Paul's writing and justifications for both continued slaveholding and abolition in the United States. The history of Pauline interpretation in Black Christian communities sometimes explicitly reflects on Paul as an ambiguous figure. Allen Dwight Callahan has examined the "creative, complex, and sometimes contradictory African American hermeneutics" that has allowed some interpreters to find "the voice of freedom in some ostensibly antiemancipatory tones" expressed by Paul.[21] On his analysis, interpreters like Hubert Danford Maultsby do find liberatory promise in Paul's teachings about Christ who frees us from sin, including sins like racism.[22] Still other Black New Testament scholars seek to reclaim an "authentic" Paul and his message from the grip of later interpreters like the author of Acts and imitators like the Pastor.[23] Yet many interpreters, like Clarice J. Martin, are attentive to aspects of intersectional identities, drawing attention to the multiple layers of Pauline teaching about gender and power for Black women readers, layers that complicate the possibility of finding a freeing message.[24] All predominantly white Christian communities in the United States engaging with Paul's image "slave of Christ" would benefit from direct and deep engagement with Black biblical theology and hermeneutics, an interpretive tradition to which I cannot do justice in this short study.

My intention in what follows is to draw attention to some additional dimensions of the U.S. and global context that may shape the way individuals who seek belonging in the household of God experience the Pauline epistles and Paul's image of the believer as enslaved. I offer some questions designed to provoke introspection about how Christian communities today can authentically pursue Pauline ideals of equality and mutual support for those who suffer under slavery and its aftereffects, in the shadow of the "slave of Christ" metaphor.

PRISONS AND WAGE SLAVERY

The U.S. prison-industrial complex perpetuates the racialized oppression and inequality established during the long centuries of slavery and segregation in this country. Ava DuVernay's 2016 documentary *13th* traces the legacy of slavery and Jim Crow into the current mass incarceration of Black Americans. As of 2016, "more African-American men are incarcerated, or on probation or parole, than were enslaved in 1850, and the U.S., which accounts for 5% of the world's population, counts nearly a quarter of the world's incarcerated people." DuVernay's highly acclaimed film takes as its starting point a clause in the Thirteenth Amendment to the U.S. Constitution, which abolished slavery and involuntary servitude, "except as a punishment for crime whereof the party shall have been duly convicted."[25] Historians, public figures, and political activists weigh in on important moments since the amendment was passed, highlighting white supremacist campaigns to villainize Black men and racialized media messaging about "urban" (read: Black) criminal threats to public safety. The overall picture that emerges is one of the intentional and fear-based criminalization of Black Americans, especially Black men, leading to disproportionate rates of arrest, prosecution, and incarceration.

In a complementary project, the Equal Justice Initiative (EJI), spearheaded by lawyer and civil rights activist Bryan Stevenson, has created the Legacy Museum in Montgomery, Alabama. The museum uses "interactive media, sculpture, videography, and exhibits to immerse visitors in the sights and sounds of the domestic slave trade, racial terrorism, the Jim Crow South, and the world's largest prison system" to trace through-lines from slavery, to Jim Crow legislation, to the mass incarceration of Black Americans in the present day.[26] Both DuVernay and the EJI are drawing attention to the long history of racial discrimination, the oppression and marginalization that persist.

One major problem concerns the prison labor allowed under the Thirteenth Amendment, which can be totally unpaid (in states like Alabama, Arkansas, Florida, Georgia, and Texas) or paid at shockingly low rates. Statistics from 2017 indicated that "incarcerated people assigned to work for state-owned businesses earn between 33 cents and $1.41 per hour on average—roughly twice as much as people assigned to regular prison jobs," that is, jobs like maintenance, food service, and custodial tasks on prison grounds.[27] These rates do not factor in the sometimes mandatory deductions taken from prisoners' wages, which can vary by state. In any event they can provide a helpful benchmark when measured against known expenses, such as the cost of commissary items like phone cards or the exorbitant fees for video calling. Basic needs like contact with loved ones can take an incredibly long time to finance with the exploitative rates of pay; sometimes services like phone calls are "provided by private for-profit companies who split the revenue with the prison itself."[28] This is not to mention the fact that people released from prison without the financial resources for transportation, work-appropriate clothing, childcare, food, and so on are more likely to struggle reintegrating into society. How does this dynamic hold up against Christian teachings about restorative justice? What is the relationship between exploitation of prisoners and the Pauline idea that Christ seeks to free people from enslavement to sin?

Paul's teachings about demonstrating loyalty to Christ by serving members of the community might offer a guide for the way forward. For example, the U.S. Conference of Catholic Bishops (USCCB) frequently publishes guidance and public statements recommending support for legislation like the Second Chance Act and the Second Chance Reauthorization Act of 2017, on the basis that such laws "fund programs that give hope to those with a difficult path in front of them, including needs for employment assistance, substance abuse treatment, housing, family programming, mentoring, victim support, and other services to individuals returning to the community from prison or jail."[29] How can Christian communities get involved in both national and local advocacy for restorative justice? Where can churches cooperate with other local organizations that provide practical support for people being released from prison and their families?

Combating Christian complicity in the exploitation of the incarcerated can even take subtle forms. Indeed Paul, in the Letter to Philemon, recognized the economic position of the enslaved Onesimus and put his own credit on the line to protect the man. Although today's prisoners typically do not profit from their work, National Public Radio reporting indicates that prison labor is "a multi-billion-dollar industry with incarcerated people doing everything from building office furniture and making military equipment to staffing call centers and doing 3D modeling."[30] Could Christian communities make a commitment to divest from vendors and companies that exploit the labor of incarcerated persons? How and where can the treasure of churches be rerouted to ensure those incarcerated and their families receive necessary financial support?

FORCED LABOR AND CHILD LABOR

Another serious issue, present in the United States but even more prominent globally, is forced labor, which may be considered a form of modern slavery. Coercion is almost always a factor in forced labor, which can be found in both private and state-owned industry. Forced labor includes sexual exploitation. A 2016 report notes that "an estimated 3.8 million adults were victims of forced sexual exploitation and 1.0 million children were victims of sexual exploitation in 2016. The vast majority of victims (99 per cent) were women and girls."[31]

One in four persons involved in forced labor is a child.[32] The International Labour Organization (ILO), in cooperation with UNICEF, issued a report in June 2021 detailing global instances of child labor, work done by children between the ages of five and seventeen. As of 2020, the report states, "Worldwide, 160 million children are engaged in child labour; 79 million of them are performing hazardous work."[33] Hazardous work may include night work or long hours of work; exposure to physical, psychological, or sexual abuse; work underground, under water, at dangerous heights, or in confined spaces; work with dangerous machinery, equipment, and tools, or which involves the manual handling or transport of heavy loads; and work in an unhealthy environment that may, for example, expose children to hazardous substances, agents, or processes, or to temperatures, noise levels, or vibrations damaging their health.[34]

For many of the children engaged in these types of work, the proximate cause of their entry into the labor force is extreme poverty. The majority are contributing to family business, either on family farms or in family microenterprises (72.1 percent). Most child labor happens in rural settings, and the overwhelming majority of child labor is in the agricultural industry (70 percent).[35] In all countries, there are more boys than girls in the labor force, although girls are disproportionately involved in uncompensated domestic labor that can be "invisible" outside the home.[36]

A not insignificant number of children performing labor are part of a debt-based arrangement such as bonded labor, when people submit themselves to slavery in order to repay a loan or a debt incurred by a loved one. CNN reporting from March 2021 profiled a mother and daughter who "were forced by their 'master' to work 11 hours a day, for which they earned just 200 rupees (about $2.75) to repay a 100,000-rupee (about $1,370) loan that had since doubled in size."[37] The women described their fear, including fear of losing the house the man holding their debt was allowing them to live in. With their lack of funds, it would be impossible for them to leave and find a better living situation, leaving them feeling trapped and despairing. This story illustrates that indentured servitude has devastating consequences for physical, mental, and emotional health. Often those working off a debt are separated from their families and community support systems, a circumstance that allows for even greater abuse and damage. Kiran Kamal Prasad, who founded the organization Jeevika to combat bonded labor, notes the psychological effects of this exploitative system: "It is very difficult to convince the bonded laborers (to go to authorities), because they feel that they are beholden to the masters or to the landlords who have helped them in the hour of their need."[38]

Shockingly, the percentages of children involved in labor and hazardous labor did not change significantly between 2016 and 2020, and the absolute numbers increased. The apparently steady percentages worldwide mask some progress combatting child labor in particular regions of the world. Some headway has been made against the exploitation of children through the work of the International Programme on the Elimination of Child Labour (IPEC), particularly in cooperation with businesses. As businesses become increasingly concerned about the issue of child labor, whether because it threatens their self-image and sense of company values, or because it endangers their ability to retain workers, or because it undermines their supply chain (children can be found at almost every stage of the typical supply chain, from agriculture, to manufacturing, to retail), groups like IPEC can step in to recommend specific interventions.[39] In general, the group encourages corporate social responsibility, the idea that business leaders accept responsibility for learning about child labor, children's rights, and strategies for preventing the exploitation of children. If such ethical considerations become a regular part of business development and strategy, it is hoped that a kind of collective care for the protection of vulnerable children will suffuse global business practices.

Despite these types of progress, a further special report from the ILO notes that the fight against child labor is likely to lose ground in the wake of the COVID-19 pandemic. A number of the risk factors that tend to lead to increased child labor or other forms of forced labor will be exacerbated by the global economic downturn. Those who are already most vulnerable are likely to face the greatest risks. "An estimated 42–66 million children could fall into extreme poverty as a result of the crisis this year, adding to the estimated 386 million children already in extreme poverty in 2019," according to the report.[40] Children without access to education or who lose their access to education because of shutdowns and a dearth of distance-learning options may be driven to take on work. If those children come from families that have experienced job losses or major health problems in the face of COVID-19, it is even more likely they could be pressured to take on work to help support their households. This pressure might be especially strong for children who are heads of household, those who belong to marginalized minority groups, and those who are refugees, migrants, or internally displaced persons. The ILO estimates that another 8.9 million children could be engaged in labor by the end of 2022.

Given that the ILO has named 2025 as the target year to end child labor globally, how might U.S. Christian communities participate in advocacy and systemic efforts to support this goal? Paul framed the Letter to Philemon as a matter of concern for the entire Christian community (Phlm 1–2) and pointed out that Philemon's treatment of Onesimus had bearing not just on their personal relationship but on "the good that we may do for Christ" (Phlm 6). Keeping in mind the interconnected nature of individual activism and collective effort, it could be beneficial for Christian communities to partner with advocacy groups that can move the levers of power. For example, the ILO suggests that "debt relief should be extended and debt re-structured in already heavily indebted countries so that social spending is not crowded out by increasing debt service payments."[41] As an initial step, today's churches might commit to spreading information, positioning themselves as learners who can benefit from the practical wisdom of secular groups like the ILO or

UNICEF. In what ways might it be helpful to reflect on Paul's claim that Christ-believers owe a debt of care to one another because of their obligations to Christ and God?

SEX TRAFFICKING AND VIOLENCE AGAINST NATIVE WOMEN

"In 2015 the National Congress of American Indians found that an estimated 40% of women who are victims of sex trafficking identify as American Indian, Alaska Native, or First Nations."[42] Yet those who identify as American Indian or Alaska Native make up only 1.7 percent of the U.S. population (based on the 2010 census).[43] These deeply troubling statistics highlight that the long history of U.S. abuses against Native peoples has created a legacy of vulnerability, leading to continued exploitation and mistreatment of this maligned population. Valaura Imus-Nahsonhoya, a Hopi expert of the subject of human trafficking in Indian country, indicates that a whole range of factors make Native women particularly vulnerable. Not only are they associated with fetishes, but many of these women come from communities experiencing poverty, historical trauma, substance abuse, and a high incidence of involvement with the foster care system.[44] Casinos and casino resorts, one of the federally protected sources of income available to tribes seeking financial self-sufficiency, are also hot spots for sex trafficking. "Nationally, a person being sex trafficked in a hotel/resort setting is forced, coerced, or intimidated to perform sex acts on an average of 5 to 10 customers per day."[45]

More broadly speaking, the statistics about violence against indigenous women, including missing and murdered indigenous women and girls, are staggering. A 2016 report from the National Institute of Justice concluded,

> Results show that more than four in five American Indian and Alaska Native women (84.3 percent) have experienced violence in their lifetime. . . . This includes 56.1 percent who have experienced sexual violence, 55.5 percent who have experienced physical violence by an intimate partner, 48.8 percent who have experienced stalking, and 66.4 percent who have experienced psychological aggression by an intimate partner.

> Overall, more than 1.5 million American Indian and Alaska Native women have experienced violence in their lifetime.[46]

These numbers might be compared to national statistics that state about one in three women will experience sexual or physical violence at the hands of an intimate partner, a percentage that has held steady for at least a decade.

Native groups have created a wealth of resources to advocate for increased accountability for perpetrators and to support the healing of survivors and their communities. The National Indigenous Women's Resource Center (NIWRC) seeks "to provide national leadership to end violence against American Indian, Alaska Native and Native Hawaiian women by supporting culturally grounded, grassroots advocacy." In service of this goal, the group produces *Speaking Our Truth, Podcast for Change* as a vehicle for women to share their stories and for the organization to build a coalition for direct action.[47] How might contemporary U.S. Christian groups create openings for hearing these stories and supporting the direct actions recommended by Native women?

As the NIWRC points out, the violence indigenous women experience exists on a spectrum, and preventing harms to indigenous women and girls must be approached with awareness about the complexity of factors involved, from dating and domestic violence to sexual assault to trafficking. The organization also advocates for the reform of Federal Indian Law to ensure local communities maintain jurisdiction and sovereignty without undue interference from the U.S. government. This last item plays more of a role than many nonindigenous Americans realize. The 1978 Supreme Court decision *Oliphant v. Suquamish Indian Tribe* ruled that tribes did not have jurisdiction over non-Indian perpetrators and cannot prosecute those offenders, even if they commit crimes in Indian Country. Instead, tribes must request intervention from the U.S. Department of Justice, and federal prosecutors may choose to prosecute or to decline such cases. In 2013 the Violence against Women Reauthorization Act (reaffirmed in 2021) did provide "federally recognized tribes with special domestic violence criminal jurisdiction, which allows tribes that meet certain conditions to prosecute certain cases involving non-Indian offenders."[48]

Despite this, rates of violence perpetrated by non-Indians against indigenous women and girls have not decreased, and in 2018, 65.2 percent of Department of Justice declinations by federal prosecutors involved physical or sexual assault and instances of sexual exploitation.[49] As a result, the NIWRC notes that indigenous women and communities are denied justice because of "limited federal prosecutions of perpetrators and the high rate of federal case declinations by U.S. Attorneys in crimes of domestic violence, sexual assault, sex trafficking and murder in Indian country."[50] Given that many Christian denominations played an active role in the forced religious conversion and violent enculturation of Native populations, including the seizure of indigenous lands and sponsoring Indian boarding schools that became sites of terror and abuse for many Native children, how can today's Christian communities make reparations? Paul asked the whole community of Christ-believers, the *ekklēsia* in Philemon's household, to stand as witnesses to the call for Philemon to accept Onesimus not as a slave but as a beloved brother (Phlm 16). What would it look like for churches today to collectively accept responsibility for the harms our (sometimes very immediate) predecessors inflicted on Native communities? How can Christians respectfully acknowledge and actively affirm the dignity of American Indian, Alaska Native, and Hawaiian Native populations, beloved siblings in the household of God?

PERIL AND PROMISE: SLAVES IN THE HOUSEHOLD OF GOD

With all these accumulated centuries of hardship and oppression, with the weight of ongoing discrimination, mistreatment, and racialized violence that are the legacy of institutionalized slavery in the United States, Paul's image "slave of Christ" seems irredeemable. This is no longer a metaphor that can create space for belonging in the Christian household of God. Yet there may be something fruitful in facing head-on the weight of the history of interpretation that has accompanied Paul's language and this specific image.

Christian communities should pay attention when the biblical translations selected for use in their congregations elide "servant" and "slave." It is perhaps preferable to choose translations that have not softened the language, so we cannot look away. Any promise of repair and reconciliation lies in our ability to stand up to the text, requires introspection and real attention to the legacy of Christianity's founding in the ancient world and white Christian complicity in a history of oppression. As awareness and discomfort come to the forefront, a number of questions may help shape white communal actions. How can the jarring nature of enslavement to Christ or God challenge our existing perceptions of authority and power? What are the effects of using the language metaphorically and insisting on its figurative nature in communities where it was decidedly not a metaphor for a significant number of people and their ancestors? Does anything change if we increase our awareness that forms of slavery persist today under other names?

As this book may demonstrate, there are other powerful metaphors Christian communities can use to reenvision the household of God in a form that allows for greater belonging. Someone might object, "But we don't want to lose the Pauline idea that a figuratively enslaved person gains honor by association with God" or "But only the image of being enslaved encapsulates the sort of loyalty human beings ideally owe to Christ." Yet perhaps their attention can be drawn to the problematic and harmful history of Paul's "slave of Christ" image, and they can also be invited to consider alternative language and images within the New Testament epistles: disciple, apostle, emissary.

In the next part of this book, we examine a metaphor with a different but related troubling legacy: the image of the conquering Christian soldier. Through close attention to Paul's language of battle, armor, and military might, we will gain a deeper understanding of how connection to Christ's power has often been used to justify the subjugation of others but could instead be used to build solidarity within a community committed to cultivating belonging.

PART 3

GOING TO WAR AS SOLDIERS OF CHRIST

Martial Metaphors for Fellowship

In 2004, Joshua Casteel was deployed to Iraq with the Army's 202nd Military Intelligence Battalion, to the military prison at Abu Ghraib. Just six weeks earlier, news sources exposed the site as a place where U.S. military personnel had shamed, abused, and tortured prisoners, and Josh was getting ready to work there as an Arabic translator and Army interrogator. On May 4, he sent an email to a friend expressing his thoughts about his position:

> So, I guess you've heard about the controversy at the prison in Iraq…the abuse of Iraqi prisoners. It's been a strange past two days since I first heard. That's the same prison I'm heading to. A wave of feelings has rushed through me. Mostly contempt, bewilderment. The photos are horrific, and that's not what I was trained to do.…The angry side of me wants on the first plane, and to be pinned my sergeant stripes as soon as possible so that I can have some authority and ensure that

> nothing of the sort happens under my watch. Then the "what the hell am I doing" side of me shows up, wondering what a blond, blue-eyed Iowa boy is doing in Iraq in the first place.[1]

Given this inauspicious start to his deployment, it may not be surprising that Josh's time at Abu Ghraib occasioned great internal turmoil and deep introspection. His reflections on politics, religion, and military life are captured in a collection of emails sent to family, friends, and spiritual advisors between 2004 and 2005, in a slim volume published as *Letters from Abu Ghraib*.

Finally, Josh identified that, for him, a life in alignment with the gospel of Christ was not compatible with military service. He pinpointed the moment of crystallization as a particular interview with a Muslim POW, when he asked the young man why he had come to Iraq in order to kill. In response the prisoner turned the same question back on Josh, which he experienced as a challenge to his faith. He recounts their exchange:

> "Your Lord, our prophet Isa, tells you to turn the other cheek, to love those who hate you. Why do you not do this?" I replied, "You're right," and then asked him when he would "go and do likewise."...I lacked the power to challenge him in any way that I did not challenge myself, because such ideas of "love" and "forgiveness" and "compassion" are not fully manifest and incarnate in me.[2]

The ensuing process of self-reflection, prayer, and conversation led him to submit an application to be registered as a Conscientious Objector (CO), a servicemember who has "religious, moral, or ethical grounds for not participating as a combatant in war."[3] The formal Department of Defense definition of a conscientious objection is "a firm, fixed, and sincere objection to participation in war in any form or the bearing of arms, by reason of religious training and/or belief."[4] While some COs continue military service in noncombatant roles, Josh sought to be discharged from the military entirely.

This soldier's internal turmoil over the compatibility of military service and Christian identity finds an intriguing counterpoint in Christian interpretation of the Pauline martial metaphor "soldier of Christ." The epistles encourage Christ-believers to take on the role of a soldier of Christ, committing themselves to follow the orders of their heavenly commander and figuratively arming themselves for spiritual battle. Members of the community from diverse backgrounds can find common ground in their war against sin, despair, and death. Chapter 5 explains how the Pauline martial metaphor might have allowed first-century believers to unite around a shared goal and shared disciplines to build an alternative empire that belonged to God rather than Caesar.

Chapter 6 will examine early Christian concerns about the morality of participating in military service and the early development of a Christology that positioned Christ as imperial commander. Turning to the contemporary United States, the chapter will present some of the challenges active-duty military personnel and veterans face, including high rates of PTSD, death by suicide, and moral injury, raising questions about where and how today's Christian communities might intervene to prevent harm and support healing. The discussion concludes with a summary of the peril and promise wrapped up in the Pauline image "soldier of Christ" and an assessment of its potential for creating belonging among those who have been most deeply harmed by war.

Chapter 5

SOLDIERS EXPANDING GOD'S EMPIRE

THE IMAGE IN THE UNDISPUTED PAULINE EPISTLES

Paul's first letter to the Thessalonians is considered by most scholars to be his earliest extant letter. It was sent in about 51 CE to Thessalonica, an ancient port city in Macedonia, right on the trade route of the Via Egnatia.[1] The Thessalonians were subjects of the Roman Empire but maintained the rule of Greek law in their city, and the Christ-believers there were most likely converts from Greek polytheistic religions rather than from Judaism. It is evident that these Christ-believers had established and maintained a close relationship with Paul. His tone throughout the letter is warm and approving. He praises the Thessalonians for how they "became imitators of us and of the Lord, for in spite of persecution you received the word with joy inspired by the Holy Spirit, so that you became an example to all the believers in Macedonia and in Achaia" (1 Thess 1:6–7). Despite their exemplary faith, the Thessalonians have raised a challenging question for Paul to answer: If Christ's second coming is imminent, and that is the time when he will raise all the waiting Christ-believers to eternal life with him, what will happen to those members of the community who have recently died? Did they miss out on the reward for their faithfulness?

His answer is to remind the Thessalonians to hold on to hope as a counterbalance for grief, "for the Lord himself, with a cry of command [*keleusma*], with the archangel's call and with the sound of God's trumpet [*salpinx*], will descend from heaven, and the dead in Christ will rise first. Then we who are alive, who are left, will be caught up in the clouds together with them to meet the Lord in the air; and so we will be with the Lord forever" (1 Thess 4:16–17). This picture of Christ's return would likely have been reassuring for the Christ-believers. Not only will those who have "fallen asleep" (a euphemism for death) rise first, but those who are still living will be united with their loved ones who have passed and are with Christ. The language Paul uses in this passage depicts Jesus as the one ordering a military engagement; his *keleusma* is a "summons to carry out a procedure, e.g. battle engagement, rowing, hunting."[2] The accompanying trumpet blast would have been recognizable as a military signal to get in battle formation or begin a maneuver. It seems that Paul wants to evoke not only Jesus's control but also the military precision of the resurrection event. Like a planned battle, the Parousia is inevitable and will be orderly. The faithful, both living and dead, will be assembled like troops.

Paul provides further encouragement while the Christ-believers wait, urging them on with additional martial imagery, that of arming for battle. He writes,

> But since we belong to the day, let us be sober, and put on the breastplate of faith and love, and for a helmet the hope of salvation. For God has destined us not for wrath but for obtaining salvation through our Lord Jesus Christ, who died for us, so that whether we are awake or asleep [here he means alive or already dead at the time of the Parousia] we may live with him. Therefore encourage one another and build up each other, as indeed you are doing. (1 Thess 5:8–11)

The breastplate (Greek *thōrax*) and helmet (*perikephalaios*, literally "thing around the head") are referred to using standard military terminology. These items, together with a shield and short sword, were considered essential items for ancient soldiers entering battle. Virtues are symbolically equated with ways of guarding and protecting oneself. Faith and love are essential protections. Hope is needed in the particular context because the Thessalonians are worried about their companions who have passed away. In another letter, the Roman Christ-believers are also exhorted to put on armor. In Romans, Paul advises, "Let us then lay aside the works of darkness and put on the armor of light." He implies that protection is needed to keep community members on the right side of an impending battle (Rom 13:12). Then he says, "Put on the Lord Jesus Christ," equating Christ himself with the soldier's armor (Rom 13:14).

But Paul does not stop with the figurative armor; he also reminds his readers to prepare mentally and emotionally. Exhorting the Thessalonians to "encourage one another and build up each other," Paul refers to a common practice among military troops. Like the members of an army, the Christ-believers are comrades in arms, responsible for boosting collective morale while working toward a collective goal. This idea of shared commitment to a common cause appears elsewhere in the Pauline corpus. Paul occasionally addresses or refers to one of his missionary partners as a "fellow soldier," *systratiōtēs* in Greek (Phil 2:25; Phlm 2). His understanding of a soldier as one who works among equals would have made good sense in the context of the first-century Roman Empire.

In the first century CE, the military was one of the only institutions open to men from all socioeconomic classes and backgrounds, where elites in command would mingle with those from working-class backgrounds. Even emperors were known to portray themselves as "fellow soldiers" (Latin *comilito*) and make a show of "consuming the same food and drink as the men, and joining in with their physical hardships of toil and exposure to the elements."[3] This created the perfect setting for male homosociality, the cultivation of friendship and mentorship relationships among men that might reinforce the patriarchal power structures in Roman society. That is, military masculinity and male fellowship could become a path to social power, even for men who started out without much authority or cachet.

Records show that each legion usually had an attachment of civilian "specialists and craftsmen, known collectively as *immunes*, those 'exempt from normal duties': surveyors, medical and veterinary orderlies, armourers, carpenters, hunters, even soothsayers."[4] Noncitizens could join as part of auxiliary troops, and in Paul's time auxiliaries who served for twenty-five years became eligible for citizenship.[5] Enslaved people were not allowed to be soldiers in most parts of the army; the main exception was the navy, where enslaved men were enlisted to do the hard and dangerous manual labor of rowing warships. Enslaved people also frequently accompanied military units on campaign; sometimes this meant enslaved women serving as "camp followers," a euphemism for forced prostitution. In this environment, one might find soldiers planning to make a lifelong career out of their service alongside newly conscripted recruits looking forward to being discharged. For many the military facilitated upward social mobility. A legate, probably a man from the equestrian class, who was put in command of a legion for a short period might proceed to a political career as governor of a province, on the basis of his service record. Those who served in the intermediate command post of centurion might be promoted to the equestrian class, which offered more opportunities for gaining wealth and prestige. Almost all soldiers received benefits like property and pensions at the end of their service. Becoming a soldier meant taking on a new social role.

Similarly, Paul's metaphorical soldiers were encouraged to see their participation in the Christian community as offering them a new identity. He remarks several times on their turning to a new way of life: "You became imitators of us and of the Lord" (1 Thess 1:6); "For you, brothers and sisters, became imitators of the churches of God in Christ Jesus that are in Judea" (1 Thess 2:14); and "We ask and urge you in the Lord Jesus that, as you learned from us how you ought to live and to please God (as, in fact, you are doing), you should do so more and more" (1 Thess 4:1). Paul finds it praiseworthy that the readers have apparently modeled themselves after existing exemplars in the Christ-believing community, namely Paul and those who were part of the earliest group of Jesus's followers. In so doing, they have themselves become "an example to all the believers not only in Macedonia and Achaia…but in every place your faith in God has become known" (1 Thess 1:7–8).

Some evidence for soldiers' experiences of taking on a new identity comes from ancient letters, written on papyrus and preserved in arid parts of the Egyptian desert. Scholars have retrieved some of these letters from piles of waste where they were discarded in the ancient world. These texts are generally referred to as documentary papyri to distinguish them from papyrus copies of literary works. Many of the so-called documentary papyri contain business contracts, marriage and divorce contracts, records of property or land disputes, and personal letters. From these everyday materials, we can reconstruct much about life in the ancient world, including the work, travels, and home lives of soldiers. Apion, a native Egyptian, writes to his father to inform him that he has arrived in the Roman port of Misenum, where he signed on for his military service and received an initial payment to reimburse him for travel expenses (Latin *viaticum*, literally "provision for a *via* or way/journey"). Offering friendly greetings to his family and various other people from his hometown, he informs them about his new mailing address, providing information about his military company, the Athenonica. Additionally, he notes that they should begin addressing letters to him as Antonius Maximus, a Roman name that he has adopted instead of his traditional Egyptian name. His military service is obviously a source of pride; Apion/Antonius writes that he has sent a portrait of himself home in the hands of a messenger.[6]

In writing to the Thessalonians, Paul employs additional, subtle military language to talk about how members of the community should cultivate personal virtues. He links their faith and his success, saying, "For we now live, if you continue to stand firm in the Lord" (1 Thess 3:8). He uses the Greek verb *stēkō* for "standing firm." Abraham Malherbe has pointed out that this was a verb commonly used for military exhortation.[7] Paul uses the verb similarly at 1 Corinthians 16:13, where the believers are also advised to "be courageous, be strong." These instructions accord with the image of the ideal Roman soldier, who was to be courageous in service to the republic and later the state. As the Roman statesman and scholar Cicero (106–43 BCE) put it, "Man's peculiar virtue is fortitude, of which there are two main functions, namely scorn of death and scorn of pain."[8] Courage was an essential attribute for soldiers, and Paul calls the Christ-believers to cultivate it.

As established in chapter 1 on the image of athletes, Paul's letter to the Philippians combines athletic and military imagery to describe the Christ-believers as engaged in an *agōn*, a contest or struggle against earthly and cosmic enemies. In this battle, members of the community "are standing firm [from *stēkō*] in one spirit, striving side by side with one mind for the faith of the gospel, and are in no way intimidated by your opponents" (Phil 1:27–28). Just as the image of a cohort standing firm can apply to trained athletes facing off against competitors, it can appear in military contexts where the opponents are a foreign army and combatants faced some very real dangers. When the Christ-believers are told, "For freedom Christ has set us free. Stand firm, therefore, and do not submit again to a yoke of slavery" at Galatians 5:1, Paul refers to one possible outcome of military defeat: enslavement.

We see enslaved captives in a number of material artifacts from the Roman imperial period. The famous *Judaea capta* coins minted under the Emperor Vespasian commemorated his son Titus's 70 CE military victory against the first Jewish revolt. The coins show a female figure, hands bound behind her body, representing the province of Judea brought to its knees by the might of the Roman army. Though Paul's earliest readers would not have seen this specific coin, the basic image would have been familiar from public art and other coinage throughout the empire. One particularly rich example appears in the lower register of the *gemma Augustea*, a small but highly detailed cameo (7.5 by 9 inches) carved by an artisan in the second or third century CE. It depicts Roman soldiers and battle captives, the latter shown bound and humiliated, perhaps in preparation for a triumphal parade. The imperial and divine figures in the upper register quite literally sit enthroned above the crushing military force that has secured their power. Such degradation was the potential cost for soldiers in defeat, but military service also had its rewards.

Paul draws on the metaphor of payment for military service to talk about his own work as an apostle of Christ, perhaps offering some insight into what is involved in serving as a "soldier of Christ." Indignant about challenges to his authority, he poses a string of rhetorical questions to the Corinthians:

> This is my defense to those who would examine me. Do we not have the right to our food and drink? Do we not have the right to be accompanied by a believing wife, as do the other apostles and the brothers of the Lord and Cephas [Peter]? Or is it only Barnabas and I who have no right to refrain from working for a living? Who at any time pays the expenses for doing military service? Who plants a vineyard and does not eat any of its fruit? Or who tends a flock and does not get any of its milk? (1 Cor 9:3–7)

While Paul explains that he has not made use of these rights and privileges, preferring to "endure anything rather than put an obstacle in the way of the gospel of Christ," he seems to insist that in principle those who do the work of evangelization deserve recompense (1 Cor 9:12). He compares an apostle's rightful reward to being paid for military service and reaping the benefits of agricultural labor. That is, he can safely assume that his readers think it entirely fair for a soldier to receive wages and other benefits in exchange for risking life and limb.

Indeed, Roman soldiers were well paid. Veterans were often granted land and property, a way the emperor could show benevolence while ensuring loyal citizens populated the growing empire. Many soldiers were stationed in provinces or colonies, often near the still-disputed borders of Roman territory. While in these areas, they were not only maintaining and protecting boundaries, but they may also have acted as emissaries of Roman culture, intentionally or by happenstance. When Romans settled military personnel in the colonies, they often set up some of the amenities these soldiers would have been accustomed to in more central parts of the empire: theaters or arenas, baths, and temples to Roman deities. If Paul and his earliest readers associated the expansion of their communities with working as soldiers of Christ, what implicit instructions might this have carried for readers? Were they to spread a new, Christ-focused culture throughout the known world as they shared the gospel with new communities? Were those who belonged colonizers?

Paul did encourage the Christ-believers to think of themselves as participating in Christ's military triumph. A triumph (Greek *thriambos*, an apparent transliteration of the Latin *triumphus*) was a public parade, a display of imperial power, and a celebration of military victory. The procession typically included victorious generals and commanders, with representatives bearing the standards with symbols designating various units. Captured booty like looted riches and human prisoners featured prominently. Paul describes the Christian equivalent:

> But thanks be to God, who in Christ always leads us in triumphal procession [*thriambeuō*], and through us spreads in every place the fragrance that comes from knowing him. For we are the aroma of Christ to God among those who are being saved and among those who are perishing; to the one a fragrance from death to death, to the other a fragrance from life to life. (2 Cor 2:14–16)

Paul speaks in the plural but seems to refer to himself. Although he undergoes hardships and frequently has to change his plans, he asserts this is under God's control. He is led by God in Christ and is himself emblematic of the divine punishments and rewards that await people who respond to the gospel message negatively or positively, respectively. Biblical interpreters taking a postcolonial perspective have read this passage as evidence that Paul envisioned God triumphing over the empires of the world and instituting a new kind of rule. Richard A. Horsley argues, "Paul suggests that God is ultimately in control of history and is taking action precisely in Paul's own mission both to deliver those in the movement (from the imperial 'salvation' imposed by the saviour Caesar) and to condemn 'those who are being destroyed' in the divine judgment of the imperial order."[9] In this view, even as Paul undermines the authority of Rome, his use of military imagery to describe the believers as "soldiers of Christ" means that members of the Christ-believing communities participate in a new empire, controlled by God.

Any struggle the Christ-believers in God's empire undertake at God's command will succeed, according to Paul. He tells the Corinthians, "Indeed, we live as human beings, but we do not wage war according to human standards [Greek "according to the flesh"]; for the weapons of our warfare are not merely human, but they have divine power to destroy strongholds. We destroy arguments and every proud obstacle raised up against the knowledge of God, and we take every thought captive to obey Christ" (2 Cor 10:3–5). Note that the believers should figuratively enslave, or "take captive," their own thoughts, and they should do this on behalf of their commander Christ. Paul reinforces again and again that Christ is the victor and the Christ-believers, his foot soldiers, share in the victory:

> But each in his own order: Christ the first fruits, then at his coming those who belong to Christ. Then comes the end, when he hands over the kingdom to God the Father, after he has destroyed every ruler and every authority and power. For he must reign until he has put all his enemies under his feet. The last enemy to be destroyed is death. For "God has put all things in subjection under his feet" [quoting Ps 8:6]. (1 Cor 15:23–27)

Christ enforces and benefits from the power and might of God, as in Philippians 2:9–10, where Christ is exalted and then all beings kneel to him.

Paul applies martial imagery to the Christ-believers, imagery that would create a sense of shared purpose and devotion. As soldiers commanded by God, the Thessalonians could envision themselves as equipped with the strength of mind and heart they needed to face persecution or despair. They could also look forward to sharing in homosociality, upward social mobility, and the reward of belonging to God's powerful military. The believer-soldiers, taking on a new identity defined by their allegiance to Christ the commander, might also think of their evangelizing work as colonization on behalf of a divine empire.

THE IMAGE IN OTHER EPISTLES ATTRIBUTED TO PAUL

Authors of the Deutero-Pauline epistles employed the image of soldier of Christ in ways that were largely similar to what we find in the undisputed letters. The slightly later time period in which these letters were composed may have influenced the ways Christ-believers writing and reading the letters would have thought about the immediate nature of the Parousia and therefore the urgency of advancing the gospel message through evangelizing colonization. Nevertheless, the epistles evince an attachment to martial imagery that might create belonging for those looking for purpose.

At 2 Thessalonians 1:6–8, God's military might is evoked. According to Paul's apocalyptic vision in 1 Thessalonians, Christ the commander would call up the troops of believers to join the ranks of the resurrected. Here, though, the letter's author envisions God repaying those who "afflict" the Christ-believers with affliction, when Jesus is "revealed from heaven with his mighty angels in flaming fire, inflicting vengeance on those who do not know God and on those who do not obey the gospel of our Lord Jesus."[10] The image of military might has expanded to include retribution against the enemies of the gospel. Confident in God's victory on their behalf, the believers can "stand firm [*stēkō*] and hold fast to the traditions that you were taught by us, either by word of mouth or by our letter" (2 Thess 2:15). Their share of the victory is here explicitly attached to adherence to tradition and authoritative teaching, as opposed to the kinds of attitudinal requirements (hope, faith, courage) referenced in the undisputed letters.

The Letter to the Ephesians, too, is considered pseudepigraphic, although there is not full scholarly agreement on this point. The letter shares a martial metaphor with the undisputed Pauline epistle to Thessalonica, but the author's development and application of that metaphor adds some striking components. The author encourages the community to "put on the whole armor [*panoplia*] of God" (Eph 6:11). The exhortation to don an entire military kit is immediately followed with a justification: "so that you may be able to stand against the wiles of the devil" (Eph 6:11). Rather than seeing the armor of spiritual virtues as necessary in light of flagging hope or the delay of the Parousia, the assumptions operating in Thessalonica, this author proposes that the armor of God will protect Christ-believers from hostile external forces. The letter continues with an explanation: "For our struggle is not against enemies of blood and flesh, but against the rulers, against the authorities, against the cosmic powers of this present darkness, against the spiritual forces of evil in the heavenly places" (Eph 6:12). The word for "struggle" here is a term from wrestling matches, demonstrating again the close connections between athletics and military service in the ancient Mediterranean. One biblical interpreter, Michael E. Gudorf, has argued convincingly that the author may have had in mind a heavily armored soldier also skilled in wrestling; this kind of figure, the *hoplitopalas*, is described in passages from Aeschylus, Greek playwright, and Plutarch, the famous biographer. Such a fighter would have key attributes like the ability to remain standing, the ability to throw an opponent in a close hand-to-hand struggle, and the ability to use tricks or cunning to defeat enemies.[11]

As in 1 Thessalonians, the pieces of armor are delineated and linked to particular virtues:

> Stand therefore, and fasten the belt [in verb form: *perizōnnumi*] of truth around your waist, and put on the breastplate [*thōrax*] of righteousness. As shoes for your feet put on whatever will make you ready to proclaim the gospel of peace. With all of these, take the shield [*thureos*] of faith, with which you will be able to quench all the flaming arrows of the evil one. Take the helmet [*perikephalaia*] of salvation, and the sword [*machaira*] of the Spirit, which is the word of God. (Eph 6:14–17)

The other military language in Ephesians is related to victory and dominion, which in Paul's world was enforced by military power. The author writes about Christ's resurrection and exaltation in military terms:

> God put this power to work in Christ when he raised him from the dead and seated him at his right hand in the heavenly places, far above all rule and authority and power and dominion, and above every name that is named, not only in this age but also in the age to come. And he has put all things under his feet and has made him the head over all things for the church, which is his body, the fullness of him who fills all in all. (Eph 1:20–23)

This unification is enforced by military might, aligned with what looks like divine imperial power.

Similarly, 2 Thessalonians highlights God's victory, by contrast with the humiliating and terrible punishment that awaits the enemies of Christ, "those who do not obey the gospel of our Lord Jesus" (2 Thess 1:8). Their punishment is to be "separated from the presence of the Lord and from the glory of his might, when he comes to be glorified by his saints and to be marveled at on that day among all who have believed" (2 Thess 1:9–10). Note that the glory and might of an enthroned, emperor-like God/Christ is in view here, too.

Christ's ability to enforce peace is linked to his blood being shed on the cross. This would resonate with Roman ideas of military might and enforcement: peace is always ensured through the exercise of power. God is the one who ensures peace in Colossians: "For in him [Christ] all the fullness of God was pleased to dwell, and through him God was pleased to reconcile to himself all things, whether on earth or in heaven, by making peace through the blood of his cross" (Col 1:19–20). This heightened focus on the spiritual nature of Christ-believers' opponents draws attention again to a link between belonging and devotion to ultimate causes in a struggle that goes beyond the earthly. Christians were not alone in attaching cosmic significance to military identity. Soldiers, like others in the Roman Empire of the first century, participated in a variety of religious cults. They were expected to offer sacrifices to the Capitoline triad and to make sacrifices on behalf of Caesar's *genius*, for the emperor's well-being and, by extension, the well-being of the empire's inhabitants. This civic religion was particularly important for military personnel since the emperor was their commander in chief and the Roman gods could choose to ensure the success of their military campaigns.

Many soldiers also participated in cults focused on deities associated with military success. The most traditional of these was for the god Mars (Greek Ares), who was thought to govern war. However, in the first century many soldiers were devoted to a god newer to the empire, Mithras. Mithras appears to have been a god adopted from Persian (Iranian) religion, and his was a mystery cult reserved for male initiates. Through a series of rituals, most taking place in caves decorated with cosmic imagery, devotees could advance through successive ranks, learning more of the divine mysteries associated with the deity. Mithras's central myth featured him defeating a primal bull to ensure fruitfulness on earth, fighting then aligning with the sun god, and proceeding to heaven, whence he was expected to return.[12] His great power over life and death meant that by attaching themselves to this cult, the Roman soldiers sought to ensure not only earthly victories but also a happy afterlife.

The early Christ-believing communities had a similar expectation for their attachment to Christ; through his power, they would achieve the ultimate victory. The Letter to the Colossians illustrates this mindset. The letter's author thinks the believers will be able to stand up against enemy forces that might enslave them: "See to it that no one takes you captive through philosophy and empty deceit,...according to the elemental spirits of the universe, and not according to Christ" (Col 2:8). They will be so empowered because Christ has shown the way. The letter says, "He disarmed the rulers and authorities and made a public example of them, triumphing over them [*thriambeuō*] in it" (Col 2:15). While God led Paul as a captive in God's triumphal procession, the Christ-believers of this later generation are to imagine themselves watching on as Christ parades their defeated enemies before them.

The Pastor adds one more valence to the Pauline "soldier of Christ" image, the idea that Christ-believing soldiers are marked by their ability to follow orders. Again we see that the communities of the early second century were preoccupied with developing sustainable structures to ensure the longevity of the Christian movement. In 2 Timothy, the Pastor outlines the following expectations: "Share in suffering like a good soldier of Christ Jesus. No one serving in the army gets entangled in everyday affairs; the soldier's aim is to please the enlisting officer" (2 Tim 2:3–4). Like athletes (mentioned in the very next verse), figurative Christian soldiers are to be disciplined and focused, attending solely to the will of their commander, Christ. The understanding of soldiers as single minded does seem to reflect the military ideal. The life of a soldier in the Roman Empire was highly disciplined. The Roman standing army had been constituted under Octavian, also known as Caesar Augustus, emperor from 27 BCE to 14 CE. He initially set a sixteen-year term of active service followed by a period of four years as a reservist, though this was later expanded to twenty years of active service with an unspecified reserve term.[13] Soldiers were not allowed to marry while on active duty, though the men posted at forts around the empire sometimes defied this rule and started families. These expectations of extended, faithful service exemplify the dedication that was a hallmark of the Roman military. Like the ideal military man, the Christian "soldier of God/Christ" was to be completely dedicated to their life's divine mission: service that is pleasing to God.

The early Christian letter writers who followed Paul in the late first and early second centuries developed his image of a Christ-believing soldier serving in the empire of God. By emphasizing God's power to defeat cosmic forces, these authors also shifted attention from the homosociality and cooperation of fellow soldiers to the might of the metaphorical commanders, God and Christ. This shift may reflect a growing concern for developing communities that were united in an ecclesial structure that could be juxtaposed against the structure of Roman imperial power. To be a soldier of Christ now meant belonging to a defined community, following the orders passed down by an earlier generation of teachers.

EFFECTS OF THE IMAGE FOR EARLY AUDIENCES

The image of a soldier of Christ does not appear frequently in Paul's letters, but it captures something essential in Pauline theology: the embattled nature of the gospel and its preachers, and their dedication to a victorious Christ who is a conqueror. Paul might have been pleased to know that in the second century, the author of the Acts of Paul and Thecla depicted him as a stereotypical military general. The physical description reads as follows: Paul was "a man short in stature, with a bald head, bowed legs, in good condition, with eyebrows that met, a fairly large nose, and full of grace. At times he seemed human, at other times he looked like an angel."[14] Leaving aside the talk about his occasional angelic appearance, the description does not seem especially flattering to modern readers! Yet in the author's time, features like these were admired as signs of manliness, particularly in military generals. Robert M. Grant points out that a very similar description about the ideal general's physique, down to being bowlegged, can be found in the poetry of Archilochus, and it is echoed by Greek orators like Dio Chrysostom and the Greek physician Galen.[15]

In Paul's earliest letters, the Christ-believers were invited to think of themselves as soldiers preparing to join the divine ranks in resurrection to eternal life. Fifty years later, the Pastor reinforced the idea that soldiers in God's army should be totally dedicated to their cause. Those ordered to "stand firm" in the face of enemies and to work as fellow soldiers to spread the gospel throughout the known world could have taken an active role in expanding and enculturating the earthly "colonies" of God's empire. By arming themselves with faith and hope, the diverse readers of these New Testament epistles could take on a new identity and find a place to belong in that advancing empire. For some, especially women and enslaved people, perhaps being welcomed to serve in the metaphorical army of Christ afforded a kind of fellowship they could not achieve in the world of the Roman Empire and its military.

Chapter 6

CHRIST AS COMMANDER AND THE COST OF WAR

AFTERLIFE OF THE IMAGE: EARLY CHRISTIAN INTERPRETATIONS

As we turn to New Testament interpreters in the early Church, we will explore how theologians adapted the image of a soldier of Christ to conceptualize the growing power of the Christian community, envisioning themselves as embattled but destined for victory. Authors in the second through fifth centuries increasingly identified Christ as an almighty *kyrios* (Greek "lord") whose ascendancy could be explained using imperial and martial imagery. This dimension of the Pauline soldier of Christ metaphor took the early Church beyond a model of fellow soldiers who were equals in spiritual battle and drew them toward a vision of divine power that required Christians to serve as foot soldiers in the Christian imperial army.

THE POWER OF CHRIST ON DISPLAY

In the early second century, the Christian bishop Ignatius of Antioch took up Paul's martial image. He wrote to Polycarp (the later martyr) and Polycarp's congregation in Smyrna to encourage them. Ignatius advises, "Please him whom you serve as soldiers, from whom you receive your wages." The "wages" in view are presumably the heavenly reward Christians will receive in return for their lives of earthly service. He reinforced the idea that an eternal reward must be earned, urging his readers, "Let none of you be found a deserter [Greek *desertōr*, a Latin loan word from a military context]. Let your baptism serve as a shield, faith as a helmet, love as a spear, endurance as armor. Let your deeds be your deposits, in order that you may eventually receive the savings that are due you."[1] Leaning into a fiduciary metaphor at the end of his statement, Ignatius echoed Paul's understanding that those who perform a service will receive recompense (1 Cor 9:7). He also adopted the language of 1 Thessalonians, where spiritual qualities are protective armor that allow the Christian to endure hardship while remaining faithful. Perhaps most significantly, Ignatius carried forward one more subtle implication of the Pauline martial metaphor: if the Christians are faithful soldiers, Christ is the commander they serve, who controls the dynamics of judgment and reward. For Ignatius, Paul, and their readers, the Roman emperor was the military commander around whom they built their analogy.

Ignatius, executed under Roman law and remembered as a martyr, is perhaps a surprising mouthpiece for an image of Christ imbued with authority like the emperor's. But many theologians, authors, and artists made comparisons between Christ and the emperor in the early Church. One area of significant overlap was in the use of the title "savior," Greek *sōtēr*. Christians who lived in the empire were under the protection of the powerful "savior of the empire and world," the emperor *sōtēr*. This title captured the emperor's role as protector and guardian of the people in his territory. The emperors were portrayed as saviors particularly in their dual role as imperial high priest (*pontifex maximus*) and military commander. Two statues of the Emperor Octavian, aka Augustus (ruled 27 BCE–14 CE), illustrate the complementary nature of the ruler's saving power. The Via Labicana Augustus depicts the emperor prepared to make sacrifices to the gods on behalf of his subjects, a mediator who will secure the safety of the empire; his head is covered as a sign of piety. The Augustus of Prima Porta depicts the emperor in military dress, his cuirass (chest plate) carved with an image of a Parthian surrendering to a Roman soldier while deities look on; the detail symbolizes the emperor's responsibility for Roman might and conquest.[2] Later carved reliefs from the Sebasteion, a temple complex in the city of Aphrodisias set up to honor the Julio-Claudian emperors, show Claudius and Nero crowned as military victors, looming over the bound bodies of women and men representing conquered territories, from Judea to Britannia. In these reliefs the emperors appear nude, an iconographic indication that they are to be honored like the gods, who typically appeared nude in Greek and Roman statuary. Depictions of imperial power like the Arch of Titus, commemorating Roman victory over Jerusalem in 70 CE, included symbols of military might: swords, victims of conquest, crowns, and images of booty carted away in a celebratory triumph. The early Christians surrounded by these visual representations of imperial power and hearing Christ called *sōtēr*, would quite logically associate martial power with their savior.

When Christians applied the title *sōtēr* to Christ, it carried the cosmic valence of salvation from sin and death, or preservation for eternal life in the resurrection, a dimension developed in Paul's writings. Christ the savior was a ruler whose authority exceeded that of Caesar. The iconography used to portray Christ is particularly fascinating in this regard. Two sorts of images predominated up through the Byzantine period: Christ the Good Shepherd, often found in catacomb frescoes, and Christ the Enthroned Ruler, often displayed in the apse mosaics of churches. Both, explains Jennifer Awes Freeman, symbolized power and rule. The Good Shepherd, although it might seem like a humble image, was actually deployed to depict kings (including David in the Hebrew Bible) and gods (like the Greek deity Hermes) in the ancient Mediterranean. As such, it "carried connotations of both gentle caretaking and protection by violence into its Early Christian spaces."[3] The late second-century theologian Clement of Alexandria emphasized that Christ, in his role as shepherd, was an authoritative lawgiver, writing, "For the Word is 'the power and the wisdom of God' (1 Cor 1:24). Again, the expounder of the laws is the same one by whom the law was given; the first expounder of the divine commands, who unveiled the bosom of the Father, the only-begotten Son."[4] Christ's power to command and enforce the good was becoming cemented in Christian thought.

Scholars of early Christianity who use a postcolonial lens point out that Paul and the theologians who followed him in depicting Christ as savior, ruler, and commander were presenting early Christians with an alternative portrait of power and leadership, in terms and images that were familiar and easily understood. That is, naming Christ savior, and *kyrios* or "Lord," and talking about his Parousia, putting him at the head of a spiritual militia, or depicting him as an enthroned ruler would have set him up in competition with the emperor by using the same images and terms typically applied to that leader of the Roman Empire. This mixing of iconography and vocabulary is an example of hybridity, a "fluid, multivalent…state of identity" that is "produced by the interaction of the cultures of the colonizer and the colonized. Each affects the other, synthesizing people into a hybrid that mixes both cultures."[5] This mixing reached its zenith when Christians in the fourth century portrayed Christian emperors like Constantine and his successors in word and image. Eusebius, a historian writing in praise of Constantine, described the emperor as "a faithful shepherd" who offers to God "the souls of that flock which is the object of his care, those rational beings whom he leads to the knowledge and pious worship of God."[6] The image that had come from portrayals of rulers to signify Christ's commanding power was applied again to Christian rulers.

In a development that might have delighted Paul, narrative portraits of the apostle began to align him, too, with the imperial Christ. Margaret M. Mitchell, in her study of John Chrysostom's homilies about Paul, points out that Paul was painted with an imperial brush in the early Christian world. Chrysostom described Paul like an artist sketching and filling in a gradually more elaborate portrait of himself through his public ministry and said that this self-portrait was also an imperial portrait, because Paul presented himself on the model of Christ. What's more, Mitchell notes that Chrysostom called Paul soldier, general, and a soul prepared for combat, "to make Paul a one-man army, a soldier who fought on all fronts, against all enemies, using all the strategic maneuvers known to military science."[7] In these images and texts that portray Christ and his imitator Paul on the model of the emperor, Christians might have found a compelling alternative to Roman imperial power. If the emperor's power was a source of oppression, they could look instead to a superior ruler and commander in heaven. This affected the lives of soldiers in complicated ways.

ECCLESIOLOGY: A (RELUCTANT?) CHURCH MILITANT

The Life of Gregory Thaumaturgus, a fourth-century biographical narrative, praises Gregory Thaumaturgus, a third-century wonder-working bishop of Neocaesarea, for his military savvy. But Gregory (ca. 210/215–ca. 270/275 CE) never went to war in a literal sense. Instead, he rallied the Christian community and provided them necessary encouragement when they faced persecution by Roman forces.[8] The author notes that the Romans particularly sought to capture Gregory, who was "like a general [*stratēgos*]," so that "they might shatter the whole battle line of the faith." But the bishop "advised the church to pull back a little from the fearful attack, thinking it better that they should save their lives by flight than that, by standing in the battle line of the contest, they should become deserters from the faith."[9] This passage exemplifies an attitude quite different from that held by some of the early martyrs discussed in our chapter on athletes. Here, the preferred response to Roman violence is canny self-preservation. If Christians are forced to face the threat of capital punishment, they might apostatize; by abandoning the battle line, the community may live to fight another day.

This attitudinal shift reflects a widespread change in the calculus of Christian leaders of the third and fourth centuries who were shepherding larger flocks in a church that was gaining greater power within the empire.[10] Unnecessary loss of life depleted the resources of the growing *ekklēsia*. But it was also connected to a Christian theological rejection of violence. George E. Demacopoulos points out that

> Christian authors between the second and early fourth centuries (whose works survive) consistently disapproved of Christians engaging in violence and/or participating in the Roman army. Justin Martyr, Athenagoras, Irenaeus of Lyons, and the ever-influential Egyptian theologian, Origen, all implied (contrary to the surviving historical evidence) that Christians did not serve in the army and that they did not resist the Roman soldiers sent to arrest them but, instead, willingly gave themselves over to martyrdom.[11]

Thaumaturgus's example of fleeing possible martyrdom aside, the message from many theologians was clear: Christians should not be soldiers. Part of the concern seems to have been practical. If Christians joined the Roman military, they would be expected to participate in certain aspects of civil religious observance concomitant with military life but antithetical to Christian teachings about monotheism and idolatry. Tertullian's *On Idolatry* enumerates all the ways military service is incompatible with Christian life because of religious observances and feast days, when participation in polytheistic cultic practices was compulsory for officers.[12]

Some theologians insisted that Christians should engage only in spiritual rather than physical warfare.[13] Origen of Alexandria, in his text *Contra Celsum* (ca. 248), is quite clear that Christians should not become soldiers but should be as priests in the empire, fighting on its behalf with their prayers.[14] The text relies on the Pastor's command in 1 Timothy 2:1–2, "First of all, then, I urge that supplications, prayers, intercessions, and thanksgivings be made for everyone, for kings and all who are in high positions, so that we may lead a quiet and peaceable life in all godliness and dignity." In this interpretive tradition we see early Christian thinkers leaning even more strongly into the metaphorical sense of the soldier of Christ who preserves order through acts that reflect his spiritual dedication.

Theologians offered practical advice for the Christians who did enter military service. Basil of Caesarea, bishop in fourth-century Cappadocia (modern-day Turkey), recommends that a soldier who has killed in battle must abstain from the Eucharist for a period of three years, a form of practical excommunication. Some scholars interpret this as an indication that such a soldier has experienced spiritual trauma and requires healing before fully rejoining the religious community. In a letter, Basil wrote, "Our Fathers did not reckon killings in war as murders, but granted pardon, it seems to me, to those fighting in defense of virtue and piety. Perhaps, however, it is well to advise them that, since their hands are not clean, they should abstain from communion alone for a period of three years."[15] Scholar Valerie A. Karras points out that Basil uses the Greek word *phonos* (properly "murder") for both instances of "killing," so he himself is demonstrating that he does not draw the same distinction the "fathers" did (Karras suggests he refers probably only to Athanasius and Eusebius, because there were so few earlier bishops who wrote approvingly about war for Christians).

While all this ecclesiological debate was churning, everyday Christians enlisted in the army, and some soldiers from polytheistic backgrounds converted to Christianity. There are stories about Christian soldiers who became military martyrs under the Emperors Decius (r. 249–51 CE) and Diocletian (r. 284–305 CE). The existence of these stories contradicts claims made by third-century writers Origen and Celsus, who suggest that there really were not many Christian soldiers at all. The Christian historian Eusebius of Caesarea, writing his *Ecclesiastical History* in the early fourth century, praised military exploits of the Christian soldiers. Christians under and after Constantine began taking on roles in imperial government, meaning they even became responsible for running military campaigns. The more pacifistic tendencies of theologians like Basil did not carry the day.

In 439, the Christian Emperor Theodosius II passed laws that allowed only Christians to serve in the army. This was a significant change from previous policy and led to a major transformation in the way many Christians thought about military service and associated moral questions. Around this time, there was also a strategic shift from imperial expansion to defending the borders of what had become a largely Christian empire. A significant number of Christians (though never all) became more comfortable with fighting in defense of others than had approved of expansionist policies. By the sixth century, the transition was complete: in the Byzantine army, soldiers were expected to attend Mass, confess their sins, and receive the Eucharist before battle.[16] Paul's figurative soldier of Christ had merged with the everyday image of real Christian soldiers who served under Christian commanders and Christian emperors.

CONTEMPORARY CULTURAL CONTEXT AND NEW INTERPRETATIONS

As Josh Casteel himself pointed out in many interviews, his evangelical Christian upbringing taught him to think of military service and Christian faith as complementary. We need only recall the Pastor's image of the single-minded soldier, or the picture in Colossians of a Christ who is victorious through self-sacrifice, or Paul's call to don armor as fellow soldiers: all of these have become the basis for U.S. Christian praise for soldiers and military families who are Christlike in sacrificing themselves for the good of others. In an email conversation with his father, Josh highlighted the connection and one of its potentially harmful dimensions, saying, "Soldiers are indeed a grand example of sacrifice. It's simply a tragedy that this is so…because we have built up so many thick hedges around ourselves that we covet 'security' to the point of paranoia. The most valued people in society are those who maintain this security through violence."[17] As evidenced in the early Christian world, this can pose a challenge: Should Christians engage in violent action?

In Josh's application for conscientious objector status, he wrote,

> My dilemma is not so much one of moral action, but of sheer IDENTITY....In Christ God has shown us what it looks like to operate according to the way the world is. The tension of that reality against the powers and principalities which rule is the tension that ultimately led Christ to the cross. And what are we told? "Pick up your cross and follow me today! Do not be conformed to the world, but be transformed in the renewing of your mind!"[18]

The final sentence, a quotation of Romans 12:2, illustrates the way in which Paul's conception of wholehearted, identity-changing attachment to Christ-belief has continued to shape people's thinking about the self and what it means to belong to a community of Christian faith.

Josh's conviction drove him to serve as a public speaker, writer, and peace worker back home in the United States. Upon his honorable discharge, Josh joined the board of directors for Iraq Veterans against the War (IVAW), chairing the Religious Dialogue committee.[19] He completed a master's of fine arts from the University of Iowa and wrote two plays about his experiences in Iraq, *The Interrogation Room* (2006) and *Returns: A Play in One Act* (2008). Josh also appeared in two documentary films, *Iraq for Sale: The War Profiteers* (2006) and PBS's *Soldiers of Conscience* (2007), the latter of which profiled U.S. soldiers who became COs. In cooperation with groups like the Catholic Peace Fellowship[20] and the Lumen Christi Institute,[21] Josh delivered public talks about his experience and his vision of a more peaceful world. As his mother reflected, "He asked especially that help and hope be given to the people of Iraq that had been so devastated by the war, as well as the thousands of soldiers who were so wounded physically and emotionally by the war and the burn pits."[22] Josh died of cancer in 2012 at the age of thirty-two, while he was a student at the University of Chicago Divinity School, and the Joshua Casteel Foundation was created in 2013.

Not all Christian soldiers experience a disjunction like Josh did. The long just war tradition that first emerged in the Christian Roman

Empire, and the real need to defend the innocent from harm, can just as easily lead military personnel to experience their service as a necessary part of defending basic human values or even ensuring that others may freely live out gospel teachings. Ethicist Marc LiVecche, a scholar of just war and global statecraft at the Institute on Religion and Democracy, argues that there is solid theological ground to support the use of lethal force in war, and that under certain conditions, "the resort to force is not only an option for a combat soldier, but in most cases, a moral obligation."[23] At the same time, he acknowledges that many military personnel experience deep psychological, spiritual, and emotional harms when they perceive (on his reading, wrongly) that they have violated a fundamental moral law by killing.

Against this backdrop—the fraught nature of moral decision-making in wartime, the challenge of reconciling Christian teaching with national defense interests, the heavy costs borne by soldiers and their loved ones—Paul's image of the soldier of Christ takes on new dimensions. In what follows I attempt to indicate some avenues for Christian communities to support healing and avoid occasions for causing additional hurts among those soldiers and military families who seek belonging in the household of God.

PTSD AND MORAL INJURY

It will not surprise today's readers to hear that there are many sources of trauma associated with being a soldier, including experiencing and witnessing life-threatening events. One of the possible results is post-traumatic stress disorder (PTSD). In fact the clinical definition of PTSD was developed in cooperation with sexual assault survivors, survivors of the Holocaust, and military veterans.[24] Lingering effects of a severe traumatic experience can include trouble with memory; hypervigilance; feelings of fear, anger, or helplessness; and suicidal ideation. The U.S. Department of Veterans Affairs website publishes the following statistics about PTSD among veterans, differentiated by service area:

- Operations Iraqi Freedom (OIF) and Enduring Freedom (OEF): About 11–20 out of every 100 Veterans (or

between 11% and 20%) who served in OIF or OEF have PTSD in a given year.
- Gulf War (Desert Storm): About 12 out of every 100 Gulf War Veterans (or 12%) have PTSD in a given year.
- Vietnam War: About 15 out of every 100 Vietnam Veterans (or 15%) were currently diagnosed with PTSD at the time of the most recent study in the late 1980s, the National Vietnam Veterans Readjustment Study (NVVRS). It is estimated that about 30 out of every 100 (or 30%) of Vietnam Veterans have had PTSD in their lifetime.[25]

What is most notable is that these numbers exceed the percentages for PTSD diagnosis in the U.S. civilian population, which stands at about 7–8 percent, though the diagnosis is more common for women (10%) than for men (4%).[26] The VA also points out that sexual trauma can be a major source of PTSD for both male and female military personnel. Using statistics from those who are receiving VA health care services, the National Center for PTSD reports that 23 percent of women report sexual assault while in the military, while 55 percent of women and 38 percent of men experience sexual harassment while in the military.[27]

While these numbers are all quite high, scholars and clinicians have pointed out that the Diagnostic and Statistical Manual of Mental Disorders' definition of PTSD is not always adequate to capture what soldiers have experienced.[28] Shira Maguen, research and clinical psychologist at the San Francisco VA, proposed in a 2013 report that "there is accumulating evidence that trauma types are far more diverse, involving a much wider range of emotions at the time of trauma, and varying post-trauma reactions in the aftermath."[29] Maguen and others turn instead to a category of harm called "moral injury."

In a perhaps surprising twist, the originator of this term was an interpreter of ancient texts. Psychiatrist Jonathan Shay published a groundbreaking book in 1994, entitled *Achilles in Vietnam: Combat Trauma and the Undoing of Character*. Shay drew upon the Greek epic poem the *Iliad* to highlight the particular kinds of betrayal and resultant harms experienced by U.S. soldiers, demonstrating that the same issues raised in the ancient Greek account of the Trojan War recurred in the Vietnam war and are liabilities in any field of war. He focused in particular on betrayal resulting from unethical behavior by commanders who put subordinates in danger, leading to a fracturing of the soldier's sense of him- or herself as a competent moral agent. Shay proposed that veterans returning from war had incurred "moral injury" at the hands of commanders who put them in impossible moral situations with high stakes. His analysis was based on years of clinical observation and focus groups from his work as a staff psychiatrist at the Department of Veterans Affairs outpatient clinic in Boston, and the book is replete with first-person recollections shared by military veterans.

Since Shay first published his ideas, many other people from the fields of psychology, theology, and military science have joined the conversation. In 2009, military trauma expert Brett Litz and a team of scholars and clinicians added some important nuance to Shay's theories about betrayal leading to moral injury. They proposed,

> [Moral injury] may entail participating in or witnessing inhumane or cruel actions, failing to prevent the immoral acts of others, as well as engaging in subtle acts or experiencing reactions that, upon reflection, transgress a moral code....Moral injury requires an act of transgression that severely and abruptly contradicts an individual's personal or shared expectation about the rules or the code of conduct, either during the event or at some point afterwards.[30]

Note that this locates the site of injury not just in the betrayal itself, but in the soldier's later analysis of and reactions to their experience. Put simply, "moral injury is the result of reflection of memories of war or other extreme traumatic conditions. It comes from having transgressed one's basic moral identity and violated core moral beliefs."[31]

An important takeaway from the ongoing conversation about moral injury is the idea that the United States' contemporary wars continue to exacerbate the problem. With the increasing mechanization of war and the normalization of extended military operations on foreign soil, the general public has become more and more unaware of soldiers' experiences. Frequently soldiers do not feel connected to the general public back home in the states. Pulitzer Prize–winning military field reporter and pacifist David Wood has written specifically about the type of moral injury sustained by soldiers in Iraq and Afghanistan who see a disconnect between the tasks they have been asked to undertake quite explicitly "for the good of the country," and the attitudes of some segment of the public who consider the war unnecessary or downright immoral. As Josh wrote in one frustrated email to his mother, "I can't avoid politics here, I AM the front line of US foreign policy."[32] In the immediate aftermath of the August 2021 withdrawal of U.S. troops from Afghanistan, this disconnect has again come to the fore, creating for some soldiers and veterans feelings of betrayal.

Wood summarizes yet another source of conflict: the sense that in our most recent wars those in charge not only betrayed their subordinates but did so knowingly. He writes, "The generation of Americans who fought in Iraq and Afghanistan did so under a military high command that was trashing its own code of ethics in an astonishing and demoralizing display" by going to war on the basis of fabricated evidence and sanctioning the abuse of detainees at Abu Ghraib.[33] All of this adds to the sense that soldiers stand apart from regular society, bearing the physical, mental, and emotional costs of violence alone and unsupported. What can be done?

Shay includes a call to action at the end of his introduction: "Learn the psychological damage that war does, and work to prevent war. There is no contradiction between hating war and honoring the soldier. Learn *how* war damages the mind and spirit, and work to change those things in military institutions and culture that needlessly create or worsen these injuries."[34] In practical terms, this can mean making sure that veterans are not invisible and disregarded once they return. When and how can faith communities make space to listen to the stories military personnel have to share, even when these bring up feelings of discomfort, guilt, or helplessness? Through such acts of compassionate listening, can contemporary Christians step into empathy and acknowledge the humanity and integrity of individuals who have been put into impossible situations on behalf of all of us? Doing so could be one way of taking seriously the idea that all members of the Christian community, noncombatants included, are "fellow soldiers" who owe a debt of listening and acceptance to those we have pushed to the front lines.

CARE AND HEALING

Without community support and treatment, a shocking number of veterans die by suicide each year. The 2020 National Veteran Suicide Prevention Report, which included numbers for 2017–18, noted an average of 17.6 veteran deaths by suicide per day in 2018 and concluded that the rate of death by suicide for veterans who received VA support decreased by only 2.6 percent.[35] It was only in 2005 that the Defense Department made it mandatory for soldiers back from deployment to receive physical and mental health screenings, but Wood points out that "there was no system to track whether individuals who were flagged with serious mental health concerns ever got help."[36] The problem is compounded by a lack of adequate resources to support the successful management of mental health struggles. During the COVID-19 pandemic, such difficulties have increased, and preliminary numbers suggest there was a 25 percent increase in deaths by suicide among military service members October through December 2020, compared to the same time period in 2019.[37] Yet there is much reason to be hopeful. House Resolution 1656, appearing before the 117th Congress (2021–22), is called the Treat PTSD Act, and it seeks to make stellate ganglion block, a treatment for PTSD, more readily available for military personnel.[38]

Progress is not just medical but grounded in forms of community care that can help veterans reintegrate into civilian life and find sources of support. Shay's follow-up to *Achilles in Vietnam* engages with the experiences of military veterans who return to civilian life. Using another ancient Greek epic as a jumping-off point for comparisons, he published *Odysseus in America: Combat Trauma and the Trials of Homecoming* in 2002. In this book, Shay highlights parallels between contemporary war veterans and the tale of Odysseus, a soldier struggling to find a path home who confronts unexpected dangers and experiences compounding losses. The book highlights some of the hardships veterans face when they attempt to reintegrate into civilian society after being psychologically wounded in war: addiction, survivor's guilt, hypervigilance, self-medicating, anger, and inability to connect with others. Fully two-thirds of the book are dedicated to the topics of "Restoration" and "Prevention," an outgrowth of Shay's work with veterans' groups.

Rita Nakashima Brock, currently senior vice president and director of the Shay Moral Injury Center at Volunteers of America, is a leader in the ongoing conversation about ways to address moral injury among military veterans. She was founding director of The Soul Repair Center in Fort Worth, Texas, established in 2012 and "dedicated to equipping religious leaders and professional caregivers to respond to veterans and all affected by moral injury."[39] Together with Gabriella Lettini, a professor of theological ethics, Brock published *Soul Repair: Recovering from Moral Injury after War* in 2012. They outline an absolutely central component of repair and healing, which is for noncombatants to accept responsibility for healing the aftermath of war. On their assessment, such a task involves taking clear stock of the major moral issues at stake and being ready to listen to those who have experienced moral anguish caused by war. The book concludes with a call for families, communities, and society to take seriously the many costs of war, to come to understand "what it would require of every one of us to send any one of us to war."[40] How can Christians today draw on Paul's image of spiritual armor—garbing themselves in hope, love, and faith—as they prepare for such difficult work?

Many clinicians and scholars highlight the powerful role religious communities can play in providing substantive, transformative support for military personnel who have experienced injury and trauma. Marketing for the PBS documentary *Soldiers of Conscience* specifies that directors and producers intended the film to be shared with military-focused groups like the VA and the National Conference on Ministry to the Armed Forces, but also more broadly with a long list of religion-focused groups, like the Association for Clinical Pastoral Education, the Episcopal Diocese of California, and the Presbyterian Church USA Peacemaking Program.[41] The distribution list illustrates the expectation that faith groups have a vested interest in the work of repair. But what would this look like?

Faith groups can provide a space for ritual actions that might alleviate guilt and help the injured move toward self-forgiveness.[42] David Wood opens his book *What Have We Done* by describing a ritual of symbolic cleansing that one military chaplain led in Iraq in May 2006.[43] Christian faith groups, in particular, can draw on a rich theological tradition to start the work of healing preemptively by discussing just war and moral injury, providing guidance for soldiers before they see combat. Marc LiVecche calls on multiple communities to provide a more robust moral and theological education for soldiers, to help them recognize that their use of lethal force need not make them morally culpable. He recommends a thoroughgoing and collaborative approach:

> We need to come alongside our uniformed religious leaders—most especially the chaplaincy—to better equip, prepare, and train them to care for our warfighters downrange over the course of deployment. And we need to renovate our families,

> congregations, schools, civic organizations, and hometown communities to provide a home worth redeploying home to. This will include theological depth to help our warfighters address the sometimes disturbing questions with which they return.[44]

By making the work of care and healing a task shared by multiple stakeholders, perhaps faith communities can find a new way to live out Paul's call to serve as fellow soldiers for those who turn to the household of God for help.

There is a growing movement within the academic fields of biblical studies and religious studies more broadly to think about how sacred texts and living religious communities can provide support for those healing from moral injury. *Exploring Moral Injury in Sacred Texts*, a 2017 collection of essays edited by Dr. Joseph McDonald, offers case studies illustrating how the authors of texts from Jewish, Christian, Muslim, and Buddhist traditions have grappled with the question of moral injury. Brad Kelle's 2020 book *The Bible and Moral Injury: Reading Scripture alongside War's Unseen Wounds* provides some key insights about the way biblical texts can become newly meaningful for those who have served. While these scholars focus primarily on Old Testament narratives, like the stories of David and Joshua, it seems that the New Testament letters attributed to Paul should be part of the conversation. When Christian communities in the United States are reading these texts, even at the level of a small church Bible study, how can leaders and participants be more attentive to the traumatic or healing potential of Pauline texts about soldiers, armor, and God the military commander?

RECRUITMENT DISPARITIES

Briefly we might consider the system of military recruitment. I have vivid memories of stumbling across a Memorial Day parade in downtown Chicago in 2008. While the crowds on the sidewalk cheered and applauded, row after row of high school students in their Junior ROTC uniforms walked past. Overwhelmingly these young kids (probably ages fourteen to eighteen) were students of color. As the U.S. Army JROTC website states, "The US Army's JROTC program currently operates in more than 1,700 public and private high schools, military institutions, and correctional centers throughout the United States and overseas. Approximately 40% of JROTC programs are in inner city schools, serving a population of 50% minorities."[45] In light of this robust structure for early onboarding, a pipeline for recruitment, it is not surprising that the disparities bear out in the composition of troops. Brock and Lettini point out that while military service without the draft is technically voluntary, "a study in 2007 found that troops who died in Iraq were disproportionately poorer than the rest of Americans....New Army recruits come primarily from lower- to middle-class communities, southern states, and Black, Hispanic, and Asian communities, according to official US Army data."[46]

For such groups, historically marginalized and excluded from some other avenues for flourishing in the United States, the military may provide desirable things like stability, income, and the opportunity for advancement. Yet there seems to be a fine line between affording minoritized groups opportunities for advancement and exploiting members of those groups. While first-century Christ-believers might have associated upward social mobility with the New Testament metaphor of the soldier of Christ, making a Christian evangelizing mission attractive, today there is a high cost for minoritized communities when military service becomes the only, or the only attractive, option. There are even extreme instances in which military recruiters target prospective servicemembers under the age of seventeen, a violation of the United Nations Operational Protocol on Children in Armed Conflict.[47] Knowing this, how might Christian communities create additional and supplementary avenues for belonging to best support those who might consider military service their only option? What might it look like, on a practical policy level, to stand in solidarity as metaphorical fellow soldiers with groups that have been under-resourced and combat the unjust, discriminatory practices that disproportionately push young people of color toward harm?

PERIL AND PROMISE: SOLDIERS IN THE HOUSEHOLD OF GOD

In the first century, Paul outlined an active role for Christ-believers as fellow soldiers serving Christ. Within his historical context, this image of an evangelist equipped for spiritual battle might have called to mind the Roman promise of upward social mobility through honorable service. The "soldier of Christ" also captured the homosociality of the Roman military, opening fellowship and belonging for believers from a broad range of social contexts. While theologians and interpreters in the second through fourth centuries raised complicated questions about the morality of military service, they also helped develop a view of Christ that made him a powerful, just commander calling Christians of the Church militant to serve. Today the real experiences of soldiers and their loved ones challenge the idea that any soldier returns from war spiritually unscathed. If Christians today don the armor of hope, perhaps we can work toward the fellowship that comes of listening to those harmed by war, seeking forgiveness for our role in putting soldiers in harm's way, and advocating for effective paths to healing. What would it mean to truly be fellow soldiers to those who serve in the military and who belong in the household of God?

Continuing a conversation about care and communal responsibility, we turn next to the Pauline metaphor "body of Christ." In tracing the contours of this image and its interpretation, we come face-to-face with questions of human vulnerability and interconnectedness, features of our shared life that may hold promise for the embodied work of facilitating belonging.

PART 4

CARING FOR THE BODY OF CHRIST

Belonging as a "Member" of the Household

The COVID-19 pandemic that broke out worldwide, starting in 2019, brought the profound fragility and vulnerability of the human body to the forefront of our minds. It has also highlighted the fragility and vulnerability of the various social "bodies" we inhabit, from our families, communities, and nations to the whole human family. Many of us have recognized in new ways that we rely on one another for care, support, and advocacy. When safety and security seemed more uncertain than usual, our collective understanding of what it means to be embodied changed. Something taken for granted, like attending a worship service or liturgy in person, became suddenly more involved, providing insight into how important the body is for ritual practice and how challenging ritual practice becomes when the body is unruly. Innovations like livestreamed services allowed those in quarantine or isolation to join the community from the safety of home. The fact that such accommodations developed quickly when abled people needed them was experienced as a slap in the face by many people who live with disabilities and would have found such accommodations beneficial even before the pandemic. There is also a risk that many measures that increased accessibility will go away with a widespread return to "normal," if those measures are not seen as "necessary" for abled people.

Our collective human struggle with the effects of COVID-19 has the potential to raise awareness about equity and help us interrogate how our contemporary U.S. culture considers only certain bodies normal and worthy. How might this prolonged period of collective uncertainty continue to shape Christian attitudes to and language about the body going forward? How could a renewed appreciation for accommodations and community care shift Christian thinking about accessibility? In particular, how might increased awareness of all our bodies' vulnerability and need for care affect how the household of God prioritizes care, access, and belonging for disabled people, who live constantly with unruly bodyminds? I use the term *bodymind* intentionally, as it is designed to push back against a particularly Western conception of mind-body dualism that is somewhat at odds with early Christian thinking grounded in Judaism; Buddhism, too, has a well-developed conception of the holistic bodymind, or *namarupa*. The English term was popularized by, among others, American writer and activist Eli Clare, and it is often used in discourse about disability justice.[1]

Conflicting impulses to point out the need for sweeping social change, on the one hand, and to advocate for a return to "normalcy," on the other, stand out in media coverage of the pandemic's effects on disabled people and disabled bodies. Mainstream media outlets like the *Washington Post* and National Public Radio occasionally cover stories about the caregivers[2] whose spouses, elders, or children have experienced discrimination when seeking medical care and workplace or classroom accommodations[3] during the pandemic. Frequently these stories focus on the caregivers and the hardships they experience, rather than on the disabled people facing discrimination. But it is books, articles, and podcasts by disabled people that have consistently drawn attention to the deeper inherent inequalities of an ableist American society and its typical ways of talking about disability.

Imani Barbarin digs into the complex nature of the media's response to COVID-19, a response deeply shaped by ableist assumptions about health, privilege, and disability. Barbarin recalls the first wave of understaffed ICUs and overwhelmed hospitals in cities like New York: "The disability community have been lambs to the slaughter in regard to the COVID-19 crisis. Early medical rationing guidelines diverted resources from disabled patients to those with a 'greater return on investment.'"[4] The assumption that some bodies are more worthy than others comes with grim costs. As someone who has studied media depictions of people with disabilities for many years and as a disabled person herself, Barbarin is acutely aware of how media stereotypes about disability proliferate and how, in her words, "they often dictated how people would treat and react to me—and how much they would think my life was worth."[5] Indeed, the way a society talks about bodies, health, and humanity shapes the way members of that society think about and treat one another.

Barbarin summarizes the situation all bodies face because of the pandemic, particularly in light of unpredictable outcomes associated with long COVID or post-acute COVID syndrome:

> "Healthy" people were expected to recover from the virus after 14 days, but weeks after the virus hit the US, reports began flowing in of "otherwise healthy" and "relatively young people" needing double lung transplants, amputations, kidney transplants, dialysis, and oxygen.
>
> Non-disabled people only saw the potential outcomes of the virus as either life or death—they didn't account for the gray. Disabled people live in the gray. Even after the virus has left the system and patients are in "recovery," about one in three COVID-19 patients experience long-term symptoms and disability. They live in the gray now with us too.[6]

These observations apply not just to the pandemic, of course, but to all situations where accommodations that facilitate access for a variety of bodyminds could become a higher priority: workplaces, schools and colleges, state and local government centers and meetings, and community centers.

The Pauline epistles simultaneously addressed those in need of greater awareness and those in need of care. To highlight the absolutely transformative nature of belief in Christ, Paul and his imitators drew on the image of a collective "body of Christ," an *ekklēsia* of diverse individuals inextricably bound together in a new communal and cooperative whole. Each Christ-believer had become one "member" (Greek *melos*) of this body, contributing particular gifts and taking actions that affected the other members. This Pauline image of a single Christian body opened new avenues for people from different parts of society to come together and experience mutual support. At the same time, the letters tackled the relationships between spirituality, sinfulness, ritual, resurrection, and the body, highlighting ways that individuals could either contribute to or undermine care for the body of Christ.

Chapter 7 will bring forward several key dimensions of the image of the body of Christ in the New Testament letters attributed to Paul, with an eye to how each facet of the metaphor might have facilitated belonging for members of the Christ-believing communities in the first and second centuries. In particular, the Pauline material emphasizes the possibility of unity among people from quite diverse social locations. Chapter 8 begins by studying two moments in early Christian reception of this metaphor, demonstrating that the Christian body, especially the female body, became a site for theological reflection about perfection, boundaries, and spiritual reproduction. Turning to contemporary case studies focused on communal care for all bodies, the chapter will close with some suggestions about the benefits and harms that may come from continuing to deploy the Pauline image of the body of Christ as a tool for creating belonging in today's churches.

Chapter 7

MANY PARTS, ONE BODY

THE IMAGE IN THE UNDISPUTED PAULINE EPISTLES

Paul sent the letter we call 1 Corinthians in about 53 or 54 CE, during the most active period of his ministry. Although he writes from Ephesus,[1] he appears to have good knowledge of what has been going on in the city of Corinth, right down to the level of who was engaging in bad behavior and how various members of the community were trying to resolve local disagreements. In fact there is evidence of an extended and extensive two-way correspondence that sustained the relationship between Paul and the community of Christ-believers at Corinth. He probably first visited them to preach his gospel in 51 CE and then maintained an active interest in the growth of the Christ-believing community even as he continued his itinerant mission in other parts of the Mediterranean region. For example, Paul writes in 1 Corinthians 7:1 that he is responding to "the matters about which you wrote," implying there was at least one letter that came to him from the city, and in 5:9 he says, "I wrote to you in my letter," probably referring to a previous missive, parts of which may or may not be preserved in 2 Corinthians.[2] We also know he had received additional reports at the hands of messengers representing various groups (e.g., "Chloe's people" in 1 Cor 1:11). What has survived of this ongoing correspondence is a set of two letters from Paul, although many scholars speculate that both 1 and 2 Corinthians may be composite letters, collecting sections from multiple pieces of mail Paul sent to the *ekklēsia*.[3]

Corinth was a cosmopolitan hub near Athens on the Greek peninsula, a center for trade and a city whose Christ-believers reflected its ethnic, cultural, socioeconomic, and religious diversity. It was a prominent Greek city and a historic center of Hellenistic culture and learning. By the first century CE, Corinth was the capital of the Roman province of Achaia and therefore an important imperial asset. The city was also important to Paul, who maintained contacts among the small house churches he had established there. When Paul receives a report from Corinth that there is a growing schism within the *ekklēsia*, he writes an impassioned, lengthy letter designed to encourage unity. He puts forward the physical human "body" (Greek *sōma*) as an image that can help the Christ-believers think about their community.

Paul proposes, "For just as the body is one and has many members, and all the members of the body, though many, are one body, so it is with Christ. For in the one Spirit we were all baptized into one body—Jews or Greeks, slaves or free—and we were all made to drink of one Spirit" (1 Cor 12:12–13). Through the ritual action of baptism, the believers are initiated into a new identity; it replaces other ways of thinking about themselves—based on gender, class status, ethnicity, or ancestral religion—that might have kept them divided. Through the power of God's Spirit, they have become a single community.

Paul writes about how the diverse members of this community, figuratively different "parts" of the body, must work in tandem. He argues against making distinctions among members of the community in two ways. First, being a particular kind of body part is less significant than being a part of the one body. It is not acceptable to reject one's connection to the whole: "If the foot would say, 'Because I am not a hand, I do not belong to the body,' that would not make it any less a part of the body" (1 Cor 12:15). Second, being a particular kind of body part does not make it acceptable to reject the *other* parts of the body: "The eye cannot say to the hand, 'I have no need of you,' nor again the head to the feet, 'I have no need of you'" (1 Cor 12:21). Paul's collectivist thinking was likely inspired by Hebrew Bible texts, many of which portray the individual as a moral actor deeply embedded in kinship relationships, including the family and the broader religious community. As Robert A. Di Vito puts it, "The community provides the *raison d'être* for individual action and concrete behavior."[4] In short, the Corinthians must accept that they are in this *ekklēsia* together. Their shared body renders them mutually dependent.

For this shared body is not really *theirs* at all; it is the body of Christ. Paul explains, "Now you are the body of Christ and individually members of it" (1 Cor 12:27). Within this single body, God is in control. God has distributed gifts and positions of authority to members of the community, the one body. Whether a believer is an apostle, a teacher, a prophet, or someone who can speak in tongues, their gift comes from God and is to be used in the service of others. Belonging, then, is a gift that carries obligations.

In the first century as today, people's understandings of bodies—their own and others'—were shaped by society. Many of Paul's readers in the first-century Mediterranean world would already have been familiar with the idea of the body as a composite organism, made of parts organized in a hierarchical structure that work together and share a common fate. This informed many metaphorical uses of the "body" image, especially in philosophical and political texts. Stoic philosophers understood human beings to be a part of a larger world organism. In one of his letters, the Stoic philosopher Seneca explained, "All that you behold, that which comprises both God and man, is one—we are the parts of one great body. Nature produced us related to one another, since she created us from the same source and to the same end."[5] Such macrocosmic interdependence could also apply in smaller political structures. According to the first-century Roman historian Quintus Curtius Rufus, the kingdom was like a body, but the ruler was its head and the provinces were its members, allied under the leadership of the head.[6] Thus authors could use the image to reinforce collective belonging while maintaining hierarchical social structures. Sometimes the figurative presentation of the body would also organize the members or parts of the body along a spectrum from shameful to honorable, ascribing social or even moral value to individuals and groups that make up the whole.

Paul tackles head-on the idea that differentiation must create inequality. He responds to possible objections that not all body parts are equal by noting that "those members of the body that we think less honorable we clothe with greater honor, and our less respectable members are treated with greater respect; whereas our more respectable members do not need this" (1 Cor 12:23–24). He is most likely referring to the different treatment of sexual organs (less honorable) and parts like the head or hands (respectable). Paul points out that people actually show great care and respect in covering the "less respectable" parts of the body. He asserts that this paradox contains an important lesson about mutual obligation, writing, "But God has so arranged the body, giving the greater honor to the inferior member, that there may be no dissension within the body, but the members may have the same care for one another" (1 Cor 12:24–25). Although some members of the community may think of themselves as higher up in a typical social hierarchy, Christ-believers must reconsider whether that hierarchy ought to hold.

Paul is advocating for unity and mutual care in the face of apparent divisions. Biblical scholars have proposed a number of possible situations that might be behind the specific problem of division at Corinth. Perhaps the community members are divided because of personal allegiance, if there are Christ-believers from Jewish versus Gentile backgrounds,[7] or some of the Corinthians have chosen to follow the teachings of Apollos while others prioritize Paul. Maybe the issue is about variant teachings, such as whether forgiveness of sin in Christ requires asceticism or allows libertinism,[8] or whether some of the community members are teaching a proto-Gnostic gospel.[9] Perhaps the divisions can be mapped along socioeconomic lines, with the wealthy elite living out their religion differently from the poor and marginalized.[10] Whatever the problem, Paul uses the metaphor of a unified body to indicate that divisions have a terrible cost: "If one member suffers, all suffer together with it; if one member is honored, all rejoice together with it. Now you are the body of Christ and individually members of it" (1 Cor 12:26–27).[11]

Recall an important analogue in Greco-Roman philosophical and political thinking, namely the image of the body politic. Margaret M. Mitchell's 1991 book *Paul and the Rhetoric of Reconciliation: An Exegetical Investigation of the Language and Composition of 1 Corinthians* demonstrates that the letter as a whole treats the Corinthian *ekklēsia* as a political entity in need of unity. She compares the epistle to a type of deliberative speech called the *homonoia* (concord) speech, designed to convince the audience to "all agree and allow no schisms to exist among yourselves, but that you be mended together in the same mind and the same opinion" (1 Cor 1:10; note the echo in 1 Cor 12:25). The remedy for schism and division is to reinforce the proper social hierarchy, and in Paul's letters this hierarchy places Christ above all human beings, regardless of class or social position.

And Christ is physically present to the community through the presence of his messenger and representative, Paul. As he proclaims to the Galatians, "It was before your eyes that Jesus Christ was publicly exhibited as crucified!" (Gal 3:1). Paul says that he bears "the marks [Greek *stigmata*] of Jesus, branded" in his own body (Gal 6:17). In the message and in the person of Paul the evangelist, the Christ-believers gained some sort of access to the image of Jesus at the center of the gospel, who was crucified and raised from the dead. Commentator Sam K. Williams proposes that the letter's vivid imagery about a public display before their eyes "reminds the Galatians of the vividness with which Paul had initially presented the crucified one."[12] His teaching was so impactful that the new Christ-believers could practically see the events of Golgotha unfolding in their midst. Paul seems to hold that his physical body can act as a conduit for encountering Christ because, as he puts it, "it is no longer I who live, but it is Christ who lives in me. And the life I now live in the flesh I live by faith in the Son of God, who loved me and gave himself for me" (Gal 2:20). Jesus's saving act has so transformed Paul that Paul now cannot help but make Jesus known, in word and deed, with his whole body.

Because he is empowered by Christ, Paul can even boast that his weakness and suffering allow Christ's perfection to be more visible for the Christ-believers. On a psychological level Paul explains that Jesus assured him, "My grace is sufficient for you, for power is made perfect in weakness." So with confidence he writes, "I will boast all the more gladly of my weaknesses, so that the power of Christ may dwell in me" (2 Cor 12:9). Jennifer A. Glancy points out that in Paul's first-century context, his decision to boast about receiving beatings or being whipped in public (as in 1 Cor 11) would have set him up for ridicule. Unlike a soldier who earned his wounds in battle, Paul got his scars in a shameful and humiliating way. Yet his physical experience of humiliation is exactly what unites him to Jesus, who had a "condemned, flagellated, and ultimately crucified body."[13] Glancy reminds readers that Paul "believes that the story of Jesus' death is legible in the scar tissue that has formed over welts and lacerations inflicted by rod and whip. Paul's share in the sufferings of Jesus is a source of corporal knowledge and ultimately of personal power."[14] Showing up before the *ekklēsia* with vivid preaching, visible scars, and manifest bodily weakness, Paul makes Christ and Christ's power tangible. His letters teach that the body of a Christ-believer becomes a tool for pointing to Christ, the head of the community.

For Paul the body is not just a metaphor for the community. It is also a means of communication, a tool more effective than language.

Paul himself is a man of words, written and spoken. His rhetorical skill allows him to write powerful, persuasive epistles that continue to speak meaningfully to communities today. Yet at several points he disavows rhetoric in favor of physical proofs. His dismissal may be an example of excessive humility; nevertheless the fact that he asks his readers to shift their focus away from words and toward sense-perceptible realities reveals again the importance of the physical body for the Christ-believers' faith. He sums up his approach as follows:

> When I came to you, brothers and sisters, I did not come proclaiming the mystery of God to you in lofty words or wisdom. For I decided to know nothing among you except Jesus Christ, and him crucified. And I came to you in weakness and in fear and in much trembling. My speech and my proclamation were not with plausible words of wisdom, but with a demonstration of the Spirit and of power, so that your faith might rest not on human wisdom but on the power of God. (1 Cor 2:1–5)

On the one hand, it's clear that Paul experiences physical suffering. In several letters he thanks the addressees for showing care for him when he was in need (e.g., Gal 4:13–15). He describes receiving "a thorn…in the flesh" at 2 Corinthians 12:7, as a means of keeping him humble in the face of having received special revelation; scholars have debated what this "thorn" might be, and their suggestions include physical illness, mental illness, persecution, or spiritual trials. Even his opponents note that "his letters are weighty and strong, but his bodily presence is weak, and his speech contemptible" (2 Cor 10:10). On the other hand, his bodily weakness affords him an opportunity to emphasize that God is the true source of power and strength behind the gospel and those who proclaim it. Writing to the Philippians, he expresses the expectation that whether he lives or dies, "Christ will be exalted now as always in my body," that is, the actions of his ministry may point to Christ, whatever the cost to himself (Phil 1:20).

Perhaps the most important takeaway is that anyone's body may be put in service of the community. Indeed, in his extended discussion of the gifts that each individual brings as a member of the one body, Paul explains that these gifts are "manifestations of the Spirit" (1 Cor 12:7). As George T. Montague puts it, "The gifts are visible, outward evidences of the work of the Spirit. They are not merely internal graces of prayer."[15] Paul even insists that manual labor, which wealthy elites would have looked down upon, is dignified when it is undertaken on behalf of the *ekklēsia*. He tells the Thessalonians that he worked to cover his own living expenses "so that we might not burden any of you while we proclaimed to you the gospel of God" (1 Thess 2:9).[16] A Christian document from around the end of the first century, the Didache, or Teaching of the Twelve Disciples, establishes a baseline expectation that missionary apostles and prophets who visit church communities must support themselves financially. For example:

> If he wishes to settle among you and is a craftsman, let him work for his living. But if he is not a craftsman, decide according to your own judgment how he shall live among you as a Christian, yet without being idle. But if he does not cooperate in this way, then he is trading on Christ. Beware of such people.[17]

Paul's approach led at least some early Christians to expect their ministers to avoid burdening the community, using the body instead to teach and serve.

On the flip side, the body may also become a site of pollution. Although Greeks and Romans had a concept of spiritual pollution or miasma that could attach to a person who had committed a crime or heinous act, it is more likely that when Paul uses the language of pollution and blemish, he expects his readers to think about the concept of moral impurity as explained in Jewish Scriptures.[18] Michael J. Gorman points out that Paul's conception of holiness is grounded in the biblical idea that those people called to be in covenant relationship with the God of Israel are marked out by "difference from the life of Gentile nonbelievers" and "non-conformity to this age."[19] It is through their distinctive conduct, in conformity with divine law, that God's people can bear witness to the reality of God's existence as the one, true God. Ruptures of the covenant relationship, instances of transgression or sin (specifically idolatry, bloodshed, and sexual immorality), result in a state of impurity that can be repaired through repentance, amended behavior, and sometimes atoning sacrifice. Embodied behaviors driven by a negative internal state lead to rupture; that rupture can be repaired through a combination of internal repentance and embodied action.

Within this cultural milieu Paul argues that an individual Christ-believer, who is in relationship with God and Christ, possesses a body that can be harmed by sin. What's more, the collective figurative body may be endangered or harmed by the actions of one member. For example, in 1 Corinthians 5, Paul tackles a tough situation in the community, the case of a man who has taken up with his father's wife, presumably his own stepmother. He recommends, "You are to hand this man over to Satan for the destruction of the flesh, so that his spirit may be saved in the day of the Lord" (1 Cor 5:5). While this may seem like a drastic solution, a few paragraphs later Paul explains just what is at stake for those who engage in sexually immoral behavior: "Do you not know that your bodies are members of Christ? Should I therefore take the members of Christ and make them members of a prostitute? Never!...Every sin that a person commits is outside the body; but the fornicator sins against the body itself" (1 Cor 6:15, 18).[20]

The obligations to show respect for one's body also extend to using one's body in ways that reflect respect for other members of the *ekklēsia*. In Corinth, the matter apparently came to a head around the type of food people were eating, specifically "food sacrificed to idols" (1 Cor 8:1). What did this mean? Paul might be talking about the meat shared by Christ-believers who belonged to voluntary societies or private associations, affiliation groups almost like medieval guilds whose members might share a certain profession. In general, a voluntary society would be dedicated to a particular deity from the Greco-Roman pantheon, and its members would pay dues in order to enjoy certain benefits, such as having the group cover their funeral expenses. These groups would gather in a sort of "supper club" format that involved sacrifice, sometimes even meeting at the temple of their patron deity.[21] If Corinthian Christ-believers continued to attend their social groups, they might very well be eating meat that had been sacrificed to a god other than the God of Israel, that is, to an idol.

Paul could also be referring to regular meat purchased in a typical Greco-Roman marketplace, which often reached the market by way of a local temple, where parts of the animal carcass had been sacrificed to a god or goddess and the rest—including most of the edible parts—made available for human consumption.[22] Some of the Corinthians who have the necessary knowledge are able to proclaim, "'No idol in the world really exists,' and that 'there is no God but one,'" so they can eat the food like any other food, knowing it brings them no spiritual harm (1 Cor

8:4). However, Paul points out that there are other members of the community whose consciences are weak and who will be led to think that the Christ-believers are taking part in the cult of polytheistic deities and mistakenly think such behavior is permissible. It is crucial to be aware that one person's bodily practices affect others in the group and changing one's own behaviors can create an important benefit for others. In this way an individual can enact care for the whole body of Christ.

Of course, the "body of Christ" is also the food Christ shared in the eucharistic meal. Paul's recounting of the Lord's Supper (1 Cor 11:23–27) includes Jesus's statement over the bread: "This is my body [*sōma*] that is for you" (1 Cor 11:24). He reminds the Christ-believers that whenever they participate in this meal, they proclaim the death of the Lord until his Parousia. It is a ritual of remembrance and hope that binds the community together in the present. In Corinth, where people are divided from one another, the sharing in a single meal, the body of Christ, should create unity in the *ekklēsia*: "Because there is one bread, we who are many are one body, for we all partake of the one bread" (1 Cor 10:17).

Paul's writing about the eucharistic meal carried a double valence for his earliest readers. Not only was he explaining a ritual way the community could be united with one another and with Christ, but he drew their attention to the symbolic value of any shared communal meal. Ways of sharing food can reflect views people have of other members of their community. It appears the wealthy in Corinth were bringing their own food to the communal meal and the poor are being excluded from full participation (1 Cor 11:17–22). Paul offers corrective guidance, in part, by using body language in 1 Corinthians 12 to explain the proper attitude of those at the top of the social hierarchy toward those at the bottom. All Christ-believers must show appropriate care for those who are typically considered the least and do so concretely, nourishing their bodies.

Paul's assumption that the external body can reflect a person's internal state would have been quite common in his cultural context. In fact, there was a whole (pseudo-)science devoted to the study of physical characteristics and the ways they corresponded to character traits: physiognomics. Practitioners like Polemo, the second-century CE author of a physiognomic manual, assumed a direct link between internal character and external appearance. He wrote, "You should know, moreover, that the heart, from which the impulses of the soul originate and have their secret start, is the seat of thought. For the eye is joined to the seat of the heart and experiences the disturbance of [the heart's] thoughts and anxieties so that the discourse of the soul shines through."[23] For Paul, a Christ-believer's physical body ought to reflect internal unity with Christ.

As Paul puts it, he himself is "always carrying in the body the death of Jesus, so that the life of Jesus may also be made visible in our bodies" (2 Cor 4:10). The body's simultaneous connection to life and death is likely grounded in Paul's conception of baptism, which he describes as a means of dying with Christ so as to join in Christ's resurrection: "We know that our old self was crucified with him so that the body of sin might be destroyed, and we might no longer be enslaved to sin" (Rom 6:6). He contrasts two ways of life: the life according to the flesh and the life in accordance with the spirit. Living according to the flesh leads to death, but "if by the Spirit you put to death the deeds of the body, you will live" (Rom 8:13). Paul frames this fundamental dichotomy not to reject the body but to emphasize that the body can become a conduit for bringing Christ's presence and abundance into the community.

In 1 Corinthians, Paul frames a challenge to those who engage in sinful behaviors: "Or do you not know that your body is a temple of the Holy Spirit within you, which you have from God, and that you are not your own? For you were bought with a price; therefore glorify God in your body" (1 Cor 6:19–20). Not only are the actions of an individual body relevant for the good of the community as a whole, but those actions have an impact on the individual's relationship with the divine. The body as "temple" or "sanctuary" (the Greek is *naos*) sets up a sort of obligation for any person with a body. The Christ-believer should avoid engaging in the kinds of immoral actions that would "dishonor" (Greek *atimazō*) the body (Rom 1:24).

Finally, Paul insists that the believer's earthly body is not the fullest expression of the self; that will not be known until the resurrection. Paul understands that the resurrection body will be rooted in but noticeably different from a person's earthly body, comparing the earthly body to a seed and the resurrection body to the resulting plant (1 Cor 15:35–38). This body will be imperishable, spiritual, glorious, powerful, and more perfectly Christlike. He can confidently proclaim that Christ "will transform the body of our humiliation that it may be conformed to the body of his glory" (Phil 3:21).

The image of a unified body, made up of many parts, was an effective tool in Paul's evangelizing mission. If all Christ-believers become part of the one body of Christ, they incur corresponding privileges and obligations that are unlike what they might expect from the hierarchical, patriarchal society of the Roman Empire in which they are accustomed to think of themselves. As members of the body of Christ, the believers are called to share their unique gifts for the benefit of the whole group. They are reminded that their actions, both moral and immoral, have real effects on the flourishing of their neighbors within that community. The call to show mutual respect and to actively take care of the body implies an approach to community life grounded in physical realities and real physical needs. Those who experience physical, emotional, or mental suffering may find encouragement in Paul's message that every person's body, regardless of how it may be assessed in earthly terms, can be unified to Christ and may reveal Christ to others. What is more, the Christ-believers may look forward to the time when their resurrected bodies will reflect Christ's glory even more fully.

THE IMAGE IN OTHER EPISTLES ATTRIBUTED TO PAUL

In the Letters to the Ephesians and the Colossians, the image of a single body of Christ signifies not just ecclesial unity but the transformative effects of redemption. Community members who are part of the body can look ahead to their future glorification. God raised Christ from the dead, placed him on a throne, "and he has put all things under his feet and has made him the head over all things for the church, which is his body, the fullness of him who fills all in all" (Eph 1:22–23). As in the undisputed epistles, the Church is the body of Christ but here it is a glorified body, and belonging to it offers a foretaste of the resurrection. This forward-looking stance is possible because Christ's suffering body was a site of reconciliation.

The author of Ephesians focuses on reconciliation between Jews and Gentiles, which took place not only in the symbolic action of the eucharistic meal (as Paul told the Corinthians), but in the crucifixion. The letter says of Christ,

> For he is our peace; in his flesh [*sarx*] he has made both groups into one and has broken down the dividing wall, that

> is, the hostility between us. He has abolished the law with its commandments and ordinances, that he might create in himself one new humanity in place of the two, thus making peace, and might reconcile both groups to God in one body [*sōma*] through the cross, thus putting to death that hostility through it. (Eph 2:14–16)

The focus is less on the actions or obligations of those who participate in Christ than on the work of Christ himself. The "hostility" mentioned here is not the ideological or social division that plagued the Christ-believing community in Corinth. Instead, the author seems to be digging into the mechanics of how diverse persons can become a single body to begin with. The undisputed epistles referred to early Christian practices like baptism and Eucharist, rituals that take place in the community and that bring the believers together by uniting them to Christ. Ephesians describes instead the earlier historical moment of the crucifixion, pointing out that Christ's death created the conditions for the unified Christian body to exist.

The author of Colossians also links Christ, the "head" of the body, with reconciliation, but he focuses on reconciliation between God and sinners, not between diverse groups within the community. According to this letter, Christ's crucifixion effected a transformation of the believers: "And you who were once estranged and hostile in mind, doing evil deeds, he has now reconciled in his fleshly body through death, so as to present you holy and blameless and irreproachable before him [God]" (Col 1:21–22). The author insists the community will remain reconciled "provided that you continue securely established and steadfast in the faith" (Col 1:23), highlighting a concern that seems better suited to a community facing a delayed Parousia than a group still awaiting Christ's imminent return.

There are other indications that the communities addressed by these two letters may be part of a later generation. For example, the author of Colossians envisions a different symbolic role for the evangelist's physical body. Speaking as Paul, the author claims, "in my flesh I am completing what is lacking in Christ's afflictions for the sake of his body, that is, the church" (Col 1:24). Paul's body, as understood here, is not just a vessel making Christ's suffering visible as a form of gospel proclamation. Rather than a reflection of Christ, here Paul's body is an extension, the implication being that the community of the author's day requires things that the historical Christ did not provide.[24] This shift at least suggests that the writer is less concerned about establishing a fledgling *ekklēsia* than meeting the changing needs of an established community.

In addition to the image of a body of reconciliation, both letters touch on the theme of development and growth. We can see a hybrid metaphor combining the body of 1 Corinthians 12 with the image of children growing to maturity. The Ephesian Christ-believers must use their individual gifts in order to "build...up the body of Christ" (Eph 4:12) so that the whole might reach maturity: "We must grow up in every way into him who is the head, into Christ, from whom the whole body, joined and knit together by every ligament with which it is equipped, as each part is working properly, promotes the body's growth in building itself up in love" (Eph 4:15–16). Among the Colossians, maturity is for those who hold fast to the head, "from whom the whole body, nourished and held together by its ligaments and sinews, grows with a growth that is from God" (Col 2:19). As in the undisputed letters, Christ is the head of the body. Whereas the image of Christ-as-head was a way for Paul to "flatten out" the customary social hierarchy in Corinth, here the authors seem to suggest that Christ-as-head provides a particular kind of direction for the members of his body. Rather than working together and displaying care for the dignity of the other members (1 Cor 12), the individual Christ-believers addressed in Ephesians and Colossians are to focus on their connection to the head.

In Ephesians, even the idea of caring for the body comes to signify something different than the mutual obligations incurred by Christ-believers; care is instead enacted out of obligation directly to Christ. In an oft-quoted passage, the author forges a link between a marriage relationship and ecclesiology. Wives are to obey their husbands, "for the husband is the head of the wife just as Christ is the head of the church, the body of which he is the Savior" (Eph 5:23). Husbands are to love their wives with a love that mimics the self-sacrificial love Christ showed for the Church (Eph 5:25) and to treat their wives with the care they show their own bodies, "for no one ever hates his own body, but he nourishes and tenderly cares for it, just as Christ does for the church, because we are members of his body" (Eph 5:29–30). Note that for this image to be effective, the audience must be familiar with the typical hierarchical relationship between the partners in an ancient Mediterranean marriage and then transfer that understanding to their thinking about Christ and the Church. Rather than members of the one body caring for one another, the body is understood to rely on Christ and submit to him.

Care for the body is discussed in a slightly different way in Colossians. For this author, as for Paul, spiritual discipline and right attitude are symbolically visible in the way one carries one's body. A person's dedication might be made known through symbolic acts like adorning the body with spiritual qualities, as when the believers are instructed to "clothe yourselves with love.…Let the peace of Christ rule in your hearts, to which indeed you were called in the one body.…Let the word of Christ dwell in you richly" (Col 3:14–16). The goal for each Christ-believer is to create alignment between the internal life of faith and the external acts of daily life in community.

The Pastor's usage of bodily imagery seems focused on the dangers and threats from external forces and false teachings. As we have seen, these are common themes in the Pastoral Epistles. Preserving the health of the Christian community is a matter of nourishing the collective body with the proper tradition. On the whole in fact, the body is less relevant than proper spiritual orientation, especially for Timothy the minister. The Pastor advises him, "Train yourself in godliness, for, while physical training is of some value, godliness is valuable in every way, holding promise for both the present life and the life to come" (1 Tim 4:7–8). In contrast to Paul's message about food sacrificed to idols, in the Pastoral Epistles the author seemingly rejects the idea that physical practices are spiritually harmful. The Pastor preemptively rejects teachings of those who would "forbid marriage and demand abstinence from foods, which God created to be received with thanksgiving by those who believe and know the truth" (1 Tim 4:3). We see here a rather significant shift from concern about embodied acts to concern for right knowledge of gospel teachings.

The three letters also teach that embodied practices reflect internal dispositions, a pattern already noted in the undisputed Pauline epistles and Colossians. The types of conduct the Pastor discusses have to do with community and household structures. People who seek leadership positions should demonstrate that they can control their physical desires, like the bishop who is "not a drunkard, not violent but gentle, not quarrelsome, and not a lover of money" (1 Tim 3:3). Even bodily adornment can be indicative of one's spiritual state, and the Pastor teaches that "women should dress themselves modestly and decently in suitable clothing, not with their hair braided, or with gold, pearls, or expensive clothes, but with good works, as is proper for women who profess reverence for God" (1 Tim 2:9–10). Immoral behaviors and false teachings are characterized as physical infirmity: "Avoid profane chatter, for it will lead people into more and more impiety, and their talk will spread like gangrene," the death of the body's tissues (2 Tim 2:16–17). This symbolic threat to the communal body can be stamped out through proper adherence to the authoritative teachings that come from Paul and commitment to Jesus, "who gave himself for us that he might redeem us from all iniquity and purify for himself a people of his own who are zealous for good deeds" (Titus 2:14).

EFFECTS OF THE IMAGE FOR EARLY AUDIENCES

The New Testament authors adopting Paul's powerful body of Christ image certainly recognized its utility for drawing the diverse members of a Christian community into cooperative relationship. The first readers and hearers of the Deutero-Pauline and Pastoral Epistles probably would have understood the emphasis on Christ, the head of the body, as an indication that their individual conduct had an impact on their relationship to that head. Adhering to proper teachings, conducting their lives outwardly in ways that reflected their internal beliefs and values, these Christ-believers could expect to grow closer to Christ. They received reassurance that Christ would care for them the way they cared for their own bodies. Following the many role models available—Christ, Paul, leaders like Timothy, the bishops, and deacons—all members of the community could hold onto the hope that their collective body would participate in Christ's glory at the resurrection.

Chapter 8

CARE FOR THE BODY

AFTERLIFE OF THE IMAGE: EARLY CHRISTIAN INTERPRETATIONS

The epistles attributed to Paul share a clear sense that the human body can be a site for expressing abstract spiritual realities and revealing a person's internal disposition, especially one's commitment to living in accord with the gospel of Christ. As time passed and the changing Christian community developed a variety of understandings about what it could mean to be Christlike, Christian views of the body also changed, yet threads of this Pauline understanding are woven into later conceptions of embodied Christian faith.

DISCIPLINING THE BODY: ASCETICISM

In the sixth century, a compelling text began to circulate among Christians in the monastic communities of Northern Africa. The text, attributed to Sophronius, the bishop of Jerusalem, begins by introducing readers to Zossima, a pious Palestinian monk who believes he has exhausted the teachings of his local Christian community. The exceedingly ascetic monk muses, "Is there a monk on earth capable of affording me benefit or passing on to me anything new, some kind of spiritual achievement of which I either do not know or in which I have not succeeded as a monk?"[1] In order to learn more about holiness, he travels to a monastery near Jerusalem, on the bank of the Jordan River. There, in the company of his fellow monks, he continues his life of devotion, especially practices of renunciation and asceticism: "For all of them there was only one aim to which all were hastening: to be in the body as a corpse, to die completely to the world and everything in the world."[2] By disciplining his body and shaping the habits of his daily life to center on prayer, Zossima feels assured that he is fulfilling his religious calling.

One year during Lent, when all the brothers leave the monastery for their customary forty days of fasting and solitude in the desert, Zossima comes across a mysterious figure who challenges all his conceptions of himself, of true holiness, and of living a Christlike life. He sees "a woman and she was naked, her body black as if scorched by the fierce heat of the sun, the hair on her head was white as wool and short, coming down only to the neck."[3] The woman notices Zossima and immediately flees. Captivated by the mysterious fugitive, Zossima sets off in pursuit. When he finally catches up to his quarry, she stands at a modest distance, addresses him by name, and requests that he give her his cloak, so that she may cover her "woman's weakness" and greet the monk properly; she offers him a blessing.[4] When she prays before him, Zossima notices "that she had risen a cubit from the ground and was standing praying in the air."[5] This is Mary of Egypt.

Although Mary is initially reluctant to speak with Zossima, she is eventually convinced to share her backstory. Drawing a connection between physical appearances and spiritual realities, she says, "As you have already seen my naked body, I shall also lay bare before you my deeds, so that you may know with what shame and contrition my soul is filled."[6] She recounts with great shame her youthful life of licentiousness, including her decision to board a ship full of Egyptian and Libyan men heading from Alexandria to Jerusalem, in hopes that she might find "more lovers for my lust" in a new city.[7] When she eventually made her way to Jerusalem, just in time for the Feast of the Exaltation of the Holy Cross, Mary found herself unable to enter the church. She realized it was her sinfulness that was holding her back. Retreating sadly into the courtyard, Mary encountered a holy icon of Mary the mother of Jesus and prayed fervently, "I beg you, from whom Christ took flesh, to guarantee my promise, which is, that I will never again defile my flesh by immersing it in horrifying lusts. As soon as I have seen the cross of your Son, holy Virgin, I will go wherever you as my mediator for salvation shall order and lead."[8] The sinful Mary experiences the holy mother's compassion and embarks on a life of self-denial. She heads out into the wilderness, where she starves her lust by avoiding the company of other people and denying her body sensual pleasures like food and fine clothing, devoting her time instead to prayer. Mary reports that during her entire sojourn in the desert—a period of about forty-seven years—she consumed only the two and a half loaves of bread she brought with her across the Jordan.

By the time Zossima meets her, she is utterly transformed. Through the extreme asceticism that separates her from her past life, Mary has become a holy being. Her physical form now reflects her spiritual state, whereas before her fleshy body led her toward spiritual ruin. As the text explains it, her body no longer looks or behaves like the bodies of other human beings. The author of the text clearly implies that the text's readers, like Zossima, should wonder at the glorious transformation of Mary's physical body, which signifies the transformed state of her immortal soul. And indeed, Mary is a figure revered as patroness of penitents in the Roman Catholic Church, while in the Eastern Orthodox Church she is commemorated on the fifth Sunday of the Great Lent. When she appears in iconography, her body is depicted as sun-browned and she is emaciated, her physical form providing secure evidence of her self-discipline. Within the *longue durée* of the Christian tradition, Mary has become a symbol of holy renunciation. Yet as modern scholar Peter Anthony Mena points out, another reading is possible: "Her abundant desires have persisted in the desert and they have grown to include an unrestrained desire for the divine."[9] Asceticism brings her back around to a holy desire that she can express with new bodily practices.

The story describes two more encounters between Mary and Zossima, both of which position her as an authority and role model for the monk who had mistakenly believed he knew all there was to know about holiness. They met again during the following Lent, on the banks of the Jordan River. As Zossima looked on, Mary "stepped on to the water and walking over the flowing waves she came as if walking on solid land."[10] Zossima offered Mary communion, the consecrated body and blood from the Holy Thursday liturgy commemorating the Last Supper. She also deigned to take just three lentils as sustenance before heading back into the wilderness. Another year passes, and when Lent arrives, Zossima heads out to look for Mary, praying, "Shew me, O Lord, that angel in the flesh of whom the world is not worthy."[11] There in the wilderness Zossima finds Mary's corpse and an inscription that notes the time of her death, which took place just hours after she received the communion at their last encounter. Though deceased, Mary has left her physical body to become the site of yet more holy wonders, not the least of which is the inscription itself: Mary had told Zossima she was entirely uneducated! As Zossima bemoans his inability to provide the holy woman with an adequate burial, a wild lion appears, licks Mary's feet, and gently digs a grave. Even the creatures of the natural world recognize and honor her holiness.

For the earliest readers of this text, Mary of Egypt demonstrated without a doubt that the body is malleable, subject to rational and spiritual control. The flesh can be disciplined in such a way that it transforms a person's spiritual nature. The wonders Mary can perform are not simply superhuman feats, they are signs of God's favor, bestowed on the sinner who embodies true repentance. We might see this story as one narrative manifestation of Pauline teachings: the body of a Christian may be conformed to the body of Christ, and through Spirit-empowered acts of virtue, the body becomes a temple that can reflect for viewers the holiness of its soul.

THE BODY AS BIRTHPLACE: *THEOTOKOS*

We find additional reflections on the potential of the Christian body for holiness in theological claims about Mary of Egypt's patroness, Mary the mother of Jesus. She becomes known by the title *theotokos*, Greek for "god-bearer." The Greek verb *tokaō* that forms part of this compound word was used to describe someone or something about to deliver or give birth. The emphasis is on pregnant expectation, something we cannot quite capture with the English translation "bear," which could mean "carry" in a general sense.[12] At the ecumenical Council of Ephesus in 431, church leaders officially agreed to refer to Mary as *theotokos*, though the title had been used earlier by Athanasius, Eusebius, and the Cappadocians in the fourth century. They could confidently make this claim because by that time, they had also agreed to hold as doctrine the idea that Jesus was both fully human and fully divine. Because he was both God and man, it could reasonably be claimed that his mother had given birth to God. After all, the Gospel of Luke uses the title "mother of the Lord" to refer to her (Luke 1:43).

Why did the title *theotokos* only become part of Mary's image in the fourth and fifth century? Up to that point, much theological attention had been focused on the identity of Jesus as Messiah, the nature of his relationship to the God of Israel and to humanity, and the logistics of calling the crucifixion and resurrection of Christ a salvific event. When they sought to explain what it meant to say that Jesus is God but that he was also born as an incarnate human being, early Christian readers and theologians had to grapple with the fact that the four most widely read Gospels, attributed to eyewitness or second-generation apostolic sources and eventually considered part of the canonical New Testament, contained very different kinds of teachings about the birth of Jesus. Their reflections on Mary's role were sometimes incidental to the central conversation about her son.

Mary's apparent import also varies depending on which Gospel account is in view. In Mark, there is no specific discussion of the birth since the evangelist jumps into his narrative with an account of Jesus's baptism. Mark does mention that Jesus had a family; in Jesus's hometown of Nazareth the locals react to his wisdom and power with disbelief, asking, "Is not this the carpenter, the son of Mary and brother of James and Joses and Judas and Simon, and are not his sisters here with us?" (Mark 6:3). Matthew and Luke expand on Mark's story, each of them adding his own unique account of Jesus's birth and infancy. Matthew tells readers about Joseph's dreams, Herod's barbarism, Magi from the East attending the infant, and the family's flight from Nazareth to Egypt and back again. Luke includes the angel Gabriel's annunciation to Mary, crafting a nativity story that features Mary's cousin Elizabeth, mother of John the Baptist, and shepherds coming to see the infant laid in a manger outside Bethlehem. Luke's account also adds a few more details about Jesus's childhood, including his presentation in the temple and a family trip to Jerusalem when Jesus is twelve years old. John, author of the famous Gospel Prologue, explains that Jesus is the Logos incarnate, but he glosses over the details of birth and childhood in favor of explicating a lofty Christology of the Logos as preexistent God-man. In light of this patchy and disparate scriptural information, it's no surprise that some early Christians sought to expand on the story of Jesus's birth and family life, especially the person of his mother.

The Protoevangelium (Proto-gospel) of James was one influential text that focused primarily on Mary, depicting her as the perfect vessel to bring God incarnate into the world. In this noncanonical narrative from the late second century CE,[13] readers learned about Mary's parents, her childhood, her life of devotion to God even before the annunciation, her experience of childbirth, and the first hours of her life as the mother of Jesus. This story is still read as part of the liturgy in the Eastern Orthodox Christian churches, and much of its content has contributed to Christian tradition around the world. Despite its noncanonical status in the Western churches, the Proto-gospel has had a lasting impact on the view of Mary as both holy mother and perpetual virgin.

The narrative account of Mary's childhood portrays her as a model of devotion. Her parents, Joachim and Anna, out of gratitude for God's gift of a child in their barrenness, dedicate their daughter Mary to serve in the Jerusalem temple. On the model of Hannah (1 Sam 1:1—2:11) and comparing herself to Sarah in Genesis, Anna proclaims, "As the Lord God lives, whether my child is a boy or a girl, I will offer it as a gift to the Lord my God, and it will minister to him its entire life."[14] Indeed, at the age of three, young Mary goes to the temple, where she lives as a pure virgin, beloved by the whole community. When she reaches the age of twelve, the priests become anxious; she will soon begin menstruating, rendering her ritually impure, and they must find her alternative lodging. Men of the community draw lots, and Joseph, an elderly carpenter and widower with children from his previous marriage, is selected by God to take Mary into his home.[15] Joseph agreed, with some reluctance, to take Mary in and guard her purity. At this point in the story, readers encounter events familiar from the Lukan infancy narrative: the annunciation, Mary's visit to Elizabeth, and the imperial census that drives Mary and Joseph to the city of Bethlehem. The Proto-gospel adds a scene in which the priests, having discovered that Mary is pregnant, require her and Joseph to undergo a ritual test to determine that they are telling the truth about not having engaged in sexual relations; they pass, confirming that the pregnancy is of divine and not earthly origin.[16]

Peter Brown notes that this account of Mary, "a human creature totally enclosed in sacred space…set the tone for all later descriptions of the consecrated woman."[17] In her separation from earthly concerns and her absolute dedication to God, Mary models "the continuous, unbroken loyalty" that was thought to characterize the Christian virgin as bride of Christ.[18] Joseph, too, becomes a model for how individuals can live in holy, celibate community. The fourth-century theologian Jerome disputed the implication from the Proto-gospel that Joseph himself had ever had sexual relations. Instead, Jerome posited that Joseph was also a perpetual virgin and that the siblings of Jesus mentioned in the canonical Gospels (e.g., Mark 6:2–3) are actually Jesus's cousins, not biological children of either Mary or Joseph. Jerome's alternative position was probably influential in Pope Innocent I's decision to condemn the Proto-gospel in 405 CE. According to the Proto-gospel, however, Joseph's children became the stepsiblings of Jesus, a position still accepted in the Eastern Church.

In his book about two "family gospels," the Proto-gospel and the Infancy Gospel of Thomas, Chris Frilingos highlights an important feature of this genre: they are stories that can give access to early Christian questions about the connection between bodily experiences and spiritual truths. What does it mean to be a family or household in the face of the unknown or the unknowable? Relationships within the holy family and between the holy family and their community raise questions about epistemology, or what humans can know and how they come to know it. Frilingos points out that "when external or internal crises threaten to tear apart the trio, time and again Joseph, Mary, and Jesus affirm their familial bonds."[19] This is so even when Mary becomes inexplicably pregnant and when the child Jesus performs miracles. Despite experiences that challenge the typical understanding of embodied experience, the holy family chooses to remain in relationship. Perhaps the authors of these texts were inspired by Paul's image of a communal body clinging together despite differences among the members.

The second major portion of the Proto-gospel focuses on Mary giving birth to Jesus and what this event says about her own holiness. In the cave where she gives birth, Mary is overshadowed by a bright cloud. Joseph and a Hebrew midwife witness this divine sign, and the midwife proclaims, "My soul has been magnified today, for my eyes have seen a miraculous sign: salvation has been born to Israel."[20] As the cloud dissipates, they behold the infant Jesus. The midwife, Salome, is still incredulous about Joseph's claim that Mary is a virgin, and she undertakes to conduct a test. Reaching her hand out to test that Mary's hymen is intact, she finds her hand "burning, falling away....For I have put the living God to the test."[21] Mary is, indeed, still a virgin. The divinely obscured arrival of the child, a lack of narration about Mary's labor pains or any cries emitted during childbirth, and the apparently unchanged state of her body have often been taken to imply that Mary's experience of birth did not involve the pain all other women experience.[22] Her body, because it is so closely aligned with a holy mission to bring Christ into the world, seems transformed into something other than what is typically expected, into something new and worthy of admiration.

TWO MARYS AND THEOLOGICAL ANTHROPOLOGY

A common thread winds through these two early Christian visions of the body. It is the Pauline idea that the Christian's body can be a site or space for expressing spiritual identity. The care taken with the body is care to work against some of its natural tendencies in order to bring out what is more essential to its nature: the image of God. Mary of Egypt models techniques for conforming oneself to the image of God, while Mary of Nazareth models turning the self into a vessel for the image of God borne out in the world. In the stories of these two women, as in Paul's letters, early Christians assert that the body of an individual may have profound effects on the social body that is the *ekklēsia*.

There is an important caveat to be considered. Many scholars have noted that some of the most influential early Christian thinking about bodies, boundaries, and holiness appears in writings about the bodies of women from the fourth and fifth centuries. These texts were mostly written by men in positions of ecclesial authority, so it can be difficult if not impossible to reconstruct the actual experiences of women like Mary of Nazareth and Mary of Egypt and what they thought about their own bodies. Virginia Burrus summarizes the phenomenon as follows:

> The culturally dominant androcentric construction of virginal sexuality, which crystallizes out of the distinctive needs of the post-Constantinian church, functions to create and defend new communal boundaries and to reassert and strengthen the gender hierarchy; in the process, it rewrites women's bodies with an almost violent disregard for the physical knowledge and experience of women.[23]

Can a theological anthropology that uses women's stories but filters them only through the eyes of powerful Christian men really be effective at carrying out Paul's wish to include people of all genders in the one body of Christ? With this question in mind, we turn to the contemporary legacy of this early Christian adaptation of the Pauline image.

CONTEMPORARY CULTURAL CONTEXT AND NEW INTERPRETATIONS

In late summer of 2021, as debates over vaccine mandates and mask policies raged across the United States,[24] the virus continued to spread increasingly among children under the age of twelve who returned to schools with inconsistent protective measures in place. The uneven enforcement of masking and other protections like social distancing went against recommendations from the Centers for Disease Control and Prevention (CDC), which were modified repeatedly to address shifting threats from variants of the virus.[25] Much of the language deployed in the heated public debates pitted individual rights and autonomy against obligations to care for the most vulnerable in communities.

What does our regard for our individual bodies say about our care for each other and our identity as Christians? How do our ideals of unity fare when pitted against fear, whether fear of losing freedoms or fear of causing harm? In what follows, I suggest that reflecting upon intertwined issues of justice and care brings us back to embodied experience and embodied responsibility.

DISABILITY (IN)JUSTICE

When Christian churches draw on Paul's language of the body of Christ to describe themselves as inclusive and diverse communities, they are following Paul's own impulse to recognize the interdependence of all the individuals who make up the whole body. Yet exclusive and ableist assumptions about the ideal or perfect body can creep in. Particularly given that much early Christian reception of the Christlike body revolved around ascetic training that would "perfect" flawed and dangerous human bodies, becoming part of the body of Christ might seem to require having a particular type of body, or rather, not having an unruly or atypical body. The movement for disability justice, spearheaded by people whose bodies and experiences have been marginalized, should galvanize today's Christians to incorporate a more expansive and inclusive understanding of bodies into the one body that is the Church.

Each body functions as one vantage point on the world; the disabled or atypical body is an important location or vantage that is frequently ignored and treated as an outlier rather than a legitimate position. Leah Lakshmi Piepzna-Samarasinha, a queer, disabled, femme artist and organizer, pushes back on the idea that disability is synonymous with loss or lack. She writes, "The deficiency model by which most people view disability only sees disabled people as a lack, a defect, a damaged good, in need of cure. The idea that we have cultures, skills, science, and technology runs counter to all of that. In a big way."[26] It is absolutely essential to listen to the voices, stories, and experiences of those who have been marginalized, oppressed, and excluded. These groups have created effective networks of support and care and do not need such things created for them without their input.

Deborah Beth Creamer, who works on the theology of disability, proposes a "limits" model for viewing disability.[27] This model allows for the recognition that limits are a natural part of human existence, something Paul acknowledged when he noted that we cannot yet fully comprehend what resurrection life will be like (1 Cor 15). What we call disabilities exist along a spectrum of limits that all humans experience in different ways. People may move along the spectrum over the course of a lifetime, encountering more and/or different limits as time passes. Creamer's framework opens space that challenges people who are not (yet) disabled to be in solidarity with those who are experiencing limits.

Piepzna-Samarasinha, in conversation with Stacey Milbern, proposes yet another possible element: joyful evolution. In her words:

> And that is such a huge paradigm shift—to view coming into disability identity as a birth, not as a death, which is how the transition(s) are seen by ableist culture. To see it as a series of births, as our bodyminds evolve in their crip, neurodivergent, deaf, sick identities over time—to name that there are life stages and rites of passage of becoming disabled, that this

> is not a static wound, these disabled bodyminds are creative, evolving strategies.[28]

As bodies change over time, Piepzna-Samarasinha and Milbern hope people can experience support and guidance for navigating new-to-them vulnerabilities, sicknesses, and disabilities. Such guidance could take place in the context of a loving and understanding community committed to recognizing all the gifts, skills, and forms of wisdom that come from existing in varied kinds of bodies. How could the Christian community support this project? Would it look like facilitating connections between mentors and those who need assistance, providing accessible spaces for meetings? How are sick, disabled, and mentally ill members of the Church included on leadership teams, consulted about their needs, and empowered to shape community life in their own image, such that the figurative body of Christ comes to truly reflect the shape of its members?

Facilitating such a shift in the community requires also shifting attitudes toward individual bodies as they are connected to the spiritual self. In contrast to a way of thinking organized around disciplining the body, shaping it into a "perfect" reflection of some elusive and ineffable spiritual perfection, activist Patty Berne writes,

> A Disability Justice framework understands that all bodies are unique and essential, that all bodies have strengths and needs that must be met. We know that we are powerful not despite the complexities of our bodies, but because of them.…Disability Justice holds a vision born out of collective struggle, drawing upon the legacies of cultural and spiritual resistance within a thousand underground paths, igniting small persistent fires of rebellion in everyday life. Disabled people of the global majority—black and brown people—share common ground confronting and subverting colonial powers in our struggle for life and justice. There has always been resistance to all forms of oppression, as we know through our bones that there have simultaneously been disabled people visioning a world where we flourish, that values and celebrates us in all our myriad beauty.[29]

Both Piepzna-Samarasinha and Berne draw on the image of birth to imagine new ways of engaging with the body. There may be a fruitful link to the figure of Mary, the mother of Jesus, as a model for those who would bear Christ into the world. And although a movement for disability justice requires no validation in the form of alignment with Pauline teachings, as a biblical scholar I find it striking that Berne's articulated vision describes a community defined by collective care, resistance to exploitative and oppressive systems of power, and a desire for flourishing that seems a lot like the community Paul envisions for the earliest Christ-believers, living in the midst of empire.

How can Christian communities today prioritize access for all bodies that are part of the body of Christ? Can this happen in ways that respect the dignity of disabled persons as individuals who, like all people, need healing but not a cure? What are the practical steps involved in listening to the wisdom of sick, disabled, and mentally ill individuals, and how can abled people become mindful of the harmful impulse to undermine or "fix" the work existing communities do for themselves, in the name of helping? Piepzna-Samarasinha frames such an act of true solidarity as love. She explains, "I think that crip solidarity, and solidarity between crips and non(yet)-crips is a powerful act of love and I-got-your-back. It's in big things, but it's also in the little things we do moment by moment to ensure that we all—in all our individual bodies—get to be present fiercely as we make change."[30] In particular, how can faith groups go beyond thinking about access as a checklist of items for making modifications to worship spaces or providing services and engage continuously in what Peipzna-Samarasinha calls "radical love" by making "access centralized at the beginning dream of every action or event"?[31] Can they join priest Blyth Barnow in asking, "How do survivors' skills translate to ministry?"[32]

COMMUNITY CARE AND CARE WORK

Most of us have encountered the term *self-care* on a social media platform, in the news, or in conversation with a mental health professional. Listicle-style articles appear in magazines, like the May 2020 edition of *Woman's Day*, which recommends, "13 Self Care Ideas That Actually Heal Your Mind and Soul," or the December 2020 issue of *Good Housekeeping*, which touts "40+ Lab-Approved Solutions to Creating the Ultimate Self-Care Routine…all backed by scientists in the Good

Housekeeping Institute."[33] The term often refers to practices like taking a mental health day, making time to rest, carving out space for a daily workout, or organizing small treats for yourself, like drinking a hot cup of green tea or giving yourself a DIY manicure (all real suggestions from the articles just mentioned). One important theme is the idea that "you cannot pour from an empty cup." That is, care for one's own needs must precede an outpouring of care for the needs of others. Returning again to the 1 Corinthians 12 image of a unified body, Christian communities might notice a variation on the Pauline theme: showing care for all the members of the body (including the self) benefits the whole.

The effects of ubiquitous calls for self-care range from helpful to hazardous. On the one hand, an International Self Care Day was established in 2011 "to raise the profile of healthy lifestyle self-care programmes around the world" and "promote self-care as a vital foundation of health."[34] Increasing awareness about healthy habits and holistic health is certainly admirable. On the other hand, it is potentially harmful for the popular media to feed an unrealistic expectation that practices to improve physical comfort and individual mental health can fully mitigate the negative effects of social inequalities and systems of oppression. Feminist and womanist scholar Altheria Caldera highlights the fact that many of the self-care activities recommended in mainstream media are in fact harmful on a systemic level. She writes, "For me, self-care does not mean indulging in luxuries such as manicures, facials, and waxes; dining at fancy restaurants; taking expensive vacations; or shopping. In my estimation, these actions are more akin to pampering than self-care and can (but do not always) lead to extreme consumerism and materialism, which are antithetical to self-care."[35] In U.S. society, such activities are also "largely products of capitalism designed to promote debt, overspending, and exclusivity," all things that are damaging to the sort of community care and mutual support that can lead to healing.[36]

This is not to dismiss the importance of self-care, but to highlight that most pop culture engagement with the concept only skims the surface of what self-care can be. People who work in caring professions point to it as an essential component of human flourishing. Scholars and practitioners in the mental health field explain the importance of self-efficacy and self-determination in defining what self-care means for different individuals. One team of researchers argues, for example, that "to understand self-care in mental health, it is important to consider the experiences of those with mental health problems."[37] To develop appropriate services and recommend truly helpful self-care practices, professionals should partner with those whose expertise comes from their own experiences of mental health issues. The results can be profound. A 2016 review of literature about parental self-care behaviors noted that practices that increase parents' self-esteem and feelings of self-worth can be crucial for parents to establish and maintain positive relationships with their young children; developing strategies to handle individual stress is beneficial for the whole family.[38] Those in the caring professions also recognize the essential nature of self-care for themselves. For instance, social workers, whose jobs require constant empathetic engagement with clients, have noted that a lack of self-care can lead to compassion fatigue, burnout, and inadequate client care. Integrating professional and personal concepts of the self, taking time for mindfulness or humor, and workplace recreational activities are all practices that social workers have found helpful for ensuring their own well-being.[39] Such a holistic approach to self-care can provide a path toward healing and enable all individuals to engage in community care in ways that are healthy and sustainable.

Building on the work of Audre Lorde, who argued that caring for the self is not self-indulgent but a political act of self-preservation, activist and author Adrienne Maree Brown has argued for an intermediate category between self-care and community care: self-determined care. Brown explains in a blog post, "I *love* the idea of community care… but what is that, if not community supporting each other in our self-determined efforts to care for ourselves and our families?"[40] The post presents a challenging question: "How does it look to do this [community care] so that people are able to do for themselves what they need?"[41] That question might inspire Christian communities looking to provide meaningful support for all the members of the one body of Christ. If the Church is a place that provides nourishment, who is at the table, who is serving, and are the roles empowering for all involved?

Complicating the conversation around care is the important fact that care work in the United States is highly gendered. Care work performed by women and femmes tends to be overlooked and undervalued as a form of work, and it is usually unfairly compensated. In late 2020, Nicole Bateman and Martha Ross of the Brookings Institute reported on the outsized burden of care that drove many mothers out of the workforce to manage childcare, education, elder care, and family health in the face of the COVID-19 pandemic. Layoffs were also disproportionately likely to affect women, since the majority of layoffs affected low-wage and face-to-face work "that rely on interaction between customers and workers, such as retail sales and hospitality, two of the most common occupations among low-wage women."[42] Unemployment for women increased more than 12 percent between February and April 2020, compared to just under 10 percent for men, and the losses were more significant for women without college degrees.[43] Care work has a great cost for those engaged in it, who are disproportionately women and disproportionately women of color.

It seems that Christian communities today face an interwoven set of challenges. Like the Corinthian community, churches today might find themselves divided, as members juggle conflicting commitments to self, family, city, nation, and church. How can Paul's challenge to find a meaningful place for each part within the ecclesial body (1 Cor 12) inspire positive change? Who is best situated to help with identifying areas of concern, and how can their voices be raised up? What can be done to distribute care work responsibilities more equitably and to adequately compensate (and express appreciation for) those who perform care work that benefits the whole community?

PERIL AND PROMISE: THE BODY OF CHRIST AND THE HOUSEHOLD OF GOD

While we moderns are accustomed to thinking of the body as the boundary of the self, the image of a collective "body of Christ" in the Pauline Epistles offers a perspective that may helpfully challenge our individualism. The rich image in 1 Corinthians 12 can point toward greater recognition of all the diverse bodyminds present in the household of God and ways communities can make that household more welcoming for different kinds of bodies and their needs. Paul's letters also call us to attend to our bodies as places where we meet—in ourselves and each other—the divine. This valence of the body of Christ image was emphasized in narratives of the early Church about women like Mary of Egypt and Mary of Nazareth. Today the great need for communal care and mutual aid may provide another avenue for bringing Christ's caring and saving presence to bodies in need. If Christian communities begin to think in terms of care not simply as self-care but as support and meaningful advocacy for the whole community, we may reform our commitments to making worship accessible, extending community care, and correcting for the inequitable assignment of careworking roles in our churches. And of course, at the center of Paul's image is the Eucharist, the physical celebration of communion with Christ and the universal Church. What would it feel like to belong to a Christian household that is grounded in *eucharistō*, profound thanksgiving, for the many parts that make up our one, holy body?

Maintaining our focus on the well-being of all members of this body of Christ, we turn to the final part of the book and one more Pauline metaphor. Paul's image "children of God" evokes ways of belonging in the household of God that are deeply meaningful for a church in need of care, nourishment, and growth. At the same time it raises challenging questions about maturity, responsibility, and what it means to build a household where it is safe for all to belong.

PART 5

RAISING UP CHILDREN OF GOD

Kinship Language for Creating Community

Russell D. Moore's 2009 book *Adopted for Life: The Priority of Adoption for Christian Families and Churches* lays out a particularly Christian and biblical justification for the practice of adoption. Moore explains, "When we adopt—and when we encourage a culture of adoption in our churches and communities—we're picturing something that's true about our God. We, like Jesus, see what our Father is doing and do likewise (John 5:19). And what our Father is doing, it turns out, is fighting for orphans, making them sons and daughters."[1] For a Christian who identifies God as the caring spiritual father of orphans, it seems natural to join in God's work of "fighting for orphans" by adopting orphaned children.

Moore's book was published during the height of American evangelical conversations about adoption. Sermons, publications, and popular media recommending that Christian families adopt orphaned children, from the United States or abroad, proliferated in the early 2000s and continued gaining widespread attention into the mid 2010s.

A preacher and theologian, Moore previously served as president of the Southern Baptist Ethics and Religious Liberty Commission, and he was professor of theology and ethics and dean of the School of Theology at the Southern Baptist Theological Seminary (Louisville, Kentucky).[2] His widespread influence in evangelical circles made him a powerful spokesperson for the orphan care movement, and his view of adoption as a form of both activism and evangelization captured the religious imaginations of many. The act of caring for an orphan, on this model, is a way of working cooperatively with the God who wishes to save all people. Like many others in the orphan care movement, Moore articulated a key desire shared by American evangelicals: to participate in an activist movement motivated by deep and sincere commitment to religious ideals.

In his 2017 book *Growing God's Family: The Global Orphan Care Movement and the Limits of Evangelical Activism*, sociologist of religion Samuel L. Perry delves into the rationale behind the American evangelical push for Christians to adopt and develop a culture of adoption. Perry conducted interviews with 223 persons involved directly or tangentially with the orphan care movement, including members of adoptive/adopting families, church leaders, and adoption/orphan experts.[3] His research led him to conclude that perhaps the most lasting effect of the movement has been the development of a distinctive language and set of images that evangelicals use to talk about orphans and the reasons Christians choose to adopt. He calls these "evangelical vocabularies of motive," which puts the emphasis on how people *talk about* their decisions, especially after the fact.[4] One of the most striking components of the movement is its adherents' insistence that right belief or motivation preceded their choice to take action. As Perry explains, "Evangelicals, like everyone else, are influenced by the broader society and make most daily decisions with a combination of self-interested and practical concerns in mind....But within the context of other evangelicals, believers are expected to draw on community-approved vocabularies of motive to explain significant life decisions."[5] In the case of adoption, motivations like the ones articulated by Moore are ideal: to imitate God's care for the orphan, to bring more children into the Christian family.

The focus on caring for marginalized or neglected children, on creating a Christian family in the image of God's inclusive household, captured evangelical imaginations and provided a rich language for talking about belonging. This language has its roots in Hebrew Bible portraits of the God who demands justice for widows and orphans (e.g., Deut 10:18; Isa 1:17), but also finds an echo in New Testament Pauline material, especially Paul's image of the Christ-believer as a "child of God." The Pauline epistles construct an image of believers as children of God, trained to think of each other as brothers and sisters of Christ, on their way to becoming mature members of the Christian community. Any Christ-believer, regardless of socioeconomic status, begins as a spiritual infant in need of guidance, formation, and education. The metaphorical child, trained in the faith by Paul and other teachers, takes on a new identity in God's household. The Pauline childhood metaphor played an equalizing role for those in the first century CE who sought to belong among the Christ-believers. Today, the image may challenge cultural expectations about who has a right to authority and encourage the believers to imagine new, collaborative models of leadership.

We begin by examining the use of childhood metaphors in the Pauline epistles in chapter 9, with particular attention to associated concepts like adoption, character development, and education. Chapter 10 will turn to the reception of this metaphor among early Christian interpreters who were seeking ways to describe catechesis and faith formation. Finally, one complex case study from the contemporary United States will help illuminate the potential for empowering and disempowering interpretations of Pauline spiritual childhood in today's Christian communities. The chapter will address the crisis of child sexual abuse and abuse cover-ups by church authorities.

Chapter 9

CHILDREN OF GOD, SIBLINGS OF CHRIST

THE IMAGE IN THE UNDISPUTED PAULINE EPISTLES

Paul's letter to the Galatians is an emotional but carefully crafted defense of his teaching about what it means for non-Jews to become part of the chosen people of God, focused primarily on the image of believers as children in God's household. By the time he sends this letter in the early 50s CE, Paul had traveled on to another region to continue his evangelizing mission, but he has received reports that other teachers have arrived in the Galatian communities, preaching the gospel in a way that is different from what Paul had presented.[1] It appears that these other teachers[2] were urging Gentile converts to be circumcised, to follow the prescriptions laid out in God's covenant with Abraham in Genesis 17, where God states, "This is my covenant, which you shall keep, between me and you and your offspring after you: Every male among you shall be circumcised....Any uncircumcised male who is not circumcised in the flesh of his foreskin shall be cut off from his people; he has broken my covenant" (Gen 17:10–14).[3] Their position is reasonable: since Scripture teaches that God's covenant requires circumcision, it makes good sense to ask how outsiders could become part of that covenant relationship without this procedure.

In response, Paul first defends his own authority, reminding the Galatians that "the gospel that was proclaimed by me is not of human origin; for I did not receive it from a human source, nor was I taught it, but I received it through a revelation of Jesus Christ" (Gal 1:11–12).[4] Having established the authority of his evangelizing and his gospel, Paul also answers Scripture with Scripture, making an end run around the passage in Genesis 17 to point to an earlier interaction between God and Abraham in Genesis 15, claiming that the covenant relationship was actually affirmed on different grounds, before the command for circumcision. Paul summarizes the takeaway point as follows: "Just as Abraham 'believed God, and it was reckoned to him as righteousness,' [quoting Gen 15:6] so, you see, those who believe are the sons [*uioi*] of Abraham" (Gal 3:6–7, alt. trans.).[5] That is, Paul asserts believing that Jesus is the Christ is the only requirement for entering a covenant relationship with God. As biblical commentator Sam K. Williams summarizes it, "For both Abraham and the Galatians, faith was the personal response essential for the eventual blessing that the divine word had initiated."[6] One who believes becomes a child in the family line of Abraham.

In Jewish tradition, to be a child of Abraham is shorthand for belonging in the community. Hans Dieter Betz points to the Hellenistic Jewish text Sirach as one text that summarizes Abraham's important patriarchal identity; I quote 44:19–20 here:

> Abraham was the great father of a multitude of nations,
> and no one has been found like him in glory.
> He kept the law of the Most High,
> and entered into a covenant with him;
> he certified the covenant in his flesh,
> and when he was tested he proved faithful.[7]

Paul includes himself in the group of Abraham's descendants in his letter to the Romans, where he explains that the Jews are "my kindred according to the flesh" (Rom 9:3). He asserts that "to them belong the adoption, the glory, the covenants, the giving of the law, the worship, and the promises; to them belong the patriarchs, and from them, according to the flesh, comes the Messiah, who is over all, God blessed forever. Amen" (Rom 9:4–5). That is, the Jewish people have an unassailable claim to belong in God's household, but Paul must make an argument that Gentile Christ-believers can also belong.

Paul sets out to make just such an argument, first explaining how Jewish Christ-believers might think about themselves. He writes, "Now before faith came, we were imprisoned and guarded under the law until faith would be revealed. Therefore the law was our disciplinarian until Christ came, so that we might be justified by faith. But now that faith has come, we are no longer subject to a disciplinarian, for in Christ Jesus you are all sons [*uioi*] of God through faith" (Gal 3:23–26, alt. trans.). A familial connection based in faith is, for Paul, a natural extension of the connection that relied on the law. The English word "disciplinarian," used to describe the law, is a translation of the Greek *paidagōgos*. In Paul's time the title referred to a member of the household, either a slave or a freeperson, who was responsible for looking after the family's children during the early years of their education, up through adolescence. The *paidagōgos* is so-called because he is responsible for leading (*agō*) a child: in Greek, *pais* or the diminutive *paidion*. The *paidagōgos* "supervised homework and meals and baths, gave instruction in manners, as well as grammar and diction, and, ideally, both taught and modelled the moral virtues."[8] Paul invites the Galatians to think about the law as their guardian and guide, which had prepared them for a life that should now be guided mainly by faith.

Consider how Paul links childhood with concepts like education, guidance, and guardianship. Indeed that term *paidagōgos* should remind us of pedagogy, the science of teaching and learning. In Greek *paideuō* is a lexically related verb that means "provide instruction or discipline."[9] It carries the sense of training, correcting, and guiding, as well as our modern sense of academic teaching. This is consistent with the ancient conception of education as a holistic endeavor. When a Greco-Roman child received formal education, which was most likely to happen for male children of the upper classes, it encompassed instruction not only in the rudiments of reading, writing, mathematics, and natural sciences, but also training for full participation in household management and even public life, whether that be in local politics, law, medicine, or some artisanal craft.[10] Ancient education was even concerned with developing virtues of character and aspects of public decorum, particularly for members of elite male society.[11]

A good part of a child's education in the Roman Empire took place in the context of the household, overseen by parents. Many passages in the Hebrew Bible—the Scriptures for Paul and his contemporaries—also highlight the importance of the household as an educational space. Proverbs in particular outlines the importance of children being educated by their parents:

> Hear, my child, your father's instruction,
>   and do not reject your mother's teaching;
> for they are a fair garland for your head,
>   and pendants for your neck. (Prov 1:8–9)

It is also entirely in line with Jewish tradition that Paul identifies God as a disciplinarian, following texts like Psalm 32:8, where God proclaims, "I will instruct you and teach you the way you should go; / I will counsel you with my eye upon you." Paul reminds the Corinthians of God's disciplinary role and its salutary effects. He explains "when we are judged by the Lord, we are disciplined so that we may not be condemned along with the world" (1 Cor 11:32). God is a teaching parent, and human beings, the adopted children, receive an education at God's hands. As the Scriptures suggest, this education enables a person to function as an ethical, responsible adult in the religious community, even guiding others in God's ways.

So when Paul explains that the Galatians no longer need a *paidagōgos*, he says it is a sign of their maturity. Because they are no longer minors, they are ready to step into a more powerful role in the figurative household:

> My point is this: heirs, as long as they are minors, are no better than slaves, though they are the owners of all the property; but they remain under guardians and trustees until the date set by the father. So with us; while we were minors, we were enslaved to the elemental spirits of the world. But when the fullness of time had come, God sent his Son [*uios*], born of a woman, born under the law, in order to redeem those who were under the law, so that we might receive adoption as children. And because you are children, God has sent the Spirit of his Son into our hearts, crying, "Abba! Father!" So you are no longer a slave but a child [*uios*], and if a child then also an heir, through God. (Gal 4:1–7)

Again Paul describes the entirely subordinated position of enslaved persons, who have no rights to property or inheritance. He also acknowledges the governing power of the male head of the household, referred to in Roman legal terms as the *patria potestas*, or power of the father/patriarch. Note that Paul assumes (free, legitimate) children within the household occupy an intermediate position. They are both privileged and subordinate; it is ultimately up to the patriarch to decide when those children can inherit goods and begin to exercise household authority.

Near the end of the passage, Paul highlights the emotional connection forged between adopted children and God. They may call God "Abba," a familiar Aramaic term for one's father,[12] and they are acknowledged as heirs, with the ability to take over their father's goods and work. The English translation here obscures an important dimension of Paul's teaching: he speaks not of a generic "child" but of a *uios* or "son." Given the gender dynamics of the first-century Mediterranean setting, we should already imagine a superior role for male children versus female children. But Paul's choice to use *uios* also allows him to punctuate the new connection forged between the Christ-believer who has become a son of God and Jesus Christ who is also God's *uios*. It is because of this "spirit of adoption" (Rom 8:15) that believers may consider themselves "joint heirs with Christ" (Rom 8:17).

Before going further, it is worth emphasizing the fact that the concept of a household (Greek *oikos* or Latin *domus*) that Paul and his readers would have shared is quite different from what most of us picture today. While evidence from funerary inscriptions shows that sometimes families were represented by the mother-father-child grouping of the stereotypical modern nuclear family, this neglects the important function of enslaved persons in the household and the lack of a firm boundary between the private/domestic sphere and the public/economic or civic sphere common in the Roman Empire.[13] Roles in the typical household were highly stratified, with all members of the household subject to the authority of the male head of household. And the household could be thought of as a microcosm of the empire, with the Roman emperor taking on the role of the *paterfamilias*, providing for, protecting, and commanding his dependents.

Paul constructs a metaphorical household in which Christ-believers become children of God through a process of adoption. He is the only New Testament author to use the technical legal term *uiothesia*, "adoption."[14] Both Jewish and Roman law in the first century allowed for the legal adoption of children and even of adults, who would become part of an existing family line. The study of Greek legal documents from Egypt shows that "the adopted son becomes the true son of his adopted father;...the adopted son cannot be repudiated;...the adopted son cannot be reduced to slavery;...adoption leads to the right of inheritance."[15] These and other legal protections create a relationship in which the parent is obliged to provide care and support for the adopted child. One important takeaway point, then, is that adopted children belong fully to the household. For Paul and his readers, the Christ-believers—whether Jews who already had an ancestral claim to covenant relationship with God (through the Abrahamic covenant of circumcision) or Gentiles who become God's people through an act of faith (like their predecessor Abraham)—are all legitimate heirs in God's household.

In other letters, Paul implies that becoming an heir in this Christian spiritual family makes it either impossible or unadvisable for the Christ-believers to become children of other beings or things; belonging in God's household is an exclusive kind of affiliation. Those who become children are aligned with the good over and against evil: "for you are all children of light and children of the day; we are not of the night or of darkness" (1 Thess 5:5). Quoting from a pastiche of prophetic texts, Paul advises the Corinthians not to link themselves with unrighteousness, darkness, unbelievers, or idolatry:

> For we are the temple of the living God; as God said....
>
> "Therefore come out from them,
>   and be separate from them, says the Lord,
> and touch nothing unclean;
>   then I will welcome you,
> and I will be your father,
>   and you shall be my sons and daughters,
> says the Lord Almighty." (2 Cor 6:16–18)[16]

He refers to another aspect of the proper relationship between parents and children: children's obedience. This was a quality expected of children in Greco-Roman households in the time of Paul and his first readers.[17] Children are meant to conform themselves to the ideals of their household and family because they are going to inherit control of the household and its resources.

Although the early Christ-believers are to think of themselves as children of God, Paul is another parent and guide responsible for their upbringing. Indeed, Paul uses the image of childhood to reinforce his own authority.[18] He highlights his role as God's agent when he addresses Christ-believers in the communities he founded as his own children, using the Greek word *teknon*. Note that he can apply this title to individuals like Philemon's slave Onesimus when he wants to show particular favor (Phlm 10);[19] to Timothy when he appoints that protégé as a go-between (1 Cor 4:17) or when he wants to praise the way Timothy has been of assistance (Phil 2:22); and collectively to the Galatians when he aims to remind them of a bond of care (Gal 4:19). Benjamin Fiore points out that "when the word is applied to community members...it is likely to carry not friendship but familial (father-child) overtones....The term then indicates election by God and an ongoing relationship with Paul, which comprise the new reality of the spiritual life made possible by God."[20]

Paul depicts himself as both mother and father for the Christian communities he has founded. In 1 Corinthians 4:15, he declares, "Indeed, in Christ Jesus I became your father through the gospel." Paul is a figurative father in the sense that he "generates" children for the Christian community. The idea of a father as the generator or active partner in procreation aligns with some popular medical understanding in Paul's time. In his treatises on the natural sciences, Aristotle (384–322 BCE) argued that the father's "seed" was the main causal component that became a child, through a process that he compares to curdling milk. Paul appears to align with this male-centric view of fetal development, as opposed to other theories that were circulating. For example, Hippocratic treatises on embryology from the fifth-century BCE were the first to argue that the mother contributes at all to the generation of a fetus. The Greek physician Galen (129–ca. 216 CE) still taught that "the creative principle resides in the male sperm," while the mother provides some useful "seed" that contributes to the growth of the child.[21] Paul's focus on the generative power of the father may align with Scripture's teachings about God as the Father and Creator of all beings.

As a figurative mother, Paul writes, "My little children, for whom I am again in the pain of childbirth until Christ is formed in you, I wish I were present with you now and could change my tone, for I am perplexed about you" (Gal 4:19–20). This rich statement conveys important information about how Paul imagines parents relating to their children. His motherly role consists of active care and concern for the community. In 2 Corinthians he explains that this is the right order of things, for parents to supply for the needs of their children, not the other way around (2 Cor 12:14). At the same time, his priority is to serve a formative role. Like the womb where an infant's body is formed, Paul acts as a spiritual incubator. He then continues the work of formation through several stages of infancy and childhood, providing nourishment for those who need it. In the ancient world, this would have been the proper role of a mother or wet nurse, as he indicates in 1 Thessalonians, stating, "We were gentle among you, like a nurse tenderly caring for her own children" (1 Thess 2:7).

For children are in a formative stage of their development. Christ-believers, too, Paul points out, are in need of formation to reach a fully mature faith. He himself has matured, as he relates to the Corinthians: "When I was a child, I spoke like a child, I thought like a child, I reasoned like a child; when I became an adult, I put an end to childish ways" (1 Cor 13:11). This passage not only describes the typical life course of a person, but it applies, Paul says, to the human experience of spiritual growth: "For now we see in a mirror, dimly, but then we will see face to face" (1 Cor 13:12). To highlight the "unfinished" nature of fledgling believers, Paul evokes the image of infant children. He calls the Christ-believers infants (*nēpioi*) and notes that they are "being like children," using the related verb *nēpiazō*. He chides the Corinthians for being misguided, drawing on the idea that children are intellectually immature: "do not be children in your thinking; rather, be infants in evil, but in thinking be adults" (1 Cor 14:20).

He is not alone in concentrating on early childhood as a formative period. Biographical accounts from the ancient world typically included a section focused on the subject's "upbringing." The Greek term is *anatrophē*, which carries a range of meanings, from general rearing and nurture to education more specifically.[22] It was considered key to the shaping of a person's character. Greco-Roman biographies and histories frequently include a few vignettes from the subject's childhood or adolescence, on the assumption that a child's words and actions could reveal the qualities that person will have when they become an adult. Famously, the Greek historian Herodotus tells the story of a young boy named Cyrus, who, though of no apparent social status, took on the role of king in a game with his fellow children and revealed his kingly understanding of justice.[23] Later in life, Cyrus's royal parentage was revealed and he became the ruler of the Persians, demonstrating that his childhood capacity for ruling had not been a fluke. Biblical wisdom literature, too, assumes that what is learned and practiced early on has a major impact on later life; thus Proverbs 22:6 states, "Train children in the right way, / and when old, they will not stray."

The Christians must also be trained so that they may become "mature" or even "perfect." The Greek term *teleios*, which Paul contrasts with childlike or infantile thinking, could mean either.[24] This relates to an ancient conception of the ideal human being as a mature adult male. In comparison to this model, "children were...perceived to be unfinished: they were humans-to-be."[25] Therefore Paul tells the Corinthians that when he first taught them, "I could not speak to you as spiritual people, but rather as people of the flesh, as infants in Christ. I fed you with milk, not solid food, for you were not ready for solid food. Even now you are still not ready" (1 Cor 3:1–2).[26] As long as they continue to think of power dynamics and community authority in a way that is conventional for their time and place, they cannot fully understand what it means to belong to God's household.

Of course, the ideal role model for Christ-believers is Christ! Paul repeatedly admonishes his readers to imitate Christ, to conform themselves to him, as in Romans: "For those whom he [God] foreknew he also predestined to be conformed to the image of his Son, in order that he might be the firstborn among many brothers" (Rom 8:29, alt. trans.). And by becoming children of God, the Christ-believers will extend their own example outward for the benefit of others. In Romans 8, Paul states that "all who are led by the Spirit of God are children of God" (Rom 8:14), then goes on to explain that the whole of creation has been waiting for these children "with eager longing" (Rom 8:19), because "the creation itself will be set free from its bondage to decay and will obtain the freedom of the glory of the children of God" (Rom 8:21).

While the image of a Christ-believer as a child in God's household does sometimes imply a lack of maturity, Paul does not shame the community for the fact that they have room to grow. Just as the believers are children, so he is a caring parent who will provide the nourishment and teaching they need in order to become mature members of the faith community. In this formative work, Paul cooperates with God as disciplinarian, guide, and nurturer. The Christ-believers who become children are themselves authorized to take on leadership roles, exercising the authority that comes from being able to call an all-powerful God "Abba" and Jesus the Christ "brother." By calling community members "children," Paul does not diminish their standing; in fact, he uses the metaphor of adoption to create an opening for more believers to belong. Gentiles, without the burden of circumcision, become descendants of Abraham, and all believers are elevated to become heirs of the divine promise.

THE IMAGE IN OTHER EPISTLES ATTRIBUTED TO PAUL

The author of Ephesians uses the image of a child in ways that echo themes in the undisputed epistles. First, people reveal their spiritual allegiance and are thereby identified as children of God. Before converting to Christ-belief, the author says, the Ephesians were "by nature children of wrath, like everyone else" (Eph 2:3). Through faith they have been changed, "for once you were darkness, but now in the Lord you are light. Live as children of light" (Eph 5:8). Second, believers are God's children because they have received adoption (Eph 1:5). Third, they are advised to take on the child's task of imitating their parents, so they may be ready to take up a mature, Christlike role in the community: "Therefore be imitators of God, as beloved children, and live in love, as Christ loved us and gave himself up for us" (Eph 5:1–2). This maturation process is presented in the form of a challenge when the author advises that "we must no longer be infants" (*nēpioi*) (Eph 4:14, alt. trans.). Finally, the letter refers once to real rather than figurative children, reinforcing cultural expectations about mutual obligations within household relationships and about children's need for education; children are to obey, and fathers are advised not to "provoke" their children, "but bring them up in the discipline and instruction of the Lord" (Eph 6:4).[27]

It is when we turn to the Pastoral Epistles that we begin to see significant variations on Paul's ways of using "child" and "heir" language to create belonging. As established in earlier chapters, the author of the Pastoral Epistles was most likely a later Christian leader, attributing his own words and teachings to Paul to gain authority for these teachings. The Pastoral Epistles seek, in part, to establish a formal line of succession from Paul to Timothy. A metaphorical parent-child relationship between Paul and Timothy is integral to the Pastor's project.

In the letters, the Pastor writing as Paul calls Timothy "my child" (1 Tim 1:18 and 2 Tim 2:1), and "my beloved child" (2 Tim 1:2). He positions himself as the parent who provided spiritual nourishment, encouraging Timothy to "be a good servant of Christ Jesus, nourished on the words of the faith and the sound teaching that you have followed" (1 Tim 4:6). Yet the letters affirm that Timothy's family of origin also contributed to his belonging in the Christian household.[28] The author mentions that Timothy's matrilineal line reveals his Christian pedigree: "I am reminded of your sincere faith, a faith that lived first in your grandmother Lois and your mother Eunice and now, I am sure, lives in you" (2 Tim 1:5). This inheritance will allow Timothy to do the most important work of preserving accurate Christian teaching, even as false teachers seek to deceive the Christ-believers in his community. Even if Timothy endures suffering, it is a sign that he is modeling himself on Paul, who suffered in his ministry.[29] The Pastor exhorts him, "But as for you, continue in what you have learned and firmly believed, knowing from whom you learned it, and how from childhood you have known the sacred writings that are able to instruct you for salvation through faith in Christ Jesus" (2 Tim 3:14–15). As Paul's metaphorical child, Timothy has received the mantle of his mentor or figurative father and may carry out his work.

That work entails passing along the "trustworthy" and "sound" message that they have inherited from Paul, not some other teachings that may be popular in their cities. In letters that mention false teachers (1 Tim 1:6, 9; Titus 1:10), both Titus and Timothy are addressed as "true" children (the Greek is *gnēsios*): "my true child in the faith" (1 Tim 1:2, alt. trans.) and "Titus, my true child in the faith we share" (Titus 1:4, alt. trans.). The greetings focus on common faith, making that faith the measure of one's genuine connectedness to Paul. This is probably a response to divisions in the growing Christian community; to be Paul's true child is to stand united with Paul's authoritative teaching against variant teachings. The educational discipline that is part of God's parenting is also at work here. The Pastor uses the verb *paideuō* to claim that God's grace is "*training* us to renounce impiety and worldly passions" (Titus 2:12). In 2 Timothy 2:25, the leaders of the Christian community must imitate God's teaching methods, "*correcting* opponents with gentleness." That is, the believers who are children receive their education from God and share it with others in a line of faithful educational succession.

As noted in previous chapters, these three epistles evince a growing Christian concern with solidifying not just teaching content but organizational structures that could facilitate proper teaching. The Pastor's view of ecclesial authority is hierarchical and patriarchal, based on the typical Greco-Roman household structure. But the households and familial relationships described in the Pastorals have a distinctively Christian component: an emphasis on shared faith. One argument for the late dating of these letters is their "developing family ethic, which goes substantially beyond traditional injunctions of rules for the household."[30] The Pastor encourages real children to adhere to their household roles, which include being faithful Christians.[31] A passage from the Letter to Titus brings together childhood, inheritance, and faith: God saved the Christ-believers "according to his mercy, through the water of rebirth and renewal by the Holy Spirit…so that, having been justified by his grace, we might become heirs according to the hope of eternal life" (Titus 3:5, 7). Baptism, a ritual of initiation into the community, functions as a "rebirth" for the believer, who becomes a legitimate child and heir of the divine household.

While the undisputed Pauline epistles remain focused on the child's potential to inherit the family's property and authority, in the Pastorals we see a new emphasis on how children's behavior reflects positively or negatively on the parents, particularly if those parents are leaders in the Christian community. Instructions in 1 Timothy outline qualifications for a bishop, who is literally an *episkopos*, or "overseer" (1 Tim 3:1–7). The prospective bishop must demonstrate his leadership at home: "He must manage his own household well, keeping his children submissive and respectful in every way—for if someone does not know how to manage his own household, how can he take care of God's church?" (1 Tim 3:4–5). As biblical scholars point out, the Greek tradition of advice-writing "provides a precedent for drawing conclusions from a person's private life about his qualifications for office."[32] We see again in the letter's statements about those who wish to become a deacon (*diakonos*) that they must "manage their children and their households well" (1 Tim 3:12). Titus is charged to appoint elders (*presbyteroi*) in the community from among men "whose children are believers" (Titus 1:6). Young women are considered to be upstanding members of the community if they conduct themselves with self-control and "love their children" (Titus 2:4). Where children are not addressed directly, they might be lumped in with the "younger men" of the community, who should "be self-controlled" in a way that will reflect well on the Christians as a whole (Titus 2:6).

The Pastoral Epistles seem to "double down" on the way children can impact their parents, linking children's faithfulness to salvation not for the children but for the parent. The idea that the actions of one's figurative children could reflect on the parent does appear in the undisputed letters, at least to the extent that Paul sees his heavenly reward as tied up in the success and salvation of the Christian communities he has nurtured. For example, in 1 Thessalonians 2:19–20, Paul asks, "For what is our hope or joy or crown of boasting before our Lord Jesus at his coming? Is it not you? Yes, you are our glory and joy!" However, in the Pastorals, the ideal of spiritual parenthood takes on a more material dimension.

One passage in 1 Timothy pertaining to this discussion is a notorious interpretive puzzle; the Pastor links childbearing and salvation, but scholars remain divided over whether "childbearing" is a literal or figurative practice here. I will quote the full passage, to better unpack it in context:

> I desire, then, that in every place the men should pray, lifting up holy hands without anger or argument; also that the women should dress themselves modestly and decently in suitable clothing, not with their hair braided, or with gold, pearls, or expensive clothes, but with good works, as is proper for women who profess reverence for God. Let a woman learn in silence with full submission. I permit no woman to teach or to have authority over a man; she is to keep silent. For Adam was formed first, then Eve; and Adam was not deceived, but the woman was deceived and became a transgressor. Yet she will be saved through childbearing, provided they continue in faith and love and holiness, with modesty. (1 Tim 2:8–15)

These instructions for women in the community outline things to do and things to avoid. It is a passage that some interpreters have used to argue against employing female teachers and ministers in Christian communities, forbidding any authoritative role for women. Even the final sentence, which concerns us here, is unclear: the mother will be saved through childbearing, but who are the "they" that must "continue in faith and love and holiness"? Women who bear children, or the children themselves?

Biblical interpreters have proposed that the "childbearing" might be figurative, referring to the cultivation of virtues, or that it is literal, and women are encouraged to have children because some opponents in the region are suggesting an ascetic lifestyle of sexual renunciation.[33] There may be a helpful clue for interpretation later in the same letter, where the author is discussing how the behavior of community members might lead to public disapproval or judgment. In 1 Timothy 5:13–14, he writes that young women who become widows and choose not to remarry "learn to be idle, gadding about from house to house; and they are not merely idle, but also gossips and busybodies, saying what they should not say. So I would have younger widows marry, bear children, and manage their households, so as to give the adversary no occasion to revile us."[34] Here the main concern seems to be the reputation of the Church as a whole, which could be damaged if Christians like these young women are not fulfilling expected social roles as wives and mothers. We have already seen that for the Pastor "true" childhood and salvation can be measured through one's participation in the community's religious life, and it may make sense to read the caution about children/mothers continuing in faith, love, and holiness in that light.

In the Deutero-Pauline epistles, we see the mutual obligations of parents and children in relationship, both literally and figuratively. Later, the Pastor strongly emphasizes that children are subordinate members of a hierarchical household, adapting Paul's image of the child of God in a way that reflects historical realities of the first and second centuries but also outlines expectations for orderly Christian behavior. The actions of a child, especially whether or not that child remains a member of the faith, have a bearing on the reputation of the child's parents: how an individual Christian conducts herself reflects on the Christian community as a whole. Here, a figurative child, like Timothy or Titus, is seen to belong to the family line of Paul if he preserves the teaching tradition handed down by Paul. The identity one inherits is not simply affiliation with God's household but allegiance to specific Christian teachings and the authority to be a Christian teacher.

EFFECTS OF THE IMAGE FOR EARLY AUDIENCES

Paul and his fellow epistle writers relied on their audiences being familiar with typical features of a Greco-Roman childhood: the experience of formal and informal education, the expectation of obedience and household discipline, the care of parents who provide for the material and intellectual needs of a child (biological or adopted) who is not yet mature. Each of these features took on a spiritual significance for the earliest Christ-believers as they began to identify themselves as children who could belong in God's household. The letters hold out the promise of coheirship with Christ, another son (*uios*) of God, and of future full participation as adult members of the divine household. Paul's ingenious idea to link belief and adoption would have made it possible for Gentiles to envision their place among God's covenantal people, as children of Abraham. When the Pastor identified "true" children as those who faithfully hand down approved teachings, he opened the door for (some, male) believers not just to belong, but to claim authority in the growing community. At the heart of the child of God metaphor in the Pauline epistles, we find the idea of a believer as someone undergoing formation to learn how to more perfectly imitate Christ.

Chapter 10

ADULT RESPONSIBILITY IN THE HOUSEHOLD OF GOD

AFTERLIFE OF THE IMAGE: EARLY CHRISTIAN INTERPRETATIONS

Paul and his imitators used the image of the Christ-believer as a child, heir, and sibling of Christ to welcome early readers who might have experienced disempowerment in the regular course of their lives. Within the household of God these adopted children could feel a new connection to God and Christ. As the *ekklēsia* itself matured in the second to fifth centuries, eventually becoming aligned with Roman imperial power, the Pauline image "child of God" gained new and different significance for a growing group of monastics and bishops, who situated themselves as spiritual parents in the Christian community. The case studies discussed below capture the impact of child-parent metaphors on religious education or formation and ecclesial authority structures.

CHRISTIAN EDUCATION AND SPIRITUAL MATURITY

Early Christian theologians followed Paul in asserting that human beings should be constantly involved in a process of development and maturation. As Paul suggested in 1 Corinthians 3:1, the Christian must transition from the "milk" appropriate for infants (Greek *nēpios*) and fleshly people (Greek *sarkinos*) to the "solid food" meant for spiritual people (Greek *pneumatikos*). Theologians of the second to fifth centuries understood this passage as a commentary on preparing beginners to understand theological teachings of increasing complexity. Some used it as a template for formal catechesis and the education of young Christians; advancing along a course of spiritual education gave one greater access to power and authority, including the authority to become a mature teacher in the Church.

The majority of these theologians had themselves been educated in the Greco-Roman rhetorical and philosophical tradition. They were well aware that the standard reading list of their time was designed not just to teach the basics of reading, writing, and argument, but to accomplish a broader enculturation for the elite male students who experienced classical *paideia*. Those who read Homer, Herodotus, Thucydides, and Plato were absorbing teachings about virtue, vice, religion, and justice foundational to successful participation in Greek and Roman civic life. That is, education created citizens of a particular type. Therefore theologians argued that young Christians seeking spiritual and intellectual maturity must proceed with caution, because the educational material used in their formation could shape their thinking in ways antithetical to a Christian way of life. In light of the dangers of philosophical training, some theologians insisted on identifying their students as the nursing infants from Paul's metaphor. John David Penniman discusses this phenomenon. On his reading of early Christian literature, "whether figural or literal, breast milk was invested with the power to establish bonds of kinship, legitimate social identity, and intellectual potential."[1] Just as an uncritical approach to Greco-Roman texts could lead a young student astray, a proper foundation would set the stage for later generations to build a flourishing church.

Like Paul himself, early biblical interpreters found examples in the Old Testament to support a progressive, guided model for religious education. Paul had positioned Moses as a mediator whose laws provided discipline for God's people until they became "children of God through faith" (Gal 3:26). Gregory of Nyssa examined the childhood of Moses and presented him as a role model for Christian students.[2] Moses was raised by the daughter of the Egyptian pharaoh (Exod 2:5–6) but nursed by his own mother, who stepped forward as a wet nurse from among the Hebrews (Exod 2:7–9). In a figurative reading of the exodus narrative, Gregory pointed out that Moses set an example for Christians who might seek educational "nourishment" from the non-Christian world:

> An Egyptian princess, having adopted Moses, trained him in the *paideia* of her country. Yet he was not removed from the breast of his mother so long as his early age needed to be nursed by nourishment such as hers. And this is also true for our teacher [i.e. Basil of Caesarea, Gregory's older brother]. For although nourished by outside wisdom, he always held fast to the breast of the Church—growing and maturing his soul by way of the teachings drawn from that source.[3]

Apparently, Basil's early grounding in Christian and biblical teaching made him ready to consume sources and ideas from the writings of Greco-Roman philosophers, rhetors, and poets. Without the firm foundation of the Church's milk, Basil might have gone astray, ending up with an improper conception of wisdom conformed to worldly ideals. Like the Corinthians Paul calls "fleshly" (1 Cor 3:3), such an ill-formed Christian would be unfit to lead the Church.

Many bishops reflecting on education also imagined themselves in the role of Paul the teacher. From this vantage point they advised their more spiritually immature pupils about the kind of intellectual content they were consuming and commented on its nutritive value. Such writers were especially concerned with proper reading material and hermeneutics, or interpretation. Basil of Caesarea, in his treatise *Address to Young Men on Greek Literature*, recommends a discerning approach to the catalog of Greco-Roman literature. Certain topics should be engaged, others avoided. For example, Basil writes,

> Since we must needs attain to the life to come through virtue, our attention is to be chiefly fastened upon those many passages from the poets, from the historians, and especially from the philosophers, in which virtue itself is praised. For it is of no small advantage that virtue become a habit with a youth, for the lessons of youth make a deep impression, because the soul is then plastic, and therefore they are likely to be indelible.[4]

But precisely because a young person's mind is so malleable, some texts are not suitable. Catechumens or students should be advised by their Christian elders, who have greater experience in matters of education and reading and can provide guidance. Basil situates himself as such a guide when he explains that the young men must not give complete control to non-Christian authors: "Now this is my counsel, that you should not unqualifiedly give over your minds to these men, as a ship is surrendered to the rudder, to follow whither they list, but that, while receiving whatever of value they have to offer, you yet recognize what it is wise to ignore."[5] The second-century theologian Tatian took an even more cautious approach in his work *Oration to the Greeks*, recommending that Christians avoid Greek literature and education altogether, since it is full of falsehood that can be damaging to the Christian's moral formation. He takes particular issue with the behavior of Greek philosophers, which he contrasts with the standard of behavior for Christians: where Christians are not driven by a desire for profit or fame and consider God's authority paramount, Tatian says the philosophers are greedy and vain.[6]

The result of all this emphasis on formative reading practices was a thriving community of interpreters who turned their attention to Scriptural interpretation in treatises and homilies. The Pauline conception of the Christian child was carried over into a burgeoning scholastic tradition that set the stage for centuries of intellectual engagement with Christian texts and theology. As Frances M. Young puts it, "The early Church was more like a school than a religion in the social world of antiquity. The emphasis on morals and lifestyle, even the controversial and apologetic ways of differentiating their own 'dogma' from other 'options' (*haereseis*), bespeaks a school-like activity."[7]

SPIRITUAL KINSHIP AND NEW WAYS OF LIFE

The apocryphal text the Acts of Thecla illustrates another strand of Pauline reception, as early Christian communities built on Paul's image of kinship in Christ and formed faith communities that could supplement or replace believers' natal families. Although it was a popular narrative that circulated independently, the Acts of Thecla also made up part of a longer composition, the Acts of Paul, composed around 170–80 CE.[8] The narrative centers around Thecla, a young woman from the Greek city of Iconium who overhears Paul's preaching about asceticism and sexual continence. Drawn to these Christian teachings, Thecla rejects her fiancé Thamyris and expresses her desire to follow Paul and become a baptized Christian missionary. Thecla's mother, Theocleia, is enraged at the prospect that her daughter has become enamored of Paul, dismissing the young woman's religious feeling as inappropriate infatuation: "My daughter is bound to the window like a spider, seized by a new desire and fearful passion through his words."[9] Some knowledge about the precarity of women's social position in the Roman Empire of this period might have created sympathy for Theocleia. No male head of household is mentioned in the text, suggesting Thecla's mother might be a widow; this would have been a financially precarious position, and losing the promise of her daughter's marriage to a respectable young man could have thrown the family's future prospects into disarray.

Readers' sympathy was likely short lived, however. Theocleia demands Thecla be publicly punished for her obstinacy, even calling for her to be burned at the stake in the local arena. After a miraculous escape Thecla makes her way to Paul and insists on traveling with him to preach the Christian message, despite Paul's reluctance. His concern that her beauty will become a liability turns out to be prescient. In Antioch, a local dignitary, Alexander, accosts Thecla on the street. When she rejects his advances, he wishes to destroy the source of his shame and condemns her to a fight with wild beasts. The narrator records that the women of the town were appalled by this development, and "a certain wealthy queen named Tryphaena, whose daughter had died, took her into her care and was comforted by her."[10] Thecla does enter the arena but again cheats death, emerging unscathed because a lioness defends her against a fearsome lion. Female solidarity in the text is not limited to the animal kingdom, for the women of the city threw heavily perfumed herbs into the arena in an effort to deter the beast attacks.

In the midst of this terrifying activity, Thecla also performs a self-baptism in a pool of bloodthirsty seals. Divine lightning smites them and affirms the legitimacy of her ritual action. Gail P. C. Streete, commenting on the text, notes that "there is not a word about her celibacy," which had been threatened by Alexander and led to Thecla's arena trial. But "perhaps there is no need for any since in this narrative the decision for Christianity is a simultaneous decision for sexual continence. Thecla's baptism merely provides the formal 'sealing' of a body that had already dedicated its integrity to Christ."[11] Indeed the victorious Thecla proclaims before the governor, "I am a slave of the living God.... I have believed in God's Son, in whom he is well pleased. That is why none of the beasts has touched me."[12]

Tryphaena steps in as a substitute mother for Thecla. Her very name, based on the Greek root *tryph-* for "luxury" or "sumptuousness," marks her as a figure who can provide the care and sustenance Thecla's natal family denied her. Having heard the account of Thecla's trial and preservation in the beast fight (the poor woman had fainted from fear during the events), Tryphaena proclaims her newfound Christian beliefs: "Now I believe that the dead are raised; now I believe that my child lives. Come inside, and I will bequeath to you all that is mine."[13] She is a protective advocate who wholeheartedly supports Thecla's Christian missionary impulses. As Thecla gains a mother, she becomes a second daughter to comfort Tryphaena, especially by giving the woman hope that her deceased daughter, Falconilla, may participate in eternal life.[14] The narrative proposes that spiritual kinship bonds may be a positive addition to the Christian's life, building up a close-knit community that supports evangelization and an ascetic way of life.

The mutual dependence of Thecla and Tryphaena, spiritual kin, had a counterpart in the communities of desert monastics, who were referred to as "fathers" and "mothers." The wisdom such teachers gained through ascetic practices and prayerful living became a spiritual patrimony for generations of Christians to follow. As Peter Brown explains, "The total dependence of small groups of disciplines on a spiritual father, or on a group of spiritual fathers, was the *sine qua non* of survival and spiritual growth in the desert. It was through dependence on his spiritual father that the monk learned to understand his own heart, and to open that heart to others."[15] The spiritual family could reproduce its learning over successive generations and build up mature Christian thinkers. Many Christians were thinkers rather than active imitators of the ascetic desert fathers and mothers: "By the fifth century many who did not adopt the religious life themselves were also deeply influenced both by the ideals of asceticism and by the examples of individual ascetics."[16] The conception of Christian spiritual kinship also offered one answer to the problem of Christian asceticism and monastic life breaking up the "traditional" family model, especially lines of succession and inheritance. In the new, Christian household, children who might previously have been expected to carry forward the family line could pursue instead a spiritual path, raising up "children" for the future Church.

ECCLESIOLOGICAL IMPACT

The legacy of Paul's metaphor of children of God in the early Christian period was complex, leading to a multiplication of figurative child-parent relationships and models of catechetical formation that held sway for centuries. Some teachers and leaders took on spiritual parenthood, and the majority of Christians were identified as spiritual children in need of education. The developmental model that was applied to the Church's individual members was extended to the church as an institution made up of people continually in formation, under the guidance of the bishops and elders (*presbyteroi*) who oversaw the Church as fictive household, authorized by the hierarchical code outlined in the Pastoral Epistles. As a sign of how deeply the developmental model permeates Christian thinking about the Church, Catholic teaching today still describes changes to Church teaching not as transformations overturning previous understandings, but as "developments" of doctrine.[17]

CONTEMPORARY CULTURAL CONTEXT AND NEW INTERPRETATIONS

Returning briefly to the evangelical orphan care movement, it is important to note that the spread and adoption of evangelical vocabularies of motive did not seem to result in a radical increase in the actual number of adoptions. On the contrary, the number of American evangelical families adopting children through both foreign and domestic agencies remained roughly static even as literature and homilies about orphan care, along with church organizations and adoption support groups, proliferated.[18] Perry's interviews with adopting/adoptive families revealed that in fact most couples chose to pursue adoption when they struggled with infertility or subfecundity. Once people began looking into adoption, they also began to read books like Moore's about Christian adoption or work with evangelical nonprofits to start the adoption process. Perry reports, "During this process of pursuing adoption, evangelical families also begin the process of learning movement ideology and community-approved vocabularies of motives to articulate their adoption pursuit within the evangelical context."[19] That is, evangelical Christian families chose to adopt out of motives that resemble those that influence nonevangelicals, but their engagement with evangelical media and literature shaped their ways of talking about their experience and decisions.

Perry offers a key critique: in evangelical activist movements like the orphan care movement, an overriding concern about caring for orphans *in order to glorify God* can lead some in the movement to "reject the idea that strategic effectiveness at serving vulnerable children is a goal for its own sake."[20] He cites as just one example the reticence of evangelical adoption agencies to place children with unbelieving families, single parents, or homosexual couples, because such family models would not accord with a "biblical" model of family. Some organizations, facing state or federal mandates that would require them to work with all families, chose to close down rather than compromise their principles. Evangelical movements that overemphasize the need for pure motivations are likely to stall out in the face of logistical challenges; they are self-limiting.

Yet the "vocabularies of motive" that attracted (and still attract) many American evangelicals to the orphan care movement are intellectually and emotionally affecting, in part, because of the appeal to images of belonging that are already operative in evangelical circles. The Christian believer's own identity as a spiritual child adopted by God inspires empathy for children in need of literal adoption. This figurative language has the power to capture attention and shape people's ways of thinking about their behavior. Contemporary U.S. Christian groups that rely on the Pauline image of the child of God to create belonging might benefit from careful examination of how that image can also be limiting. For a Church that learns as it teaches, how might the real experiences of children create new space for conversation about belonging? In what follows, I propose one essential avenue for exploration.

CHILD SEX-ABUSE CRISIS IN THE CHURCH

In 1985, a disturbing case broke in southwestern Louisiana: the Roman Catholic priest Rev. Gilbert Gauthe admitted to having sexually abused thirty-seven children. As a Boy Scout chaplain, Gauthe had access to children in the parish troop, and he had molested children there and in at least two other parishes where he had previously been placed.[21] Public responses rightly included horror at the idea of someone in a position of authority, especially religious authority, taking advantage of the community's trust. Many members of the public questioned why Gauthe had continually been reassigned to new parishes and if his superiors knew about his acts of abuse but protected him.[22] Others wondered whether such abuses had been taking place in other parishes around the country, perpetrated by other members of the clergy. As some in the Church at the time anticipated, this first highly publicized case encouraged other survivors of clerical sexual abuse to come forward. This set off a string of investigations and inquiries that revealed a shocking pattern of child sexual abuse in the Church.

Most famously, the John Jay Report of 2004 catalogued allegations of abuse, provided profiles of victims and abusers (largely demographic information), and compiled details about what bishops knew and did in response to allegations over the period 1950–2002. The report was commissioned by the United States Conference of Catholic Bishops (USCCB) and conducted by the John Jay College of Criminal Justice, an independent body; an updated report covering 1950–2010 was published in 2011.[23] The numbers from the initial report can be summarized as follows: "The total number of priests with allegations from 1950 through 2002 was 4,392 out of a total of 109,694 priests who served in ministry during that time. The number of accused priests is equivalent to 4 percent of priests in ministry."[24] Sociologists and experts in victimology point out that these numbers probably represent an undercount. In all settings, sexual assault and rape are underreported, leaving a "dark figure" or "hidden figure" of the cases that never come to light.[25] Additional reports since 2011 have continued the work of cataloguing allegations and the identities of known abusers, at the diocesan level and within particular religious orders. Sociologists of religion point out that sexual abuse of children is not a problem that plagues only the Catholic Church. A 2018–19 investigation by the *Houston Chronicle* and the *San Antonio Express-News* uncovered that "since 1998, roughly 380 Southern Baptist church leaders and volunteers have faced allegations of sexual misconduct.... That includes those who were convicted, credibly accused, and successfully sued, and those who confessed or resigned," leaving behind more than seven hundred victims.[26] Additionally, abuse is not a problem that only affects children; vulnerable adults have also been targeted.

The 2017 Netflix documentary series *The Keepers* offers one accessible presentation of the truly expansive scope of the crisis. Ryan White's seven-episode series begins by examining the unsolved 1969 homicide of a Roman Catholic nun, Catherine Cesnik. Cesnik was a teacher at Archbishop Keough girls' high school in Baltimore, Maryland, whose homicide remained unsolved for years.[27] The documentary follows several Keough alumnae who set out to investigate the cold case. Over the course of their investigation, they talk with students who were sexually abused by the school's chaplain, Fr. Joseph Maskell, and another priest, Fr. Neil Magnus. Some of the young women had reported their abuse to Cesnik shortly before she was murdered, and the series implies that Cesnik may have been killed to cover up the priests' wrongdoing. As the documentary turns to focus more on the history of abuse, the investigators uncover evidence that despite multiple credible allegations leveled against Maskell between 1975 and 1992, the priest was simply reassigned to new ministries, including Keough and later three different Catholic parishes.[28] At one point his superiors sent him to receive treatment for depression at the Institute of Life (IOL) in Connecticut, although a therapist from the IOL reported that priests admitted they were there because of abuses they had committed and the bishops' desires to keep their abuses out of the news.[29]

By the end of the series, viewers see that threads of abuse and cover-up appear to extend throughout diocesan and civil offices in Baltimore and beyond. Sharon May, the division chief for sex offenses in the state's attorney's office in 1994, chose not to prosecute the case against Maskell, the order of the School Sisters of Notre Dame who ran Keough, the archdiocese, and a gynecologist who accepted student referrals from Maskell and allowed him to observe exams.[30] In an interview for the documentary, May also dismissed questions about why the police have no files documenting allegations made against Maskell in the early nineties, although survivors gave statements to police; May insists that it is not unusual to have missing files from the mid-nineties, when files were not "on computers."[31] The survivors seeking legal redress ran up against a statute of limitations that precluded them pressing charges so many years after the abuses took place. One of the abuse survivors, who recovered her memories of the abuses only years later, consistently faced skepticism about her testimony. Multiple survivors were offered financial settlements, which they found unsatisfactory, desiring instead evidence of the Church's changed approach to handling abuse allegations.

Although the problem may seem insurmountable, individuals and organizations both inside and outside the Church are working to put an end to the abuses. SNAP, the Survivors Network of those Abused by Priests, presents itself as "the largest, oldest, and most active support group for women and men wounded by religious and institutional authorities (priests, ministers, bishops, deacons, nuns, coaches, teachers, and others)."[32] Since 2014, SNAP has partnered with StoryCorps, an oral history project archived at the American Folklife Center in the Library of Congress. The stated purpose of StoryCorps aligns with one of the key tenets of SNAP, that telling one's story can contribute to healing for individuals and the broader community:

> StoryCorps' mission is to preserve and share humanity's stories in order to build connections between people and create a more just and compassionate world. We do this in order to remind one another of our shared humanity, to strengthen and build the connections between people, to teach the value of listening, and to weave into the fabric of our culture the understanding that everyone's story matters.[33]

SNAP also works in the realm of advocacy, specifically in support of laws that would better protect children and other vulnerable groups and to lengthen or get rid of restrictive statutes of limitations that prevent those who were abused as children from pursuing prosecutions in the present.[34]

Alongside these grassroots efforts by survivors to provide support for one another, churches have taken steps intended to prevent incidences of sexual abuse. The USCCB outlined best practices and resolutions in a 2002 document, the Charter for the Protection of Children and Young People, sometimes called the Dallas Charter.[35] This effort also included the creation of a secretariat (administrative unit) that oversees and audits the programs in each diocese that are meant to ensure a safe environment for children and young people involved in diocesan activities.[36] In a statement responding to the Pennsylvania Grand Jury Report of 2018, the USCCB acknowledged individual and institutional responsibility for harms, writing,

> The report of the Pennsylvania grand jury again illustrates the pain of those who have been victims of the crime of sexual abuse by individual members of our clergy, and by those who shielded abusers and so facilitated an evil that continued for years or even decades. We are grateful for the courage of the people who aided the investigation by sharing their personal stories of abuse. As a body of bishops, we are shamed by and sorry for the sins and omissions by Catholic priests and Catholic bishops.[37]

Many nevertheless argue that institutional responses on the part of the Roman Catholic Church and other Christian churches have been insufficient and unsatisfactory. The (mis)management of Gauthe's case is illustrative. Although the local bishop of Lafayette confronted Gauthe because of inappropriate actions in 1974, after Gauthe said the "imprudent touches" were an isolated incident, the bishop assigned him as parish Boy Scout chaplain in 1975.[38] The Houston/San Antonio report also noted that at least thirty-five of the pastors, volunteers, and employees accused of abuse were able to find continued employment at churches.[39]

Scholars and survivors agree that the crisis is exacerbated by a hierarchical web of secrecy and an insistence on internal management of the crisis, which can limit or undercut cooperation with civil authorities. As the *New York Times* reported already in 1985, "'The tragedy and scandal,' The National Catholic Reporter said in an editorial last week on the

Louisiana case, 'is not only with the actions of the individual priests—these are serious enough —but with church structures in which bishops, chanceries and seminaries fail to respond to complaints, or even engage in cover-ups.'"[40] With regard to this particular issue, Christian communities may need to confront the harmful potential of the Pauline letters. Writing to the Corinthians about lawsuits among believers, Paul advises that as far as possible they should settle grievances within the community, without seeking intervention from civil authorities, coded as "the unrighteous" and "those who have no standing in the church" (1 Cor 6:1, 4). In today's cultural context, which includes greater awareness of these terrible abuses, should people of faith not find it troubling that Paul writes, "In fact, to have lawsuits at all with one another is already a defeat for you. Why not rather be wronged? Why not rather be defrauded? But you yourselves wrong and defraud—and believers at that" (1 Cor 6:7–8). One can see how this advice might encourage cover-ups and attempts to manage crimes that the institution is not equipped to prosecute. It could also be (and has been) used to imply that Christians are obligated to submit to suffering, even suffering abuse at the hands of trusted Christian leaders.

Is there a healthier way forward for Christian communities in which the majority of members do not have a powerful voice in the hierarchy of the institutional church? In their book *The Abuse of Minors in the Catholic Church: Dismantling the Culture of Cover Ups*, Anthony J. Blasi and Lluis Oviedo point out that such a complex problem needs a cooperative, multivalent response:

> Since the phenomenon is multifaceted and involves several issues, it requires a multidisciplinary treatment: from sociology, psychology, psychiatry, legal studies, anthropology, history, and theology. Only a team of specialists in each field, committed to finding out the factors that determined such a development, can offer an adequate approach and clarify such an enigmatic and destructive process.[41]

Social scientist and social worker Marie Keenan identifies another facet of the crisis, related to the kinds of language used to discuss the abuses. Keenan points out that a dichotomous totalizing language like perpetrator and victim "is actually a limiting one, acting as a constraint and barrier in any endeavor to understand the complex issues involved, and to find a way forward."[42] She rightly notes that the words we use and the images we invoke are of great consequence.

It seems likely that a closer examination of the Pauline metaphor of the child of God and its institutional legacy have some bearing on the conversation. What avenues to power and activism appear closed off to members of the Christian community who have become accustomed to thinking about themselves as perpetual children? What would it look like to challenge the entrenched conception of bishops, priests, and community leaders as infallible spiritual parents? I do not mean to suggest that laypeople and community members who have not perpetrated abuses are culpable for the behavior of abusive priests and bishops. Rather, I propose that additional dimensions of Paul's image, including the potential for maturation and the vision of children as heirs, could empower these groups to advocate for new institutional structures. Fully formed adult members of the *ekklēsia* might think and behave differently if some of the "nourishment" they consumed as a matter of course came from the first-hand accounts of survivors seeking healing and demanding change. If Paul's letters invite us to consider our own vulnerabilities as a means of highlighting our common kinship, how might this motivate us to show greater familial care for one another as siblings and co-heirs in God's household?

PERIL AND PROMISE: CHILDREN IN THE HOUSEHOLD OF GOD

Paul's first-century Gentile readers found a foothold in the Christ-believing movement through the letters' language of adoption and heirship, joining the Jewish Christ-believers to create an *ekklēsia* where "all… are one in Christ Jesus" (Gal 3:28). The child of God image also enabled Paul to express the parental care and attachment he felt for the Christ-believers to whom he ministered. Pauline imitators in subsequent generations latched onto the realia of children's roles in Greco-Roman households and family structures and deployed the image to describe ideal hierarchical relationships within the developing institutional *ekklēsia*. As that church expanded in the second through fifth centuries, theologians capitalized on Paul's image of a spiritual parent providing immature children with age-appropriate nourishment to propose new models for catechesis and religious formation that empowered church leaders as educators. Today the traumatic experiences of children who have faced sexual abuse at the hands of church leaders should drive Christian communities to reconsider our unquestioning attachment to the Pauline image of children of God, in light of its potential disempowering effects. Taking on a role as full adults in the household of God could mean challenging the ecclesial model that suggests childhood renders us powerless or subordinate. Perhaps some promise for a future Church that is truly a safe place to belong lies in (re)claiming Paul's emphasis on children as heirs and as siblings of Christ, stepping into our authority to manage the household of God.

CONCLUSION

In each part of this book, I have outlined the kinds of questions and concerns that were crucial for Paul and his earliest readers, placing these alongside some illustrative examples from the history of Pauline reception in the earliest centuries of Christian growth. Turning to contemporary case studies and modern considerations, I have attempted to draw attention to some thought-provoking "gaps" between the way Paul would probably have intended his metaphors to be read and the way modern U.S. Christian readers are likely to experience those metaphors, given our twenty-first-century context.

Part 1 noted that while the Pauline idea of a self-disciplined athlete could inspire faithful action, modern social expectations of both amateur and professional athletes place people in danger or exploit their labor for the sake of entertainment, perhaps pushing contemporary Christians toward a redefinition of the appropriate sphere for advocacy.

Part 2 outlined the complex and troubling legacy of Paul's "slave of Christ" image; although it may have been intended to increase equality within the *ekklēsia*, a long history of reception has revealed that the metaphor is inadequate to overcome the realities of slavery as an oppressive system and may in fact cause further harms. Its perils come into sharp relief against contemporary practices like wage slavery in the U.S. prison-industrial complex and forced labor around the world, including sex trafficking and sexual violence within the United States.

In Part 3 we explored the gap between the New Testament image of an upwardly mobile "soldier of Christ" and the work that lies ahead for today's Christian communities that seek to support veterans and active-duty military personnel wounded by war. In particular, the imperial warrior Christology that developed in ancient Christianity may require revision to clear the way for healing.

Part 4 grappled with the disconnect between Pauline claims that the Church is a unified "body of Christ" and the reality in today's churches that many bodies and bodyminds—disabled, gendered, marginalized—do not find a place to belong within the *ekklēsia*. The discussion illustrated that our Christian pursuit of justice must continue so that the gifts of each member may be fully appreciated.

In Part 5, a discussion of the contemporary child sex abuse crisis in Catholic and other Christian churches indicated there is a devastating disconnect between a Pauline image designed to empower members of the community—"child of God" and "sibling of Christ"—and the current deformation of ecclesial authority that has endangered and harmed survivors of sexual abuse while adult members of the community find themselves limited to a posture of spiritual childhood.

The peril and promise wrapped up in each Pauline metaphor draw our attention to the enduring power of these ancient letters to provoke deep thinking and inspire new questions. The history of reception, where we find beautiful wisdom mingled with some of our worst human impulses to violence and discrimination, reflects the messy nature of biblical interpretation. Interpretation must be performed where we find ourselves, glimpsing truth and hope "in a mirror, dimly" (1 Cor 13:12). As Christian readers move forward into an equally complex and challenging future, it is my hope that this book might provide a model for fruitful scriptural exegesis. Like our Christian siblings in the second through fifth centuries, we have the ability to articulate a way forward for the Church that is our common household; responsive and responsible biblical interpretation can be a useful tool as we forge new models of Christian identity.

If we the *ekklēsia* choose to use the Pauline epistles and their rich metaphorical language as a guide for cocreating our lives together, we must grapple with the many ways Paul's images resonate, or fail to, in our daily lives. Where possible, members of the community may draw upon each other's varied gifts and talents, born of experience, training, and insight, to strike a balance between historical critical awareness, socially conscious hermeneutical approaches, and practical wisdom. May the interpretive gaps continue to evoke questions and inspire action as together we (re)form the household of God.

NOTES

INTRODUCTION

1. Acts 11:23 states that the believers were first called Christians at Antioch (probably around 43 CE), but I adhere to a relatively late dating for the composition of Acts (ca. 110–15 CE) and have serious questions about its reliability as an accurate historical record. We know that there was confusion about what to call the group in Rome in the 40s CE. Claudius issued an edict expelling Jews because they were "causing trouble on account of some Chrestus." He probably had in view some Jewish Christ-believers, but the group did not seem to have a fixed title distinguishing them from Judaism proper.

2. Elizabeth Drescher, *Choosing Our Religion: The Spiritual Lives of America's Nones* (New York: Oxford University Press, 2016).. The identification of "nones" may be complicated by those who should more technically be classified as "liminal," a status not adequately captured in most large-scale surveys; see Michael Hout, "Religious Ambivalence, Liminality, and the Increase of No Religious Preference in the United States, 2006–2014," *Journal for the Scientific Study of Religion* 56, no. 1 (March 2017): 52–63.

3. This is not a new issue. "Pope Concerned About U.S. Priest Shortage," *Associated Press Online*, November 26, 2004, https://advance.lexis.com/api/document?collection=news&id=urn:contentItem:4DWK-VC60-00BT-N3J3-00000-00&context=1516831.

4. Joshua J. McElwee, "Francis Declines to Answer Amazon Synod's Requests for Married Priests, Women Ministers," *National Catholic Reporter*, February 12, 2020, https://www.ncronline.org/news/vatican/francis-declines-answer-amazon-synods-requests-married-priests

-women-ministers. The Final Document of the Synod on the Pan-Amazon Region, from October 26, 2019, may be found at https://www.vaticannews.va/en/vatican-city/news/2020-02/final-document-synod-amazon.html.

5. David J. Fleming, "Toward a Marianist Future: A Marianist Spiritual Family?" in *A New Fulcrum: Marianist Horizons Today* (Dayton, OH: North American Center for Marianist Studies, 2014), 177–94.

6. The Editors, "Sex Abuse and Clericalism," *Commonweal* 145, no. 14 (September 7, 2018): 5. See recent comments by Pope Francis and others at the meeting "The Protection of Minors in the Church" at the Vatican; e.g., "Address of His Holiness Pope Francis at the end of the Eucharistic Concelebration," the Vatican, http://w2.vatican.va/content/francesco/en/speeches/2019/february/documents/papa-francesco_20190224_incontro-protezioneminori-chiusura.html.

7. For an accessible introductory presentation of Paul's life and theology, I recommend E. P. Sanders, *Paul: A Very Short Introduction* (Oxford: Oxford University Press, 1991).

8. For example, the letters mention as coworkers the wife and husband missionary pair Prisca and Aquila (Rom 16:3); the female apostle Junia (Rom 16:7); Onesimus, an enslaved man, and Philemon his master, who should become brothers in Christ (Phlm 16); Titus a former Gentile (Gal 2:3); and (though the partnership had some tense moments!) Peter, James, and John, leaders in the Jerusalem community of Jewish Christ-believers (Gal 2:9).

9. Hans-Josef Klauck, following E. R. Richards, notes that ancient authors could rely on scribes in a variety of ways, whether as mere recorders or as coauthors or even "composers," who were given the freedom to shape the letter around basic requested content. Paul most likely had a scribe recorder. See Hans-Josef Klauck, *Ancient Letters and the New Testament: A Guide to Context and Exegesis* (Waco, TX: Baylor University Press, 2006), 59.

10. Klauck refers helpfully to the "secondary orality" of letters, to highlight that first and foremost these were written compositions, even if they were subsequently proclaimed and heard. See Klauck, *Ancient Letters and the New Testament*, 208.

11. Ancient rhetorical handbooks, or *progymnasmata*, outline the purposes of this exercise. The first-century CE author Aelius Theon explains, "Personification (*prosopopoeia*) is the introduction of a person to whom words are attributed that are suitable to the speaker and

have an indisputable application to the subject discussed." See Aelius Theon, *Exercises* 8 [Spengel 10], English translation in George A. Kennedy, trans., *Progymnasmata: Greek Textbooks of Prose Composition and Rhetoric*, SBL Writings from the Greco-Roman World 10 (Atlanta: Society of Biblical Literature, 2003), 47.

12. The Latin *pastor* literally means "shepherd."

13. Full English text available at https://www.vatican.va/archive/hist_councils/ii_vatican_council/documents/vat-ii_const_19651118_dei-verbum_en.html.

14. I do use the masculine pronoun to refer to biblical authors; to the best of our knowledge, all the texts were written by men, in part because men had access to the kinds of education and wealth that enabled them to become literate.

15. Anna Rebecca Solevåg, "Salvation as Slavery, Marriage, and Birth: Does the Metaphor Matter?" in *Bodies, Borders, Believers: Ancient Texts and Present Conversations*, ed. Anne Hege Grung, Marianne Bjelland Kartzow, and Anna Rebecca Solevåg (Cambridge: The Lutterworth Press, 2016), 144–63, at 148.

16. The concept of intersectionality was introduced in Kimberlé Crenshaw, "Demarginalizing the Intersection of Race and Sex: A Black Feminist Critique of Antidiscrimination Doctrine, Feminist Theory and Antiracist Politics," *University of Chicago Legal Forum* vol. 1989, iss. 1, art. 8 (1989): 139–67.

PART 1

1. "CYO Mission Statement," San Antonio Archdiocesan webpage, accessed June 26, 2020, https://www.archsa.org/cyo.

2. Timothy B. Neary, *Crossing Parish Boundaries: Race, Sports, and Catholic Youth in Chicago, 1914–1954*, Historical Studies of Urban America (Chicago: University of Chicago Press, 2016), 72.

3. There was an initial patriotic and anticommunist thrust to the CYO, as exemplified in its 1932 charter, which states, "The Catholic Youth Organization was established to promote among youth a recreational, educational, and religious program that would adequately meet the physical, mental, and spiritual needs of boys and girls without regard to race,

creed, or color...while instilling in their minds and hearts a true love for God and country." Cited in Neary, *Crossing Parish Boundaries*, 71.

4. Neary, *Crossing Parish Boundaries*, 85.

5. Neary, *Crossing Parish Boundaries*, 85.

6. Neary, *Crossing Parish Boundaries*, 76. Neary also points out that there was an implicit element of competition. After World War I, the Vatican "warned American bishops about the YMCA and encouraged them to start Catholic societies to protect youth from the Protestant organization" (79).

7. Neary, *Crossing Parish Boundaries*, 14.

8. Neary, *Crossing Parish Boundaries*, 130–31.

Chapter 1

1. There is significant debate over the dating for this letter. Hans Dieter Betz and Richard Cassidy, e.g., situate its composition in a final imprisonment near the end of Paul's life, while Adolf Deissmann and more recently Carolyn Osiek argue the letter was written during an earlier imprisonment in Ephesus, in the mid-50s CE. See Paul A. Holloway, *Philippians: A Commentary*, Hermeneia (Minneapolis: Fortress, 2017), 19–24.

2. English translation available in Lucian, *Volume IV*, trans. A. M. Harmon, Loeb Classical Library 162 (Cambridge, MA: Harvard University Press, 1925).

3. Robert Murray, "Philippians," in *The Oxford Bible Commentary*, ed. John Barton and John Muddiman (Oxford: Oxford University Press, 2007), 1179–90, at 1181.

4. Margaret Y. MacDonald raises the possibility that perhaps the breach lies not between Euodia and Syntyche, but between the two of them and Paul. She also notes that the letter's emphasis on cooperation may indicate their rift is Paul's main impetus for writing, putting the women at the center of the correspondence. See Margaret Y. MacDonald, "Reading Real Women through the Undisputed Letters of Paul," in *Women and Christian Origins*, ed. Ross Shepard Kraemer and Mary Rose D'Angelo (New York: Oxford University Press, 1999), 199–220, esp. 204–6.

5. Troels Engberg-Pedersen, *Paul and the Stoics* (Louisville, KY: Westminster John Knox, 2000).

6. Barbara K. Gold offers a brief, helpful discussion of endurance as a gendered, feminine virtue and Seneca's role in rendering it appropriate for men. See Barbara K. Gold, *Perpetua: Athlete of God*, Women in Antiquity (Oxford: Oxford University Press, 2018), 31–32.

7. Robert Paul Seesengood, "Hybridity and the Rhetoric of Endurance: Reading Paul's Athletic Metaphors in a Context of Postcolonial Self-Construction," *The Bible and Critical Theory* 1, no. 2 (2005): 1–14, at 8.

8. Murray, "Philippians," 1179.

9. Cavan W. Concannon, "'Not for an Olive Wreath, but Our Lives': Gladiators, Athletes, and Early Christian Bodies," *Journal of Biblical Literature* 133, no. 1 (Spring 2014): 193–214.

10. Michael J. Carter, "Bloodbath: Artemidorus, Αποτομος Combat, and Ps.-Quintilian's 'The Gladiator,'" *Zeitschrift für Papyrologie und Epigraphik* 193 (2015): 39–52, at 46.

11. Anna McCullough points out that most authors from the imperial period who mention female gladiators take a moralizing bent. Such authors object to the participation of women not on principle but because of their association with unseemly displays of lavish wealth, either on the part of the emperors and private benefactors who could afford to sponsor unusual athletes or on the part of elite women who joined the games as a way of entertaining themselves; such censure is not usually applied to female gladiators of the lower classes. See Anna McCullough, "Female Gladiators in Imperial Rome: Literary Context and Historical Fact," *The Classical World* 101, no. 2 (Winter 2008): 197–209, esp. 202–3.

12. Paul addresses this particular issue in his correspondence with the Corinthians, where eating meat that has been sacrificed to idols (Greco-Roman gods) has become a point of division for the Corinthian Christ-believers (1 Cor 8, 10).

13. J. R. Harrison, "The Fading Crown: Divine Honour and the Early Christians," *The Journal of Theological Studies* new series 54, no. 2 (October 2003): 493–529, at 494.

14. Harrison, "The Fading Crown," 497.

15. Paul seems to use "Day of the Lord" and "Day of Christ" interchangeably, with some variations: "Day of Jesus Christ" at Phil 1:6, "Day of the Lord Jesus Christ" at 1 Cor 1:8.

16. For a helpful and brief discussion of the Parousia in Greco-Roman history, literature, and the material record, see Brent Kinman,

"Parousia, Jesus' 'A-Triumphal' Entry, and the Fate of Jerusalem (Luke 19:28–44)," *Journal of Biblical Literature* 118, no. 2 (Summer 1999): 279–94, esp. 280–84.

17. Paul has not invented the idea of an imperishable prize. He may be drawing on Hebrew Bible Wisdom literature. As part of an extended praise of virtue, the author of Wisdom depicts virtue itself as the victor in a contest (*agōn*), receiving prizes that are "undefiled" (Wis 4:2).

18. On the question of Corinthian factionalism, see thorough discussion in Margaret M. Mitchell, *Paul and the Rhetoric of Reconciliation: An Exegetical Investigation of the Language and Composition of 1 Corinthians* (Tübingen: Mohr Siebeck, 1992).

19. These and other examples may be found in John G. Gager, *Curse Tablets and Binding Spells from the Ancient World* (Oxford: Oxford University Press, 1992).

20. Concannon, "'Not for an Olive Wreath,'" 197.

21. Although John Chrysostom, Christian theologian of the fourth century CE, received the same "Golden Mouth" epithet, the two figures should not be confused.

22. Dio Chrysostom, *Oration* 28.12. English translation in Dio Chrysostom, *Discourses* 12–30, trans. J. W. Cohoon, Loeb Classical Library 339 (Cambridge, MA: Harvard University Press, 1939), 369.

23. Seesengood, "Hybridity," 9.

24. See a brief and still-helpful summary of key issues and Pauline concerns in Hans Dieter Betz, *Galatians: A Commentary on Paul's Letter to the Churches in Galatia*, Hermeneia (Philadelphia: Fortress, 1979), esp. 84–88.

25. Commentators point out that a Christian would make such a confession at the time of baptism or when being appointed to some office (such as bishop or deacon, positions discussed in the Pastoral epistles). See Martin Dibelius and Hans Conzelmann, *The Pastoral Epistles: A Commentary on the Pastoral Epistles*, trans. Philip Buttolph and Adela Yarbro, Hermeneia (Philadelphia: Fortress, 1972), 88.

26. Pliny, *Letters* 10.96–97. Facing Latin and English text available in Pliny the Younger, *Letters*, vol. 2, *Books 8–10, Panegyricus*, trans. Betty Radice, Loeb Classical Library 59 (Cambridge, MA: Harvard University Press, 1969).

27. *Pace* Clare Drury, who states that the three images (soldier, athlete, farmer) the Pastor uses in 2 Tim 2:1–7 "are not explained; Timothy is told to work out their meaning for himself, with the help of

the lord (v. 7), but the general sense is clear. Work is involved in all three images." See Clare Drury, "The Pastoral Epistles," in Barton and Muddiman, *Oxford Bible Commentary*, 1220–33, at 1228.

28. Not all scholars agree that the letter is pseudonymous. For a brief defense of possible authentic authorship, see Jerome Murphy-O'Connor, "Colossians," in Barton and Muddiman, *Oxford Bible Commentary*, 1191–99, at 1191–92.

Chapter 2

1. As Carly Daniel-Hughes and Maia Kotrosits point out in a recent article, Christians like Tertullian who were writing about God and martyrs in a divinely ordered forensic context perhaps appealed to a fantasy version of the Roman justice system as a way of fabricating juridical and moral clarity where otherwise ambiguity and capriciousness might reign. See Carly Daniel-Hughes and Maia Kotrosits, "Tertullian of Carthage and the Fantasy Life of Power: On Martyrs, Christians, and Other Attachments to Juridical Scenes," *Journal of Early Christian Studies* 28, no. 1 (Spring 2020): 1–31.

2. A recent English translation and commentary is available in Thomas J. Heffernan, *The Passion of Perpetua and Felicity* (Oxford: Oxford University Press, 2012).

3. Lynn H. Cohick and Amy Brown Hughes, "Perpetua and Felicitas: Mothers and Martyrs," in *Christian Women in the Patristic World: Their Influence, Authority, and Legacy in the Second through Fifth Centuries* (Grand Rapids: Baker Academic, 2017), 27–64, at 29.

4. Gail P. C. Streete, *Redeemed Bodies: Women Martyrs in Early Christianity* (Louisville, KY: Westminster John Knox, 2009), 10.

5. Eusebius, *Historia ecclesiae* 5.1. English translation available in Eusebius, *Ecclesiastical History*, vol. 1, trans. Kirsopp Lake, Loeb Classical Library 153 (Cambridge, MA: Harvard University Press, 1926).

6. Cohick and Hughes, *Christian Women in the Patristic World*, 63.

7. Gail Corrington Streete, "Women as Sources of Redemption and Knowledge in Early Christian Traditions," in *Women and Christian Origins*, ed. Ross Shepard Kraemer and Mary Rose D'Angelo (New York: Oxford University Press, 1999), 330–54, at 349.

8. Cohick and Hughes, *Christian Women in the Patristic World*, 28.

9. Candida Moss, *Ancient Christian Martyrdom: Diverse Practices, Theologies, and Traditions*, Anchor Yale Bible Reference Library (New Haven, CT: Yale University Press, 2012).

10. This is not to say that girls and young women were excluded from the CYO. There were female teams playing basketball in the first (1931–32) season, and female participation continued to grow. However, boys' sports "dominated CYO athletics coverage in the archdiocesan and city newspapers" (Timothy B. Neary, *Crossing Parish Boundaries: Race, Sports, and Catholic Youth in Chicago, 1914–1954*, Historical Studies of Urban America [Chicago: University of Chicago Press, 2016], 117). It was not until the 1950s that the girls' track team garnered the lion's share of attention.

11. Neary, *Crossing Parish Boundaries*, 83. Quotation from "Boxing Tournament Winners to Qualify for Olympic Games," *New World*, September 23, 1932.

12. Neary, *Crossing Parish Boundaries*, 98. Italics mine.

13. Neary, *Crossing Parish Boundaries*, 135–66.

14. Neary, *Crossing Parish Boundaries*, 97.

15. Archdiocese of San Antonio, "Catholic Youth Association: Evangelization," https://www.archsa.org/cyo/evangelization.

16. Associated Press, "Trump Says NFL Should Fire Players Who Kneel during Anthem," NBC Sports, September 22, 2017, https://www.nbcsports.com/boston/new-england-patriots/trump-says-nfl-should-fire-players-who-kneel-during-anthem.

17. Around the NFL Staff, "Players Send Message to League in Coordinated Video Post," NFL.com, June 5, 2020, https://www.nfl.com/news/players-send-message-to-league-in-coordinated-video-post.

18. Jason Owens, "Roger Goodell: NFL Admits 'We Were Wrong' on Player Protests, Says 'Black Lives Matter,'" Yahoo Sports, June 5, 2020, https://sports.yahoo.com/roger-goodell-nfl-admits-we-were-wrong-on-player-protests-black-lives-matter-224540686.html.

19. Jace Evans, "President Donald Trump Questions Roger Goodell's Statement to NFL players," *USA Today*, June 8, 2020, https://www.usatoday.com/story/sports/nfl/2020/06/07/donald-trump-questions-roger-goodell-message-nfl-players/3173571001/.

20. Kurt Badenhausen, "Poll: 61% of Americans Say Roger Goodell Owes Colin Kaepernick an Apology," *Forbes*, June 15, 2020, https://www.forbes.com/sites/kurtbadenhausen/2020/06/15/poll-61

-of-americans-say-roger-goodell-owes-colin-kaepernick-an-apology/#6fb564931f3e.

21. Amir Vera and Jill Martin, "Roger Goodell Encourages NFL Teams to Sign Colin Kaepernick," CNN, June 16, 2020, https://www.cnn.com/2020/06/16/us/nfl-roger-goodell-colin-kaepernick-spt-trnd/index.html.

22. Neary, *Crossing Parish Boundaries*, 131–32.

23. Allen R. Sanderson and John J. Siegfried, "The Case for Paying College Athletes," *Journal of Economic Perspectives* 29, no. 1 (Winter 2015): 115–38, at 117.

24. Sanderson and Siegfried, "Case for Paying," 124.

25. Sanderson and Siegfried, "Case for Paying," 132–33.

26. The proliferation of developmental leagues open to hiring players right out of high school may create some pressure for the NCAA to more seriously consider compensation for student-athletes. See David A. Grenardo, "The Blue Devil's in the Details: How a Free Market Approach to Compensating College Athletes Would Work," *Pepperdine Law Review* 46, no. 2 (2019): 203–76, at 249–50, https://digitalcommons.pepperdine.edu/plr/vol46/iss2/1.

27. Grenardo, "Blue Devil's," 206.

28. Brakkton Booker, "College Athletes Are Now Closer to Getting Paid after NCAA Board OKs Plan," *NPR*, April 29, 2020, https://www.npr.org/2020/04/29/847781624/college-players-are-now-closer-to-getting-paid-after-ncaa-board-oks-plan#:~:text=In%20a%20significant%20shift%20for,does%20not%20pay%20them%20directly.

29. "Board of Governors Moves toward Allowing Student-Athlete Compensation for Endorsements and Promotions," *NCAA*, April 29, 2020, http://www.ncaa.org/about/resources/media-center/news/board-governors-moves-toward-allowing-student-athlete-compensation-endorsements-and-promotions.

30. "What is CTE?," *Concussion Legacy Foundation*, accessed June 30, 2020, https://concussionfoundation.org/CTE-resources/what-is-CTE.

31. "CTE in Former College Football Players," *Concussion Legacy Foundation*, accessed July 15, 2020, https://stage.concussionfoundation.org/CTE-resources/cte-college-football.

32. Ken Belson, "Players with C.T.E. Doubled Risk with Every 5.3 Years in Football," *New York Times*, October 7, 2019, https://www.nytimes.com/2019/10/07/sports/football/football-cte-study-risk.html.

33. Ken Belson and Benedict Carey, "Abnormal Levels of a Protein Linked to C.T.E. Found in N.F.L Players' Brains, Study Shows," *New York Times*, April 10, 2019, https://www.nytimes.com/2019/04/10/health/concussion-nfl-football-cte.html.

34. Jimmy Vielkind, "New York Lawmakers Debate a Tough Topic: Kids Playing Football," *Wall Street Journal*, October 29, 2019, https://www.wsj.com/articles/new-york-lawmakers-debate-a-tough-topic-kids-playing-football-11572387276.

35. Sanderson and Siegfried, "Case for Paying," 133.

36. "NFL Issues Response to CTE Research Report," NFL website, July 26, 2017, https://www.nfl.com/news/nfl-issues-response-to-cte-research-report-0ap3000000822159.

37. For example, House Bill 25 passed in the Texas legislature in October 2021, restricting transgender athletes' ability to participate in school sports. While some transgender athletes competed in the 2020 Tokyo Olympics, their participation sparked intense debate and has led to calls for rules that are more inclusive for diverse athletes. See Rachel Treisman, "Texas' New Law Restricts Transgender Athletes' Participation on School Sports Teams," *NPR*, October 27, 2021, https://www.npr.org/2021/10/27/1049634164/texas-new-law-restricts-transgender-athletes-participation-on-school-sports-team. See also Tariq Panja and Ken Belson, "Olympics' First Openly Transgender Woman Stokes Debate on Fairness," *The New York Times*, July 31, 2021, https://www.nytimes.com/2021/07/31/sports/laurel-hubbard-trans-weight-lifting.html.

38. Decision as quoted in Franklyn Cater, "Federal Judge Dismisses U.S. Women's Soccer Team's Equal Play Claim," *NPR*, May 2, 2020, https://www.npr.org/2020/05/02/849492863/federal-judge-dismisses-u-s-womens-soccer-team-s-equal-pay-claim.

39. Jill Martin, "US Women's National Soccer Team Players Ask for Appeal and Trial Delay after Judge Dismisses Equal Pay Claims," *CNN*, May 9, 2020, https://www.cnn.com/2020/05/08/football/uswnt-equal-pay-lawsuit-appeal-spt-intl/index.html.

40. Jaclyn Diaz, "U.S. Soccer Is Offering the Same Contracts for Its Men's and Women's Teams," *NPR*, September 15, 2021, https://www.npr.org/2021/09/15/1037237343/u-s-soccer-offers-mens-womens-teams-identical-contracts.

41. Alysia Montaño, "Nike Told Me to Dream Crazy, Until I Wanted a Baby," *The New York Times*, May 12, 2019, https://www.nytimes.com/2019/05/12/opinion/nike-maternity-leave.html.

42. Allyson Felix, "Allyson Felix: My Own Nike Pregnancy Story," *The New York Times*, May 22, 2019, https://www.nytimes.com/2019/05/22/opinion/allyson-felix-pregnancy-nike.html?action=click&module=RelatedLinks&pgtype=Article.

43. Andrew Das, "U.S. Women's Soccer Team Sues U.S. Soccer for Gender Discrimination," *The New York Times*, March 8, 2019, https://www.nytimes.com/2019/03/08/sports/womens-soccer-team-lawsuit-gender-discrimination.html.

44. Adam Kilgore, "Under Fire, Nike Expands Protections for Pregnant Athletes," *The Washington Post*, August 16, 2019, https://www.washingtonpost.com/sports/2019/08/16/under-fire-nike-expands-protections-pregnant-athletes/.

45. "Our Vision," &Mother website, accessed September 26, 2021, https://andmother.org/about.

46. Taylor Dutch, "Alysia Montaño Creates Nonprofit for Professional Athlete Mothers," *Runner's World*, May 6, 2020, https://www.runnersworld.com/news/a32388733/alysia-montano-nonprofit-for-athlete-mothers/.

PART 2

1. Frederick Douglass, *Appendix to Narrative of the Life of Frederick Douglass, an American Slave, Written by Himself* (Boston 1845), Project Gutenberg, updated February 28, 2021, https://www.gutenberg.org/files/23/23-h/23-h.htm.

2. Douglass, *Appendix*.

3. Julius H. Bailey, "The Religious Life of Enslaved Americans," in *Down in the Valley: An Introduction to African American Religious History* (Minneapolis: Fortress, 2016), 25–51, at 27–28.

4. Theologian Howard Thurman shares one account. See Howard Thurman, *Jesus and the Disinherited* (Boston: Beacon, 1976), 20. His grandmother, who had been enslaved, recounted how the white minister would use Pauline texts in preaching to the enslaved, including quotations of "slaves, obey your masters" three to four times per year. Thurman quotes her: "I promised my Maker that if I ever learned to read and if freedom ever came, I would not read that part of the Bible."

5. Rosemary Radford Ruether, "Racism in the United States: White, Black, Red, Brown, and Yellow," in *Christianity and Social Systems: Historical Constructions and Ethical Challenges* (Lanham, MD: Rowman & Littlefield, 2009), 75–90, at 76.

Chapter 3

1. Ronald F. Hock points out that though some scholars suggest a later date aligned with Paul's Roman imprisonment (ca. 60–62 CE), some data like Paul's hope of traveling from Rome to Spain (Rom 15:23–24) and a note in Philemon 22 about Paul visiting Philemon's household soon mitigate against seeing this letter as so late. See Ronald F. Hock, "The Letter of Paul to Philemon, Introduction," in *The HarperCollins Study Bible*, ed. Harold W. Attridge (San Francisco: HarperOne, 2006), 2032.

2. Carolyn Osiek states, "It is possible that Apphia is Philemon's wife and Archippus his brother, or that all three are unmarried siblings in the same household, or if married, their spouses do not share the faith. It is less likely that Apphia is the wife of Archippus since wives would not normally be named before their husbands....Of course, it is also possible that only one of the three hosts the house-church and the other two are the only other members of it that Paul knows." See Carolyn Osiek, *Philippians, Philemon*, Abingdon New Testament Commentary (Nashville: Abingdon, 2000), 134.

3. In the midst of this serious proposal, Paul cannot resist including a pun on Onesimus's name, which means "useful" or "beneficial" in Greek. As a Christ-believer and figurative child of Paul, Onesimus truly lives up to his name.

4. Sara Winter has proposed that Onesimus was not a slave of Philemon, but of the Archippus mentioned in Phlm 2. Allen Callahan argues that Onesimus was not a slave at all but was instead Philemon's brother who was being wrongly treated *like* a slave (relying on verse 16). The interpretation that holds Onesimus was enslaved and ran away from Philemon's household does have the benefit of antiquity (although this is not always the best desideratum): this reading is recorded as early as the fourth century, in a homily of theologian and preacher John Chrysostom. A slightly different reading by Peter Lampe suggests that a slave who went to a known associate would not have been subject to legal penalties for running away, and that Onesimus was in

this situation. For a summary of these various positions, see Osiek, *Philippians, Philemon*, 126–31.

5. Chris Frilingos notes some important similarities between Paul's letter and a similar letter by the Roman Pliny the Younger. See Chris Frilingos, "'For My Child, Onesimus': Paul and Domestic Power in Philemon," *Journal of Biblical Literature* 119, no. 1 (Spring 2000): 91–104, at 91.

6. Hans-Josef Klauck, with Daniel P. Bailey, *Ancient Letters and the New Testament: A Guide to Context and Exegesis* (Waco, TX: Baylor University Press, 2006), esp. 73–75.

7. Scholars estimate that in the Augustan period, at least 20 percent and perhaps as much as 35 percent of the population was made up of enslaved persons. See Keith Bradley, *Slavery and Society at Rome* (Cambridge: Cambridge University Press, 1994), 12.

8. Take, e.g., the New Revised Standard Version, which is the preferred translation among scholars in the Society of Biblical Literature and which typically uses "servant" to translate the Pauline figurative uses of *doulos* and then adds a footnote indicating that the original Greek was "slave."

9. Paul presents himself as an *oikonomos* of God at 1 Cor 4:1.

10. Peter Hunt, *Ancient Greek and Roman Slavery* (Hoboken, NJ: Wiley-Blackwell, 2018), 18.

11. Anna Rebecca Solevåg, "Salvation as Slavery, Marriage, and Birth: Does the Metaphor Matter?" in *Bodies, Borders, Believers: Ancient Texts and Present Conversations*, ed. Anne Hege Grung, Marianne Bjelland Kartzow, and Anna Rebecca Solevåg (Cambridge: The Lutterworth Press, 2016), 149.

12. Aristotle, *Politics* 1.1254a 14–16. English translation from Aristotle, *Politics*, trans. C. D. C. Reeve (Indianapolis: Hackett, 1998).

13. Keith Bradley, *Slavery and Society at Rome* (Cambridge: Cambridge University Press, 1994), 43. See esp. chap. 3, "The Roman Slave Supply."

14. Hunt, *Ancient Greek and Roman Slavery*, 19. The quotation is taken from Hunt's helpful summary (at 17–29) of key terms and ideas from Patterson's *Slavery and Social Death: A Comparative Study* (Cambridge, MA: Harvard University Press, 1982).

15. Frederick W. Danker, Walter Bauer, William F. Arndt, and F. Wilbur Gingrich, *A Greek-English Lexicon of the New Testament and*

Other Early Christian Literature, 3rd ed. (Chicago: University of Chicago Press, 2000) (hereafter, "BDAG"), s.v. δουλεύω.

16. Hans Dieter Betz points out that Paul seems to ascribe to the view that, unlike the one true God of Israel, the deities of the Greco-Roman pantheon are only so-called gods whose only existence is in "the superstitious imaginations and projections of the worshippers," a view shared by the Greek writer Plutarch. Hans Dieter Betz, *Galatians: A Commentary on Paul's Letter to the Churches in Galatia*, Hermeneia (Philadelphia: Fortress, 1979), 215.

17. Moses (1 Chr 6:49; 2 Chr 24:9; Neh 10:29; Dan 9:11) and Joshua (Judg 2:8).

18. The Lex Fufia Caninia, passed under Augustus in 2 BCE, placed limits on the number of enslaved persons that could be freed through testamentary manumission. The fact that this law was part of a slate of legislation designed to limit ostentation reveals a crucial aspect of Roman attitudes about manumission: freeing one's slaves was an uncouth display of wealth. See discussion in Keith R. Bradley, *Slaves and Masters in the Roman Empire: A Study in Social Control* (Oxford: Oxford University Press, 1987), 91.

19. Henrik Mouritsen suggests this was an infrequent occurrence and a departure from the norm. See Henrik Mouritsen, *The Freedman in the Roman World* (Cambridge: Cambridge University Press, 2011), 166.

20. Epictetus (ca. 50–ca. 135) was part of the Stoic school, and his teachings are preserved in the *Discourses* and *Enchiridion*.

21. This is according to the Lex Aelia Sentia passed in Rome in 4 CE, as explained in Mouritsen, *Freedman in the Roman World*, 29.

22. For a comprehensive overview of women's legal rights in the early Christian period, see Antti Arjava, *Women and Law in Late Antiquity* (Oxford: Oxford University Press, 1996). Examples of marriage contracts may be found in A. S. Hunt and C. C. Edgar, trans., *Select Papyri I: Private Affairs*, Loeb Classical Library 266 (Cambridge, MA: Harvard University Press, 2001), 2–30.

23. Katharine P. D. Huemoeller, "Freedom in Marriage? Manumission for Marriage in the Roman World," *Journal of Roman Studies* 110 (November 2020): 123–39.

24. Mouritsen, *Freedman in the Roman World*, 20. On the flip side, sometimes male citizens would free the enslaved women who had borne their children in order to give the children legitimate status so they could become heirs. See Rachel Zelnick-Abramowitz, *Not Wholly*

Free: The Concept of Manumission and the Status of Manumitted Slaves in the Ancient Greek World (Leiden: Brill, 2005), 168.

25. Betz, *Galatians*, 203.

26. Chris L. de Wet, "Divine Bondage: Slavery between Metaphor and Theology," in *Preaching Bondage: John Chrysostom and the Discourse of Slavery in Early Christianity* (Berkeley: University of California Press, 2015), 45–81, at 49.

27. Pliny the Younger, *Epistle* 96. For an accessible English translation of Pliny's collected letters, see Pliny the Younger, *The Letters of the Younger Pliny*, Penguin New Impression Edition, trans. Betty Radice (London: Penguin, 2003).

28. Bradley, *Slavery and Society at Rome*, 171.

29. Jeremy Punt, "Not Child's Play," *Neotestamentica* 51, no. 2 (2017): 235–60, at 254.

30. There is a nearly identical passage at Col 3:22—4:1.

31. See also Titus 2:9–10, where the enslaved persons who render their service with "perfect fidelity…may be an ornament to the doctrine of God our Savior."

32. Hunt, *Ancient Greek and Roman Slavery*, 22–23.

Chapter 4

1. Gregory of Nyssa, *Life of Macrina* 11, 28. English translation available in Gregory of Nyssa, *Ascetical Works*, trans. Virginia Woods Callahan, the Fathers of the Church, a New Translation 58 (Washington, DC: The Catholic University of America Press, 1967), 161–91.

2. Gregory of Nyssa, *Life of Macrina* 11.

3. Gregory of Nyssa, *Homilies on Ecclesiastes IV*. English translation by Rachel Moriarty in Gregory of Nyssa, *Gregory of Nyssa Homilies on Ecclesiastes: An English Version with Supporting Studies; Proceedings of the Seventh International Colloquium on Gregory of Nyssa (St. Andrews, September 5–10, 1990)*, ed. Stuart George Hall (Berlin: Walter de Gruyter, 1993).

4. Lionel Wickham, "Homily IV," in Hall, *Gregory of Nyssa, Homilies on Ecclesiastes*, 179.

5. Gregory of Nyssa, *Homilies on Ecclesiastes IV*, this English translation by Andrew Maguire, Early Church Texts, accessed August 29, 2021, https://earlychurchtexts.com/public/gregoryofnyss_ecclesiastes_slavery.htm.

6. Ilaria Ramelli, "Theosebia: A Presbyter of the Catholic Church," *Journal of Feminist Studies in Religion* 26, no. 2 (Fall 2010): 79–102, at 101.

7. Chris L. de Wet, "The Cappadocian Fathers on Slave Management," *Studia Historiae Ecclesiasticae* 39, no. 1 (May 2013): 1–12.

8. His reminder about the enslaved person's humanity is almost incidental in a longer treatise actually focused on self-discipline and appropriate Christian behavior, the *Paidogōgos.* As Peter Brown puts it, "He wrote with genuine anger of those who summoned slaves by snapping their fingers: to deny slaves contact through the gentle harmonies of the human voice was to deny them their humanity." See Peter Brown, *The Body and Society: Men, Women, and Sexual Renunciation in Early Christianity*, Lectures on the History of Religions, New Series 13 (New York: Columbia University Press, 1988), 127.

9. Brown, *Body and Society*, 58–59.

10. Ignatius, *Letter to Polycarp* 4.3. Greek text and facing English translation available in Michael W. Holmes, ed., *The Apostolic Fathers: Greek Texts and English Translations* (Grand Rapids: Baker Books, 1999), 196–97.

11. Averil Cameron, *The Mediterranean World in Late Antiquity: AD 395–600*, Routledge History of the Ancient World (London: Routledge, 1993), 85.

12. Palladius, *Lausiac History* 46.4. English translation in Palladius, *Palladius: The Lausiac History*, trans. R. T. Meyer, Ancient Christian Writers 34 (New York: Newman, 1964).

13. Cameron, *Mediterranean World in Late Antiquity*, 86.

14. Chrysostom argues first that human beings do not need slaves because they are created with self-sufficiency (the Stoic idea of *autarkeia*) and second that in Christ there is no slave or free, no difference in spiritual status. See Ilaria Ramelli, "Gregory of Nyssa's Position in Late Antique Debates on Slavery and Poverty, and the Role of Asceticism," *Journal of Late Antiquity* 5, no. 1 (Spring 2012): 87–118, at 91.

15. Chris L. de Wet, "Divine Bondage: Slavery between Metaphor and Theology," in *Preaching Bondage: John Chrysostom and the Discourse of Slavery in Early Christianity* (Berkeley: University of California Press, 2015), 45–81, at 48.

16. de Wet, "Divine Bondage," 54. Quotation is from Chrysostom, *Homily on 1 Corinthians* 34.7.

17. Chrysostom, *Homily on 1 Corinthians* 40.7.

18. Chrysostom, *Homily on Philemon* 3.2.

19. Frederick Douglass, *Appendix to Narrative of the Life of Frederick Douglass, An American Slave, Written by Himself* (Boston 1845), Project Gutenberg, updated February 28, 2021, https://www.gutenberg.org/files/23/23-h/23-h.htm.

20. Ramelli points out that Augustine's position is even more harsh, taking slavery to be not just a result of the fall and all human sin, but even a specific punishment for sinful individuals. See Ramelli, "Gregory of Nyssa's Position," 92–93.

21. Allen Dwight Callahan, "'Brother Saul': An Ambivalent Witness to Freedom," in *Onesimus Our Brother: Reading Religion, Race, and Culture in Philemon*, ed. Matthew V. Johnson, James A. Noel, and Demetrius K. Williams (Minneapolis: Fortress, 2012), 143–56, at 143.

22. See esp. Hubert Danford Maultsby, "Paul, Black Theology and Hermeneutics," *Journal of the Interdenominational Theological Center* 3 (1976): 49–64.

23. Callahan, "Brother Saul," 155. Callahan mentions Latta R. Thomas's reading of 1 Cor 7:20–21 and Amos Jones, who understands Paul's message to have been corrupted and misused in white American Christianity.

24. See, e.g., Clarice J. Martin, "The Haustafeln (Household Codes) in African American Biblical Interpretation: 'Free Slaves' and 'Subordinate Women,'" in *Stony the Road We Trod: African American Biblical Interpretation*, ed. Cain Hope Felder (Minneapolis: Fortress, 1991), 206–31.

25. Amendment XIII of the U.S. Constitution, National Archives webpage, accessed September 3, 2021, https://www.archives.gov/founding-docs/amendments-11-27#xiii.

26. "The Legacy Museum: From Enslavement to Mass Incarceration," EJI website, accessed August 24, 2021, https://museumandmemorial.eji.org/. The powerful visual artifacts and individual testimonies have their complement at the EJI's National Memorial for Justice and Peace, also in Montgomery. The Memorial is a walk-through that commemorates the lives of thousands of Black Americans murdered in lynchings (extrajudicial executions designed to inflict racial terror). Learn more about the memorial at https://museumandmemorial.eji.org/memorial.

27. Wendy Sawyer, "How Much Do Incarcerated People Earn in Each State?" Prison Policy Initiative website, updated April 28, 2017, https://www.prisonpolicy.org/blog/2017/04/10/wages/.

28. The Indicator for Planet Money, "The Uncounted Workforce," NPR, June 29, 2020, https://www.npr.org/transcripts/884989263.

29. USCCB, "Letter to Congress on Second Chance Reauthorization Act of 2017," October 16, 2017, https://www.usccb.org/resources/letter-congress-second-chance-reauthorization-act-2017.

30. The Indicator for Planet Money, "Uncounted Workforce."

31. International Labour Organization, *Executive Summary, Global Estimates of Modern Slavery: Forced Labour and Forced Marriage* (September 2017), 9. See https://www.ilo.org/wcmsp5/groups/public/@dgreports/@dcomm/documents/publication/wcms_575540.pdf.

32. International Labour Organization, "Forced Labour, Modern Slavery and Human Trafficking," accessed July 23, 2021, https://www.ilo.org/global/topics/forced-labour/lang--en/index.htm.

33. International Labour Organization, *Executive Summary, Child Labour: Global Estimates 2020, Trends and the Road Forward* (June 10, 2021), 2. See https://www.ilo.org/wcmsp5/groups/public/---ed_norm/---ipec/documents/publication/wcms_800278.pdf.

34. "2020 Global Estimates of Child Labour—Frequently Asked Questions," International Labour Organization, June 10, 2021, https://www.ilo.org/ipec/news/WCMS_800333/lang--en/index.htm?ssSourceSiteId=global.

35. International Labour Organization, *Executive Summary, Child Labour*, 3.

36. Of the 160 million children estimated in the 2020 report, ILO counts 63 million girls and 97 million boys. See International Labour Organization, *Executive Summary, Child Labour*, 5.

37. Sugam Pokharel and Tom Page, "Silk Slaves: India's Bonded Laborers Are Forced to Work to Pay Off Debts," *CNN*, March 13, 2021, https://www.cnn.com/2021/03/13/asia/silk-slaves-india-the-freedom-project-spc-intl/index.html.

38. Pokharel and Page, "Silk Slaves."

39. ILO-IPEC, "Corporate Social Responsibility (CSR) and Child Labour," accessed July 23, 2021, https://www.ilo.org/ipec/Action/CSR/lang--en/index.htm.

40. International Labour Organization, "COVID-19 Impact on Child Labour and Forced Labour: The Response of the IPEC+ Flagship Programme" (May 2020), 4. Available online at https://www.ilo.org/

wcmsp5/groups/public/@ed_norm/@ipec/documents/publication/wcms_745287.pdf.

41. International Labour Organization, *Executive Summary, Child Labour*, 10.

42. Freedom United, "Why Traffickers Go After Native American Women," *Navajo-Hopi Observer*, March 19, 2019, https://www.freedomunited.org/news/why-traffickers-go-after-native-american-women/.

43. National Congress of American Indians, "Demographics, Indian Country Demographics, Population," accessed September 5, 2021, https://www.ncai.org/about-tribes/demographics.

44. Freedom United, "Why Traffickers Go After Native American Women."

45. Hawai'i State Commission on the Status of Women, Khara Jabola-Carolus, Executive Director, "Gender Impact Statement, Gambling with Women's Safety: A Feminist Assessment of Proposed Resort-Casino," January 26, 2021, 2. The full report, prepared for the Hawai'i State House of Representatives, is available online at https://humanservices.hawaii.gov/wp-content/uploads/2021/02/1.26.21-r2.1.21-GIS-FINAL_DHHL-Casino.pdf.

46. André B. Rosay, "Violence against American Indian and Alaska Native Women and Men: An NIJ-Funded Study Shows That American Indian and Alaska Native Women and Men Suffer Violence at Alarmingly High Rates," National Institute of Justice website, June 1, 2016, https://nij.ojp.gov/topics/articles/violence-against-american-indian-and-alaska-native-women-and-men.

47. See the NIWRC mission statement and access the podcast online at https://www.niwrc.org/podcast.

48. Rosay, "Violence against American Indian and Alaska Native Women and Men."

49. 2021 MMIW National Briefing, "Addressing the National Crisis of Missing and Murdered Indigenous Women: Advocacy in Action," webinar, April 29, 2021, https://www.niwrc.org/resources/webinars/2021-mmiw-national-briefing-addressing-national-crisis-missing-and-murdered.

50. "Missing and Murdered Indigenous Women (MMIW)," National Indigenous Women's Resource Center, accessed September 5, 2021, https://www.niwrc.org/policy-center/mmiw.

PART 3

1. Joshua Casteel, *Letters from Abu Ghraib*, 2nd ed. (Eugene, OR: Cascade Books, 2017), 3.

2. Casteel, *Letters from Abu Ghraib*, 68.

3. Definition from Iraq Veterans against the War, accessed October 11, 2021, https://www.ivaw.org/conscientious-objector.

4. DoD Instruction 1300.06, July 12, 2017, https://centeronconscience.org/who-is-military-co/.

Chapter 5

1. Edgar M. Krentz, "The First Letter of Paul to the Thessalonians, Introduction," in *The Harper Collins Study Bible*, ed. Harold W. Attridge (San Francisco: HarperOne, 2006), 2005.

2. BDAG, s.v. κέλευσμα.

3. Jon Coulston, "Courage and Cowardice in the Roman Imperial Army," *War in History* 20, no. 1, Special Issue on Courage and Cowardice in Wartime (January 2013): 7–31, at 10.

4. Antony Kamm, "The Roman Army," in *The Romans: An Introduction*, 2nd ed. (London: Routledge, 2008), 172–80, at 174.

5. This was a policy first enacted by the Emperor Claudius, who reigned from 41–54 CE, right during the time of Paul's letter writing.

6. "112. Letter from a Recruit at Misenum, 2nd century," in *Select Papyri*, vol. 1, *Private Documents*, trans. A. S. Hunt and C. C. Edgar, Loeb Classical Library 266 (Cambridge, MA: Harvard University Press, 1932), 304–5.

7. Abraham Malherbe, *The Letters to the Thessalonians*, Anchor Bible 32B (New York: Doubleday, 2000), 203.

8. Cicero, *Tusculan Disputations* 2.43. For more full discussion of Roman ideas about courage, see Catalina Balmaceda, "The Concept of *Virtus*," in *Virtus Romana: Politics and Morality in the Roman Historians* (Chapel Hill: University of North Carolina Press, 2017), 14–47, esp. 15–19.

9. Richard A. Horsley, "The First and Second Letters to the Corinthians," in *A Postcolonial Commentary on the New Testament Writings*, ed. Fernando F. Segovia and R. S. Sugirtharajah, The Bible and Postcolonialism 13 (London: T&T Clark, 2009), 220–45, at 241.

10. Scholars debate the authenticity of the letter 2 Thess. The hypothesis that some imitator of Paul composed the letter relies on two main observations: first, the letter reproduces almost exactly the structure of 1 Thess, suggesting the author had it as a model. Second, although the letter is similar in structure and style, its content is surprisingly different, especially when it comes to teachings about the end times. Those who argue for the pseudonymous authorship of this letter find it strange that the Christ-believers in Thessalonica, who were so concerned about their deceased community members potentially missing out on Christ's Parousia (1 Thess) would need to be advised that the Parousia had not, in fact, already taken place (2 Thess). In any event, the author of this letter draws upon military images in some intriguing ways.

11. Michael E. Gudorf, "The Use of πάλη in Ephesians 6:12," *Journal of Biblical Literature* 117, no. 2 (Summer 1998): 331–35.

12. For a helpful summary of the origin and features of the Mithras cult, as well as Christian attitudes toward its initiates, see Hans-Josef Klauck, *The Religious Context of Early Christianity: A Guide to Graeco-Roman Religion* (Minneapolis: Fortress, 2003), 139–49.

13. Kamm, "The Roman Army," 173.

14. The Acts of Thecla 3. For an accessible English translation of this text and other noncanonical gospels and acts, see Bart D. Ehrman, *Lost Scriptures: Books That Did Not Make It into the New Testament* (Oxford: Oxford University Press, 2003).

15. Robert M. Grant, "The Description of Paul in the Acts of Paul and Thecla," *Vigiliae Christianae* 36, no. 1 (March 1982): 1–4.

Chapter 6

1. Ignatius, *Letter to Polycarp*, 6.2. Greek text and facing English translation available in Michael W. Holmes, ed., *The Apostolic Fathers: Greek Texts and English Translations* (Grand Rapids, MI: Baker Books, 1999), 198–99.

2. For a discussion of the statue and cuirass, see Davina C. Lopez, *Apostle to the Conquered: Reimagining Paul's Mission*, Paul in Critical Contexts (Minneapolis: Fortress, 2010), 38–42.

3. Jennifer Awes Freeman, "The Good Shepherd and the Enthroned Ruler: A Reconsideration of Imperial Iconography in the Early Church," in *The Art of Empire: Christian Art in Its Imperial Context*,

ed. Lee M. Jefferson and Robin M. Jensen (Minneapolis: Fortress, 2015), 159–95, at 166.

4. Clement of Alexandria, *Stromata* 1.26, trans. William Wilson in *Ante-Nicene Fathers*, vol. 2, ed. Alexander Roberts, James Donaldson, and A. Cleveland Coxe (Buffalo, NY: Christian Literature Publishing Co, 1885). Full English text: Kevin Knight, ed., New Advent, accessed September 13, 2021, https://www.newadvent.org/fathers/02101.htm.

5. W. Randolph Tate, "Postcolonialism/Postcolonial Criticism," in *Handbook for Biblical Interpretation: An Essential Guide to Methods, Terms, and Concepts* (Grand Rapids, MI: Baker Academic, 2012), 329–33, at 331.

6. Eusebius, *De laudibus Constantini* 2.3, trans. Ernest Cushing Richardson in *Nicene and Post-Nicene Fathers, Second Series*, vol. 1, ed. Philip Schaff and Henry Wace (Buffalo: Christian Literature Publishing Co., 1890); rev. ed. Kevin Knight for New Advent, accessed September 13, 2021, https://www.newadvent.org/fathers/2504.htm.

7. Margaret M. Mitchell, "The Archetypal Image: John Chrysostom's Portraits of Paul," *The Journal of Religion* 75, no. 1 (January 1995): 15–43, esp. 27–28 and 32.

8. The particular episode does not specify a date, but Thaumaturgus was bishop during the time of both Decius (r. 249–51) and Valerian (r. 253–60), and both emperors instituted periods of increased prosecution against Christians.

9. Gregory of Nyssa, *The Life of Gregory Thaumaturgus* 84; my English translation. For more information on this passage, see Allison L. Gray, *Gregory of Nyssa as Biographer: Weaving Lives for Virtuous Readers*, Studien und Texte zu Antike und Christentum 123 (Tübingen: Mohr Siebeck, 2021), 178–80.

10. For discussion of the changing role of bishops, which becomes increasingly managerial during this period, see Claudia Rapp, *Holy Bishops in Late Antiquity: The Nature of Christian Leadership in an Age of Transition* (Berkeley: University of California Press, 2005), and Andrea Sterk, *Renouncing the World Yet Leading the Church: The Monk-Bishop in Late Antiquity* (Cambridge, MA: Harvard University Press, 2004).

11. George E. Demacopoulos, "Constantine, Ambrose, and the Morality of War: How Ambrose of Milan Challenged the Imperial Discourse on War and Violence," in *Orthodox Christian Perspectives on War*, ed. Perry T. Hamalas and Valerie A. Karras (University of Notre Dame Press, 2016), 159–94, at 162.

12. For a good discussion of Tertullian's objections, see Valerie A. Karras, "'Their Hands Are Not Clean': Origen and the Cappadocians on War and Military Service," in Hamalas and Karras, *Orthodox Christian Perspectives on War*, 138.

13. This view led to the classical Catholic definition of "church militant," which refers to those in the Church who are still living on earth, battling spiritual temptations and working for the triumph of love. The church militant exists alongside the "church triumphant" (those in heaven) and the "church penitent" (those in purgatory).

14. Origen, *Contra Celsum* 8.73.

15. Karras, "Their Hands Are Not Clean," 145–46; quotation is from Basil, *Epistle* 188.

16. Demacopoulos, "Constantine, Ambrose, and the Morality of War," 167.

17. Joshua Casteel, *Letters from Abu Ghraib*, 2nd ed. (Eugene, OR: Cascade Books, 2017), 61.

18. Casteel, *Letters from Abu Ghraib*, 81–82, all emphasis in the original.

19. IVAW has now become About Face: Veterans against the War. The IVAW website is archived at ivaw.org.

20. Catholic Peace Fellowship, "About CPF," http://www.catholicpeacefellowship.org/wp/wordpress/about-cpf/.

21. Lumen Christi Institute, https://www.lumenchristi.org/.

22. Kristi Casteel, "A Mother's Tribute," in Casteel, *Letters from Abu Ghraib*, 92.

23. Marc LiVecche, *The Good Kill: Just War and Moral Injury* (Oxford: Oxford University Press, 2021), 199.

24. In earlier periods, as after WWI and WWII, what was probably PTSD was referred to as "shell-shock."

25. "How Common Is PTSD in Veterans?," VA website, PTSD: National Center for PTSD, accessed July 9, 2021, https://www.ptsd.va.gov/understand/common/common_veterans.asp.

26. "How Common Is PTSD in Adults?," VA Website, PTSD: National Center for PTSD, accessed July 9, 2021, https://www.ptsd.va.gov/understand/common/common_adults.asp.

27. "How Common Is PTSD in Veterans?"

28. American Psychiatric Association, *Diagnostic and Statistical Manual of Mental Disorders: DSM-5*, 5th ed. (Washington, DC: American Psychiatric Association, 2013).

29. Shira Maguen and Kristine Burkman, "Combat-Related Killing: Expanding Evidence-Based Treatments for PTSD," *Cognitive and Behavioral Practice* 20, no. 4 (November 2013): 476–79, at 476.

30. Brett Litz et al., "Moral Injury and Moral Repair in War Veterans: A Preliminary Model and Intervention Strategy," *Clinical Psychology Review* 29, no. 8 (December 2009): 695–706, at 700.

31. Rita Nakashima Brock and Gabriella Lettini, *Soul Repair: Recovering from Moral Injury after War* (Boston: Beacon, 2012), xiv.

32. Casteel, *Letters from Abu Ghraib*, 39.

33. David Wood, *What Have We Done: The Moral Injury of Our Longest Wars* (New York: Little, Brown and Company, 2016), 66.

34. Jonathan Shay, *Achilles in Vietnam: Combat Trauma and the Undoing of Character* (New York: Scribner, 1994), xxiii.

35. Office of Public and Intergovernmental Affairs, "VA releases 2020 National Veteran Suicide Prevention Annual Report," U.S. Department of Veterans Affairs website, Office of Public and Intergovernmental Affairs, November 12, 2020, https://www.va.gov/opa/pressrel/pressrelease.cfm?id=5565.

36. Wood, *What Have We Done*, 92.

37. Stephen Losey, "Military Deaths by Suicide Jumped 25% at End of 2020," Military.com, April 5, 2021, https://www.military.com/daily-news/2021/04/05/military-deaths-suicide-jumped-25-end-of-2020.html.

38. A summary and the text of the resolution are available online at https://www.congress.gov/bill/117th-congress/house-bill/1656?s=1&r=8 (accessed September 11, 2021).

39. Soul Repair Center website, https://www.brite.edu/programs/soul-repair/.

40. Brock and Lettini, *Soul Repair*, 115.

41. Archived "POV: Soldiers of Conscience" page, http://archive.pov.org/soldiersofconscience/film-update/.

42. Nancy J. Ramsay, "Moral Injury as Loss and Grief with Attention to Ritual Resources for Care," in *Military Moral Injury and Spiritual Care: A Resource for Religious Leaders and Professional Caregivers*, ed. Nancy J. Ramsay and Carrie Doehring (Saint Louis: Chalice, 2019), 142–68.

43. Wood, *What Have We Done*, 3–5.

44. LiVecche, *The Good Kill*, 201.

45. "Army Junior ROTC Program Overview," U.S. Army JROTC website, accessed July 8, 2021, http://www.usarmyjrotc.com/general/program_overview.php.

46. Brock and Lettini, *Soul Repair*, 2.

47. Brock and Lettini, *Soul Repair*, 3.

PART 4

1. See more about Eli Clare's use of *bodymind* in "Stolen Bodies, Reclaimed Bodies: Disability and Queerness," *Public Culture* 13, no. 3 (Fall 2001): 359–65.

2. Amber Ferguson, "Unpaid Caregivers: How America Treats Women Caring for Paralyzed Partners," *The Washington Post*, August 6, 2021, available at https://www.washingtonpost.com/business/interactive/2021/caregiver-partner-paralyzed-marriage-pandemic/.

3. Cory Turner, "Education Dept. Announces Civil Rights Investigations into 5 States' Mask Mandate Bans," NPR.org, August 30, 2021, https://www.npr.org/sections/back-to-school-live-updates/2021/08/30/1032520335/education-department-civil-rights-investigations-mask-mandates.

4. Imani Barbarin, "Death by a Thousand Words: COVID-19 and the Pandemic of Ableist Media," *Refinery29*, August 30, 2021, https://www.refinery29.com/en-us/2021/08/10645352/covid-19-and-the-pandemic-of-ableist-media.

5. Barbarin, "Death by a Thousand Words."

6. Barbarin, "Death by a Thousand Words."

Chapter 7

1. This traditional idea about the place of composition depends on the prologue inscription of 1 Corinthians in the Vulgate, which says Paul is *scribens eis ab Epheso per Timotheum*, "writing to them from Ephesus by way of Timothy," with Timothy presumably being the one delivering the letter. This runs somewhat counter to information in Paul's own letters and the account of his journeys in Acts. For a fuller discussion, see Conzelmann, *1 Corinthians*, 4–5, in Martin Dibelius and Hans Conzelmann, *The Pastoral Epistles: A Commentary on the Pastoral*

Epistles, trans. Philip Buttolph and Adela Yarbro, Hermeneia (Philadelphia: Fortress, 1972).

2. Some argue that a fragment of the letter mentioned in 5:9, which was about sexual immorality, may be preserved in 2 Cor 6:14—7:1.

3. John T. Fitzgerald offers a brief but helpful overview of the primary partition theories in his introductory essay for 2 Cor in the *HarperCollins Study Bible*. See John T. Fitzgerald, "The Second Letter of Paul to the Corinthians," in *The HarperCollins Study Bible*, ed. Harold W. Attridge (San Francisco: HarperOne, 2006), 1956–58.

4. Robert A. Di Vito, "Old Testament Anthropology and the Construction of Personal Identity," *The Catholic Biblical Quarterly* 61, no. 2 (April 1999): 217–38, at 225.

5. Seneca, *Epistle* 95.52. English translation from Seneca the Younger, *Epistles*, vol. 3, trans. Richard M. Gummere, Loeb Classical Library 77 (Cambridge, MA: Harvard University Press, 2014).

6. Quintus Curtius Rufus, *Historia Alexandri* 10.6.8; 10.9.2 (reference from Conzelmann, *1 Corinthians*, 211).

7. This argument was articulated by F. C. Baur, "Die Christus Partei in der korinthischen Gemeinde," *Tübinger Zeitschrift für Theologie* 5 (1831): 61–206.

8. On libertinism, see T. W. Manson, "The Corinthian Correspondence (1)," in *Studies in the Gospels and Epistles*, ed. Matthew Black (Philadelphia: Westminster, 1962).

9. This is the position of Conzelmann.

10. Montague outlines this argument in George T. Montague, *First Corinthians*, Catholic Commentary on Sacred Scripture (Grand Rapids: Baker Academic, 2011), 190–92.

11. Paul also refers to the unity of the body, made up of diverse parts, in abbreviated form in Rom 12:1–5. Here, too, he notes that each member of the body makes an important contribution to the whole.

12. Sam K. Williams, *Galatians*, Abingdon New Testament Commentaries (Nashville: Abingdon, 1997), 83.

13. Jennifer A. Glancy, *Corporal Knowledge: Early Christian Bodies* (Oxford: Oxford University Press, 2010), 46.

14. Glancy, *Corporal Knowledge*, 47.

15. Montague, *First Corinthians*, 208.

16. The question of manual labor had apparently become a point of contention among the Corinthians. Paul crafts a lengthy defense

of his right to expect material support from those to whom he ministers, comparing the evangelizing apostle to a soldier who is paid for military service and a farmer who is fed from the produce of his field or flock. Although he believes he is deserving of payment or support, Paul reminds the Corinthian Christ-believers that he did *not* request this from the community (1 Cor 9:6–18).

17. Didache 12.3–4. Greek with facing English translation in Michael W. Holmes, ed., *The Apostolic Fathers: Greek Texts and English Translations* (Grand Rapids: Baker Books, 1999), 246–69.

18. Moral impurity should be distinguished from ritual impurity, which can occur without any evil intention on the part of the actor (e.g., someone becomes ritually impure by giving birth or touching a corpse, actions without negative moral weight).

19. Michael J. Gorman, "'You Shall Be Cruciform for I Am Cruciform': Paul's Trinitarian Reconstruction of Holiness," in *Holiness and Ecclesiology in the New Testament*, ed. Kent E. Brower and Andy Johnson (Grand Rapids: Eerdmans, 2007), 148–66, at 153.

20. Paul bases this assertion on the statement in Gen 2:24, that a man and woman become one flesh in marriage, or here, through the act of extramarital sexual intercourse, seen as a choice "to repudiate the relationship of belonging to the body of Christ" (Conzelmann, *1 Corinthians*, 111). The reasoning here probably also serves as justification for advising Christ-believers to marry within the faith where possible rather than being married to nonbelievers (1 Cor 7:12–16).

21. Klauck explains, "A major element in the life of the association was the sacrificial feast and common meal held at regular intervals, each year on the feast of the god or of the foundation, once a month or even more frequently, depending on the aim and the statutes of the association." See Hans-Josef Klauck, *The Religious Context of Early Christianity: A Guide to Graeco-Roman Religion* (Minneapolis: Fortress, 2003), 44.

22. Montague, *First Corinthians*, 142.

23. Polemo, *Physiognomy* 1.1.110ff. Quotation and excellent discussion found in Maud W. Gleason, "Deportment as Language: Physiognomy and the Semiotics of Gender," in *Making Men: Sophists and Self-Presentation in Ancient Rome* (Princeton, NJ: Princeton University Press, 1995), 55–81, at 57.

24. The author does not seem to recognize a potential conflict with his own claims elsewhere that Christ's body was unique "for in him the whole fullness of deity dwells bodily [Greek *sōmatikōs*], and you have

come to fullness in him, who is the head of every ruler and authority" (Col 2:9–10).

Chapter 8

1. Sophronius, *The Life of St. Mary of Egypt* 2. English translation in Benedicta Ward, "St. Mary of Egypt; the Liturgical Icon of Repentance," in *Harlots of the Desert: A Study of Repentance in Early Monastic Sources*, Cistercian Studies Series 106 (Kalamazoo, MI: Cistercian Publications, 1987), 37.

2. Sophronius, *Life of St. Mary of Egypt* 4.

3. Sophronius, *Life of St. Mary of Egypt* 7.

4. Sophronius, *Life of St. Mary of Egypt* 9.

5. Sophronius, *Life of St. Mary of Egypt* 10.

6. Sophronius, *Life of St. Mary of Egypt* 12.

7. Sophronius, *Life of St. Mary of Egypt* 13.

8. Sophronius, *Life of St. Mary of Egypt* 16.

9. Peter Anthony Mena, "The Holy Harlotry of *Mestizaje*," in *Place and Identity in the Lives of Antony, Paul, and Mary of Egypt: Desert as Borderland*, Religion and Spatial Studies (Cham, Switzerland: Palgrave Macmillan, 2019), 85–114, at 109.

10. Sophronius, *Life of St. Mary of Egypt* 22.

11. Sophronius, *Life of St. Mary of Egypt* 24.

12. For this general concept, Greeks used *phoreō*, and sometimes Mary and others are called "theophoros" or "Christophoros," God- or Christ-bearers.

13. The text's date of composition is uncertain, but it was known to Origen of Alexandria in the mid-second century, and possibly to Clement of Alexandria by the end of the first century, suggesting it would have been in circulation by around 150 CE. See Bart D. Ehrman, *Lost Scriptures: Books That Did Not Make It into the New Testament* (Oxford: Oxford University Press, 2003), 63.

14. Proto-gospel of James 4; English translation in Ehrman, *Lost Scriptures*, 64–72.

15. Proto-gospel of James 9.

16. Proto-gospel of James 15–16.

17. See Peter Brown, *The Body and Society: Men, Women, and Sexual Renunciation in Early Christianity*, Lectures on the History of

Religions, New Series 13 (New York: Columbia University Press, 1988), 273.

18. Brown, *Body and Society*, 274.

19. Christopher A. Frilingos, *Jesus, Mary, and Joseph: Family Trouble in the Infancy Gospels* (Philadelphia: University of Pennsylvania Press, 2017), 128–29.

20. Proto-gospel of James 19.

21. Proto-gospel of James 20.

22. Jennifer Glancy points out that although a number of early Christian theologians submit that Mary had a painless experience of childbirth, not everyone agreed or ascribed the same significance to her pain or lack thereof (Jennifer A. Glancy, *Corporal Knowledge: Early Christian Bodies* [Oxford: Oxford University Press, 2010], esp. chap. 4, "Mary in Childbirth," 81–136).

23. Virginia Burrus, "Word and Flesh: The Bodies and Sexuality of Ascetic Women in Christian Antiquity," *Journal of Feminist Studies in Religion* 10, no. 1 (Spring 1994): 27–51, at 51.

24. Lindsay Whitehurst and Colleen Long, "Mask Debate Moves from School Boards to Courtrooms," *AP News*, August 28, 2021, https://apnews.com/article/lifestyle-health-coronavirus-pandemic-school-boards-f59c2d847a8528b6ea472260f7998bd6.

25. Guidance from August 5, 2021, states, "CDC recommends universal indoor masking for all teachers, staff, students, and visitors to K-12 schools, regardless of vaccination status. Children should return to full-time in-person learning in the fall with layered prevention strategies in place." See "Guidance for COVID-19 Prevention in K-12 Schools," CDC website, https://www.cdc.gov/coronavirus/2019-ncov/community/schools-childcare/k-12-guidance.html.

26. Leah Lakshmi Piepzna-Samarasinha, *Care Work: Dreaming Disability Justice* (Vancouver: Arsenal Pulp, 2018), 69. At this point she is discussing the concept of "crip skills" or "crip science," modeled on Kim Katrin Milan's phrase "femme science," to mean "femme skills, technologies, and intelligences" (69).

27. Deborah Beth Creamer, *Disability and Christian Theology: Embodied Limits and Constructive Possibilities* (Oxford: Oxford University Press, 2009).

28. Piepzna-Samarasinha, *Care Work*, 241.

29. Words of Patty Berne, Sins Invalid cofounder and executive director; Sins Invalid "is a disability justice based performance project

that incubates and celebrates artists with disabilities, centralizing artists of color and LGBTQ/gender-variant artist as communities who have been historically marginalized." See "Our Mission," Sins Invalid webpage, accessed October 13, 2021, https://www.sinsinvalid.org/about-us. Berne is quoted in Piepzna-Samarasinha, *Care Work*, 21.

30. Piepzna-Samarasinha, *Care Work*, 75.

31. Piepzna-Samarasinha, *Care Work*, 76.

32. The question and some answers were shared on Barnow's Instagram account. Some of the answers included "boundaries, finding healing moment in texts, nuance, destigmatizing mental health, process of finding healthy self-worth, and self-grace." Image was described and quoted in Piepzna-Samarasinha, *Care Work*, 232.

33. Colleen Stinchcombe, "13 Self-Care Ideas That Actually Heal Your Mind and Soul," *Woman's Day*, May 30, 2020, https://www.womansday.com/health-fitness/wellness/g32619113/self-care-ideas/; Nicole Saporita, Good Housekeeping Institute, and Zee Krstic, "40+ Lab-Approved Solutions to Creating the Ultimate Self-Care Routine," *Good Housekeeping*, December 2, 2020, https://www.goodhousekeeping.com/health/wellness/g25643343/self-care-ideas/.

34. "International Self-Care Day," International Self-Care Foundation, accessed September 10, 2021, https://isfglobal.org/international-self-care-day/.

35. Altheria Caldera, "Challenging Capitalistic Exploitation: A Black Feminist/Womanist Commentary on Work and Self-Care," *Feminist Studies* 46, no. 3 (2020): 707–16, at 713–14.

36. Caldera, "Challenging Capitalistic Exploitation," 714.

37. Mike Lucock et al., "Self-Care in Mental Health Services: A Narrative Review," *Health and Social Care in the Community* 19, no. 6 (2011):602–16, at 603.

38. Phyllis Raynor and Charlene Pope, "The Role of Self-Care for Parents in Recovery from Substance Use Disorders: An Integrative Review of Parental Self-Care," *Journal of Addictions Nursing* 27, no. 3 (2016): 180–89.

39. M. Elena Cuartero and José F. Campos-Vidal, "Self-Care Behaviours and Their Relationship with Satisfaction and Compassion Fatigue Levels among Social Workers," *Social Work in Health Care* 58, no. 3 (2019): 274–90, at 284.

40. Adrienne Maree Brown, "How about a Beginning of Self-Determined Care?" adriennemareebrown.net, October 15, 2012, http://

adriennemareebrown.net/2012/10/15/how-about-a-beginning-of-self-determined-care/.

41. Brown, "How about a Beginning."

42. Nicole Bateman and Martha Ross, "Why Has COVID-19 Been Especially Harmful for Working Women?" *Brookings*, October 2020, https://www.brookings.edu/essay/why-has-covid-19-been-especially-harmful-for-working-women/.

43. Bateman and Ross note that the employment rate for women without college degrees dropped by 15 percent, versus 11 percent for men without college degrees (Bateman and Ross, "Why Has COVID-19").

PART 5

1. Russell Moore, *Adopted for Life: The Priority of Adoption for Christian Families and Churches* (Wheaton, IL: Crossway, 2009), 73. Moore is quoted in Samuel L. Perry, *Growing God's Family: The Global Orphan Care Movement and the Limits of Evangelical Activism* (New York: New York University Press, 2017), 75.

2. In June 2021, Moore became the director of the Public Theology Project at *Christianity Today*, a prominent evangelical magazine originally founded by Billy Graham in 1956. The media group's website claims to reach "over five million people monthly with various digital and print resources." *Christianity Today*, Media Room, accessed July 21, 2021, https://www.christianitytoday.org/media-room/.

3. Perry, *Growing God's Family*, 231.

4. Perry, *Growing God's Family*, 138. Perry indicates he is indebted to sociologist C. Wright Mills, who introduced the idea of a vocabulary of motive.

5. Perry, *Growing God's Family*, 140.

Chapter 9

1. The date for Galatians is uncertain, but on the basis of information Paul includes about expecting a collection of monetary donations from Galatia in 1 Cor 16:1, scholars conjecture it may have been written after 1 Cor but before the Letter to the Romans, where Paul still seems to be waiting for money from that collection. See, e.g., Sam K.

Williams, *Galatians*, Abingdon New Testament Commentaries (Nashville: Abingdon, 1997), 31–32.

2. I choose this neutral terminology for referring to those proposing alternate teachings. In the history of the interpretation of Galatians, they have been variously identified as Jewish Christians (F. C. Baur, 1831), Judaizing Christians/Judaizers (W. Lütgert, 1919), Galatian Gentiles (J. Munck, 1954), recently converted Gentiles (G. Wagner, 1990), Gnostics (W. Schmithals, 1956), and "agitators" (F. J. Matera, 1992). For a helpful, brief summary of the debate over who these teachers might have been, see Frank. J. Matera, *Galatians*, Sacra Pagina Series 9 (Collegeville, MN: Liturgical Press, 1992), 2–6.

3. Within the letter itself, see Paul's strenuous objections to the idea Gentile converts must be circumcised at 2:3 (Paul did not require Titus to be circumcised) and 5:2–6 (Paul warns them that if they choose to be circumcised they will "cut themselves off" from Christ).

4. Hans Dieter Betz points out that this statement is the "thesis" of Paul's letter, an exercise in deliberative rhetoric designed to persuade the Galatians. Betz notes that "Paul stands in older traditions, according to which truth in the authentic sense cannot be obtained through teaching, but only through direct revelation," which Paul claims to have received in Galatians 2:2 and elsewhere. See Hans Dieter Betz, *Galatians: A Commentary on Paul's Letter to the Churches in Galatia*, Hermeneia (Philadelphia: Fortress, 1979), 62–63.

5. Although Paul uses the masculine noun *uios*, or "son," in Greek as in many modern Romance languages the masculine plural form can refer to a group of mixed genders. Some Bible translations use the more inclusive term "children" (KJV, NABRE) or even "descendants" (NRSV). I've chosen to stick with a literal translation here to highlight how Paul uses fairly consistent language.

6. Sam K. Williams, *Galatians*, Abingdon New Testament Commentaries (Nashville: Abingdon, 1997), 86.

7. Betz, *Galatians*, 139.

8. Williams, *Galatians*, 102.

9. BDAG, s.v. παιδεύω.

10. Some essential titles for the study of Greco-Roman education include Raffaela Cribiore, *Gymnastics of the Mind: Greek Education in Hellenistic and Roman Egypt* (Princeton, NJ: Princeton University Press, 2001), and Teresa Morgan, *Literate Education in the Hellenistic and Roman Worlds* (Cambridge: Cambridge University Press, 1998).

11. On the issues involved in gendered self-presentation and education, see Maud W. Gleason, *Making Men: Sophists and Self-Presentation in Ancient Rome* (Princeton, NJ: Princeton University Press, 1995).

12. Jesus uses the term at Mark 14:36.

13. Chris Frilingos, "'For My Child, Onesimus': Paul and Domestic Power in Philemon," *Journal of Biblical Literature* 119, no. 1 (Spring 2000): 94–95.

14. BDAG, s.v. υἱοθεσία.

15. Matera, *Galatians*, 151.

16. The quotation here appears to be a mix of Ezek 37:27, Isa 52:11, and 2 Sam 7:14.

17. "Obedience was regarded in antiquity as a central virtue at all stages of life, but particularly in children's relations with parents. The obligation of obedience was due both parents, but especially the father, as household leader (κύριος, paterfamilias)." See Reidar Aasgaard, "Paul as a Child: Children and Childhood in the Letters of the Apostle," *Journal of Biblical Literature* 126, no. 1 (Spring 2007): 129–59, at 144.

18. "The exhortation not to behave like children…, and related insinuations made by means of kinship language, emphasise [*sic*] Paul's maturity and that of those in agreement with him, in contrast to his adversaries." See Jeremy Punt, "Not Child's Play," *Neotestamentica* 51, no. 2 (2017): 235–60, at 249.

19. Chris Frilingos notes that Paul may also be playing on a Greco-Roman trope that situates one's child as a mirror of the self, pointing to Dio Chrysostom's statement, "How can it be anything but a pleasure to raise up from the ground a child…a physical and mental mirror of yourself, so that, as it grows up another self is created?" (56.3.4). This could lie behind Paul's command that Philemon accept Onesimus as if he is Paul (Phlm 17). See Frilingos, "'For My Child Onesimus,'" 101.

20. Benjamin Fiore, *The Pastoral Epistles: First Timothy, Second Timothy, Titus*, Sacra Pagina 12 (Collegeville, MN: Liturgical Press, 2007), 134.

21. A helpful overview of these and other positions can be found in Jean-Baptiste Bonnard, Lillian E. Doherty, and Violane Sebillotte Cuchet, "Male and Female Bodies according to Ancient Greek Physicians," in "When Medicine Meets Gender," *Clio: Women, Gender, History* 37 (2013): 19–37, at 25.

22. Interestingly, when the term is used in the context of agriculture or husbandry, it may best be translated "cultivation."

23. Herodotus, *The Histories*, I.114–116. For an accessible English translation, see Herodotus, *The Histories*, rev. ed., trans. Aubrey de Sélincourt (London: Penguin, 2003).

24. BDAG, s.v. τέλειος.

25. Aasgaard, "Paul as a Child," 144.

26. There is an echo of this in 2 Cor 6:12–13, where Paul writes, "There is no restriction in our affections, but only in yours. In return—I speak as to children—open wide your hearts also."

27. See closely parallel passages in Col 3: 20–21 and Eph 6:1–4. Both base the need for children to be obedient on the Decalogue's command to honor one's father and mother (Exod 20:12).

28. Benjamin Fiore comments, "The recollection of Timothy's early introduction to the faith and of the tradition of belief going back to his grandmother fits the letter's conception of the church as the household of God (1 Tim 3:15). The family continues to be the social and religious context in which faith is richly nurtured." See Fiore, *Pastoral Epistles*, 140.

29. As biblical scholars Dibelius and Conzelmann put it in their Hermeneia commentary on the Pastorals, "Thus, in addition to the tradition of the apostle as teacher (2 Tim 2:2), the Pastoral Epistles also proclaim an image of the apostle, valid for all times, as the prototype of life, especially of suffering." See Martin Dibelius and Hans Conzelmann, *The Pastoral Epistles: A Commentary on the Pastoral Epistles*, Hermeneia (Philadelphia: Fortress, 1972), 98.

30. Dibelius and Conzelmann, *Pastoral Epistles*, 40.

31. Interestingly, one of the indications that Christians have entered the "distressing times" of the last days will be that children will be "disobedient to their parents" (2 Tim 3:2); this is so against the typical order of things, it can be read as a sign that the day of the Lord is near.

32. Dibelius and Conzelmann, *Pastoral Epistles*, 53.

33. Ilaria Ramelli, an expert on the third-century interpreter Origen of Alexandria, points out that the allegorical interpretation arises quite early; she writes that Origen "always allegorizes the statement in 1 Tim 2:15 that women will be saved only through τεκνογονία or childbearing: he never takes it at face value, but regularly interprets τεκνογονία as the production of Christ and virtue in one's heart (Comm. Rom. 4.6.160; Hom. Jer. 4.5; Fr. Luc. 32 Rauer)." See Ilaria Ramelli, "Theosebia: A Presbyter of the Catholic Church," *Journal of Feminist Studies*

in Religion 26, no. 2 (Fall 2010): 86. For a summary of scholarly positions, see Anna Rebecca Solevåg, *Birthing Salvation: Gender and Class in Early Christian Childbearing Discourse*, Biblical Interpretation Series (Leiden: Brill, 2013), 87–91.

34. A briefer echo of this instruction appears at Titus 2:4, which reads, "So that they [older women] may encourage the young women to love their husbands, to love their children."

Chapter 10

1. John David Penniman, "Fed to Perfection: Mother's Milk, Roman Family Values, and the Transformation of the Soul in Gregory of Nyssa," *Church History* 84, no. 3 (September 2015): 495–530. See also John David Penniman, *Raised on Christian Milk: Food and the Formation of the Soul in Early Christianity*, Synkrisis: Comparative Approaches to Early Christianity in Greco-Roman Culture (New Haven, CT: Yale University Press, 2017).

2. Gregory's interpretation has a parallel in the interpretation of Philo of Alexandria, a Hellenistic Jewish philosopher and exegete, who held Moses up as a model of the ideal philosophical life for his Jewish contemporaries. For more on this parallel, see Albert C. Geljon, "Philonic Exegesis in Gregory of Nyssa's De vita Moysis," *Brown Judaic Studies* 333 (Providence: Brown Judaic Studies, 2002).

3. Gregory of Nyssa, *Basil* 20, English translation in Sr. James Aloysius Stein, *Encomium of Saint Gregory Bishop of Nyssa on His Brother Saint Basil*, The Catholic University of America Patristic Studies 17 (Washington, DC: The Catholic University of America, 1928), 41–43. Penniman cites this passage as illustrative of Gregory's understanding. See Penniman, "Fed to Perfection," 506.

4. Basil, *Ad adulescentes* 5. English translation from Frederick Morgan Padelford, *Essays on the Study and Use of Poetry by Plutarch and Basil the Great*, Yale Studies in English 15 (New York: Henry Holt and Company, 1902): 99–120. The translation is also available online at https://www.tertullian.org/fathers/basil_litterature01.htm.

5. Basil, *Ad adulescentes* 1.

6. Emily J. Hunt, *Christianity in the Second Century: The Case of Tatian* (London: Routledge, 2003), 100–102.

7. Frances M. Young, *Biblical Exegesis and the Formation of Christian Culture* (Peabody, MA: Hendrickson, 1997), 244.

8. For comments on dating and the manuscript tradition, see Hans-Josef Klauck, *The Apocryphal Acts of the Apostles: An Introduction*, trans. Brian McNeil (Waco, TX: Baylor University Press, 2008), 48–50.

9. Acts of Thecla 9.

10. Acts of Thecla 27.

11. Gail P. C. Streete, *Redeemed Bodies: Women Martyrs in Early Christianity* (Louisville, KY: Westminster John Knox, 2009), 88–89.

12. Acts of Thecla 37.

13. Acts of Thecla 39.

14. There is no discussion of the fact that Falconilla died without having been a Christian; this is just one aspect of the text that troubled some early interpreters like Tertullian, who rejected it on the grounds that its teachings defied custom in a number of matters: "But if certain women defend the Acts of Paul, which are falsely so named, with regard to the right of women [after the example of Thecla] to teach and to baptize, let them know that in Asia the presbyter who compiled that document, thinking to complete Paul's authority by his own authority, was found out. He admitted that he had done it only out of love for Paul, and he laid down his office." Quotation from Tertullian, *On Baptism* 17.5. English translation in Klauck, *Apocryphal Acts*, 48.

15. Peter Brown, *The Body and Society: Men, Women, and Sexual Renunciation in Early Christianity*, Lectures on the History of Religions, New Series 13 (New York: Columbia University Press, 1988), 227–28.

16. Averil Cameron, *The Mediterranean World in Late Antiquity: AD 395–600*, Routledge History of the Ancient World (London: Routledge, 1993), 71.

17. The specific terminology was proposed by Catholic theologian John Henry Newman. See John Henry Newman, *An Essay on the Development of Christian Doctrine* (London: J. Toovey, 1845).

18. See Samuel L. Perry, "What Evangelical Orphan Boom?" in *Growing God's Family: The Global Orphan Care Movement and the Limits of Evangelical Activism* (New York: New York University Press, 2017), 33–65.

19. Perry, *Growing God's Family*, 154.

20. Perry, *Growing God's Family*, 212.

21. Jon Nordheimer, "Sex Charges against Priest Embroil Louisiana Parents," *The New York Times*, June 20, 1985, https://www.nytimes.com/1985/06/20/us/sex-charges-against-priest-embroil-louisiana-parents.html.

22. This does appear to be the case. In a deposition, Bishop Gerard Frey revealed that a young man made a credible accusation against Gauthe in 1974, which led to Frey confronting Gauthe. According to Frey, Gauthe "admitted that he had made a mistake, that he had been guilty of imprudent touches with this young man, that it was an isolated case, incident, that it would never happen again," and Frey subsequently appointed Gauthe the chaplain for the diocesan Boy Scout troop in 1975. See Jason Berry, "The Tragedy of Gilbert Gauthe," *The Times of Acadiana*, May 23, 1985, https://www.bishop-accountability.org/news/1985_05_23_Berry_TheTragedy.htm.

23. The full 2011 report is available online at https://www.usccb.org/sites/default/files/issues-and-action/child-and-youth-protection/upload/The-Causes-and-Context-of-Sexual-Abuse-of-Minors-by-Catholic-Priests-in-the-United-States-1950-2010.pdf (accessed July 25, 2022).

24. Karen J. Terry et al., *The Causes and Context of Sexual Abuse of Minors by Catholic Priests in the United States,1950–2010: A Report Presented to the United States Conference of Catholic Bishops by the John Jay College Research Team* (May 2011), 8. See previous note for a link to the full report online.

25. On underreporting, see, e.g., Bonnie Fisher, "The Sexual Victimization of College Women," U.S. Department of Justice, Office of Justice Programs, National Institute of Justice (2000).

26. Robert Downen, Lise Olsen, and John Tedesco, "Abuse of Faith. 20 Years, 700 Victims: Southern Baptist Sexual Abuse Spreads as Leaders Resist Reforms," part 1 of 6, *Houston Chronicle*, February 10, 2019, https://www.houstonchronicle.com/news/investigations/article/Southern-Baptist-sexual-abuse-spreads-as-leaders-13588038.php.

27. The school is now permanently closed.

28. *The Keepers*, directed by Ryan White (Netflix, 2017). See Episode 3, "The Revelation."

29. *The Keepers*, "The Revelation." The psychologist noted that when the IOL staff insisted that they would not accept more priests without full files detailing all the relevant information, the diocese stopped referring them as patients.

30. *The Keepers*, Episode 4, "The Burial."

31. *The Keepers*, Episode 6, "The Web."

32. SNAP website front page, accessed July 15, 2021, https://www.snapnetwork.org/.

33. StoryCorps website, accessed July 16, 2021, https://storycorps.org/about/.

34. "About," SNAP website, accessed July 16, 2021, https://www.snapnetwork.org/about.

35. The full text of the Charter is available online at https://www.usccb.org/test/upload/Charter-for-the-Protection-of-Children-and-Young-People-2018-final(1).pdf (accessed July 25, 2022).

36. "Protection of Children and Young People Committee," USCCB website, accessed September 22, 2021, https://www.usccb.org/committees/protection-children-young-people/committee.

37. "President of U.S. Bishops' Conference and Committee Chairman Response to Pennsylvania Grand Jury Report," USCCB Public Affairs Office, August 14, 2018, https://www.usccb.org/news/2018/president-us-bishops-conference-and-committee-chairman-response-pennsylvania-grand-jury.

38. Nordheimer, "Sex Charges against Priest."

39. Downen, Olsen, and Tedesco, "Abuse of Faith. Offend, Then Repeat," part 2 of 6, *Houston Chronicle*, February 12, 2019, https://www.houstonchronicle.com/news/investigations/article/Southern-Baptist-churches-hired-ministers-accused-13588233.php.

40. Nordheimer, "Sex Charges against Priest."

41. Anthony J. Blasi and Lluis Oviedo, eds., *The Abuse of Minors in the Catholic Church: Dismantling the Culture of Cover Ups*, Routledge Studies in Religion (London: Routledge, 2020).

42. Marie Keenan, *Child Sexual Abuse and the Catholic Church: Gender, Power, and Organizational Culture* (Oxford: Oxford University Press, 2012), xxiii. Keenan's extensive study relied on first-hand accounts from clergy sexual offenders as well as external studies like the John Jay College Report and similar reports in Australia and her focal country, Ireland.

INDEX